JOE SCHREIBE

CHASING THE DEAD

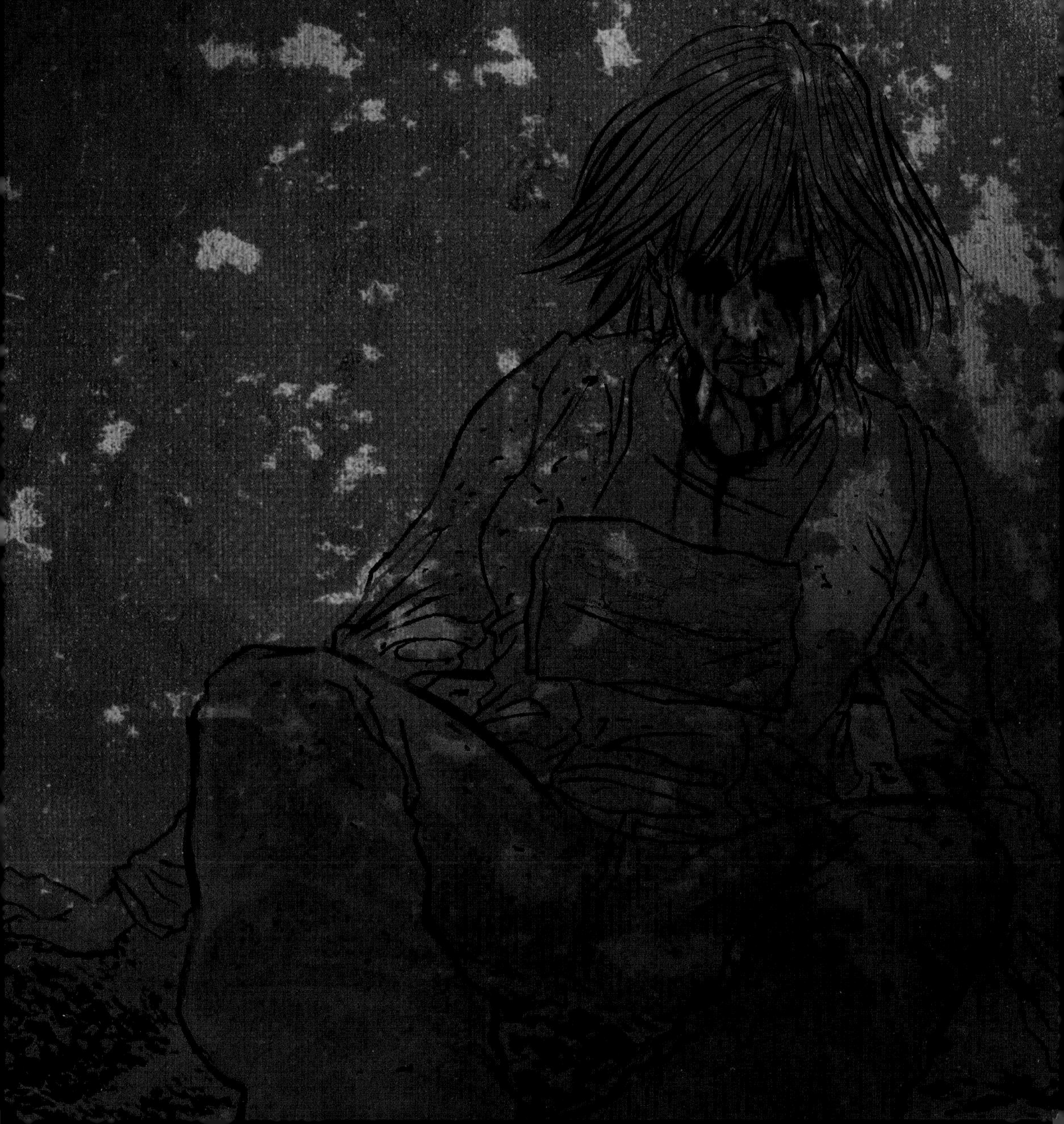

Written by
Matthew Scott and Tim Westland
Based on the Novel by Joe Schreiber

Art by
Dietrich Smith

Colors by
Sendol Arts and Matthew Scott

Letters by
Comicraft

Cover by
David Petersen

Collection Edits by
Justin Eisinger and Alonzo Simon

Collection Design by
Robbie Robbins

IDW founded by Ted Adams, Alex Garner, Kris Oprisko, and Robbie Robbins

ISBN: 978-1-61377-602-5

16 15 14 13   1 2 3 4

Ted Adams, CEO & Publisher
Greg Goldstein, President & COO
Robbie Robbins, EVP/Sr. Graphic Artist
Chris Ryall, Chief Creative Officer/Editor-in-Chief
Matthew Ruzicka, CPA, Chief Financial Officer
Alan Payne, VP of Sales
Dirk Wood, VP of Marketing
Lorelei Bunjes, VP of Digital Services

Become our fan on Facebook **facebook.com/idwpublishing**
Follow us on Twitter **@idwpublishing**
Check us out on YouTube **youtube.com/idwpublishing**
www.IDWPUBLISHING.com

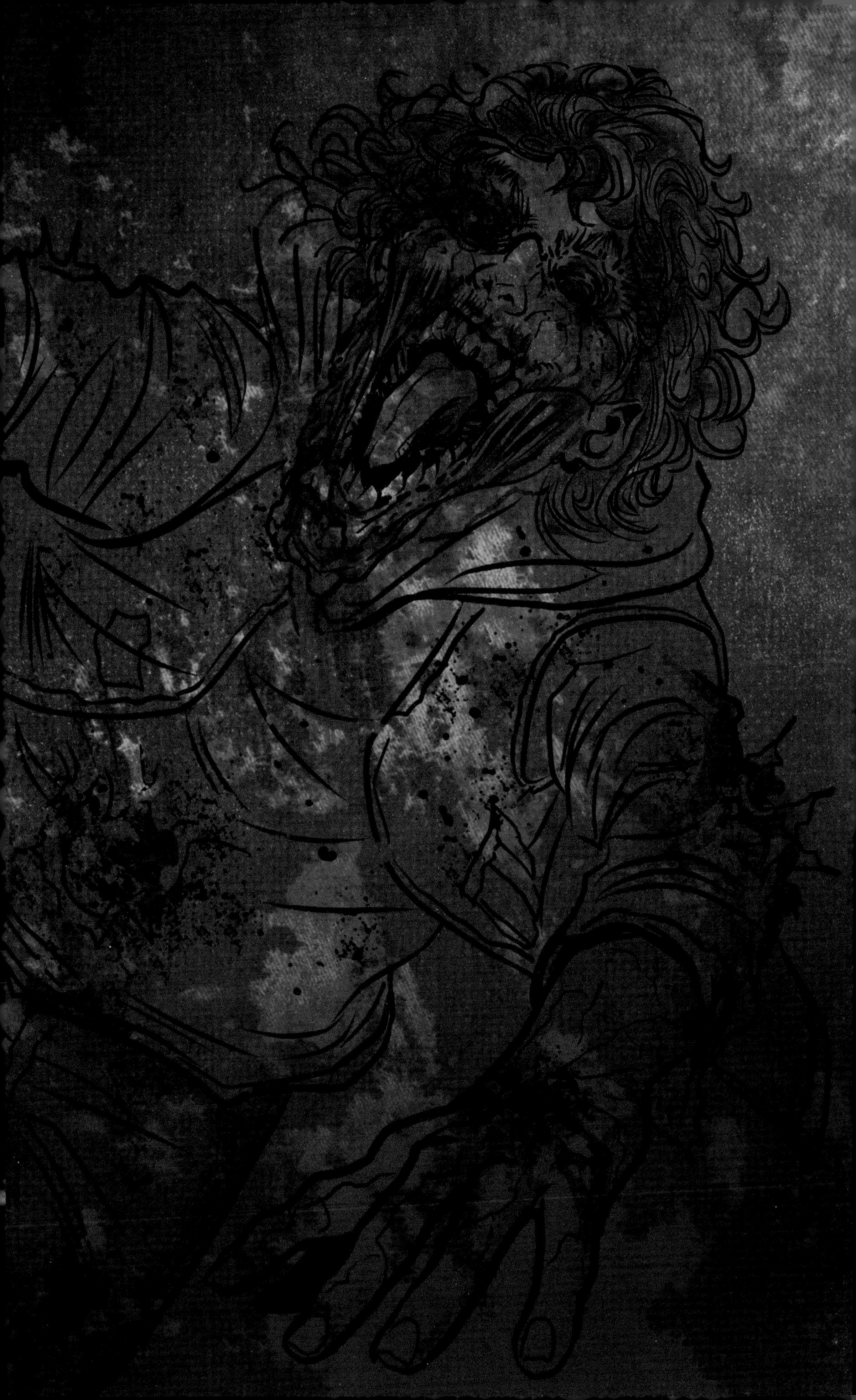

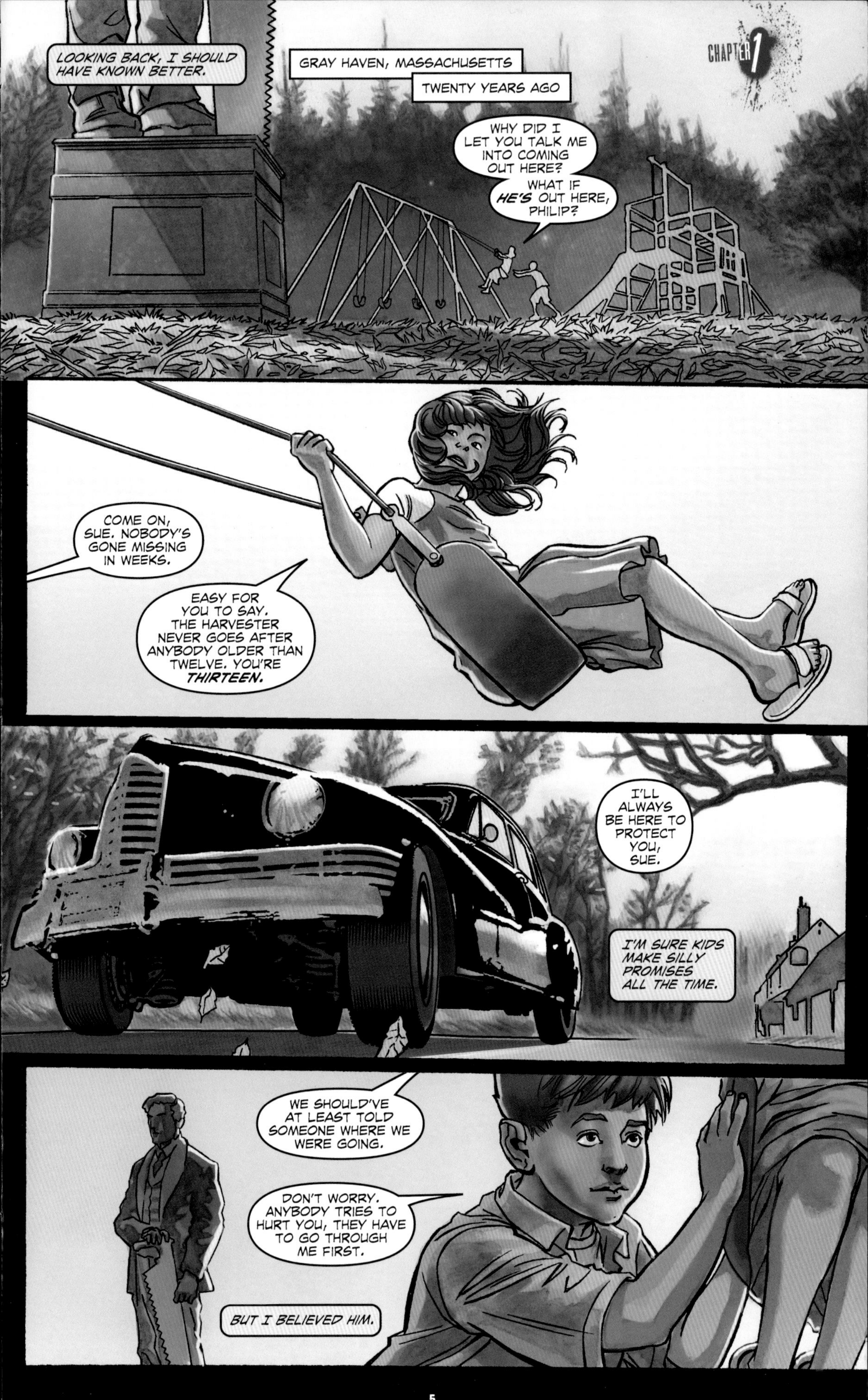
CHAPTER 1
LOOKING BACK, I SHOULD HAVE KNOWN BETTER.
GRAY HAVEN, MASSACHUSETTS
TWENTY YEARS AGO
WHY DID I LET YOU TALK ME INTO COMING OUT HERE?
WHAT IF HE'S OUT HERE, PHILIP?
COME ON, SUE. NOBODY'S GONE MISSING IN WEEKS.
EASY FOR YOU TO SAY. THE HARVESTER NEVER GOES AFTER ANYBODY OLDER THAN TWELVE. YOU'RE THIRTEEN.
I'LL ALWAYS BE HERE TO PROTECT YOU, SUE.
I'M SURE KIDS MAKE SILLY PROMISES ALL THE TIME.
WE SHOULD'VE AT LEAST TOLD SOMEONE WHERE WE WERE GOING.
DON'T WORRY. ANYBODY TRIES TO HURT YOU, THEY HAVE TO GO THROUGH ME FIRST.
BUT I BELIEVED HIM.

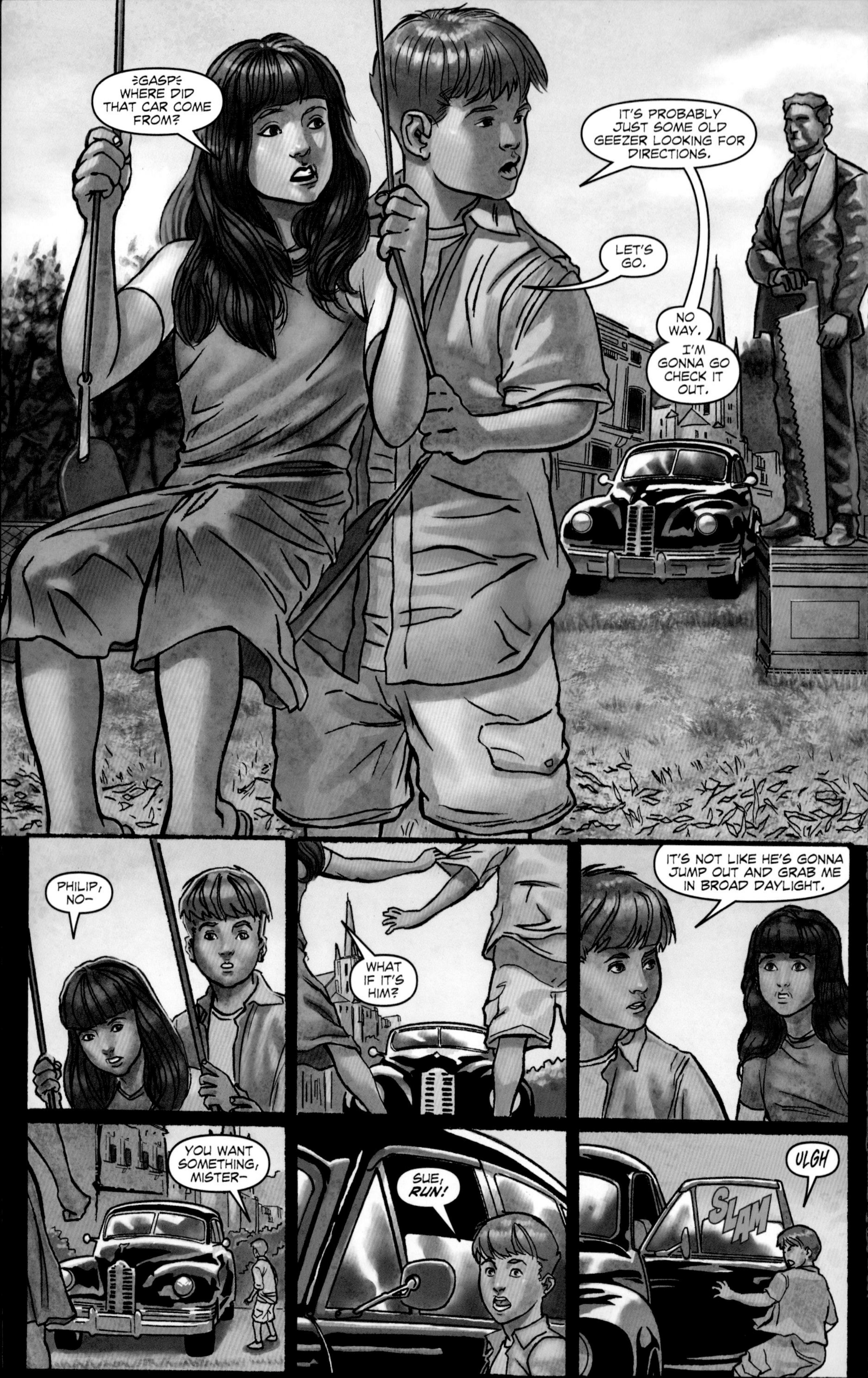

GASP WHERE DID THAT CAR COME FROM?
IT'S PROBABLY JUST SOME OLD GEEZER LOOKING FOR DIRECTIONS.
LET'S GO.
NO WAY.
I'M GONNA GO CHECK IT OUT.
PHILIP, NO-
WHAT IF IT'S HIM?
IT'S NOT LIKE HE'S GONNA JUMP OUT AND GRAB ME IN BROAD DAYLIGHT.
YOU WANT SOMETHING, MISTER-
SUE, RUN!
SLAM
ULGH

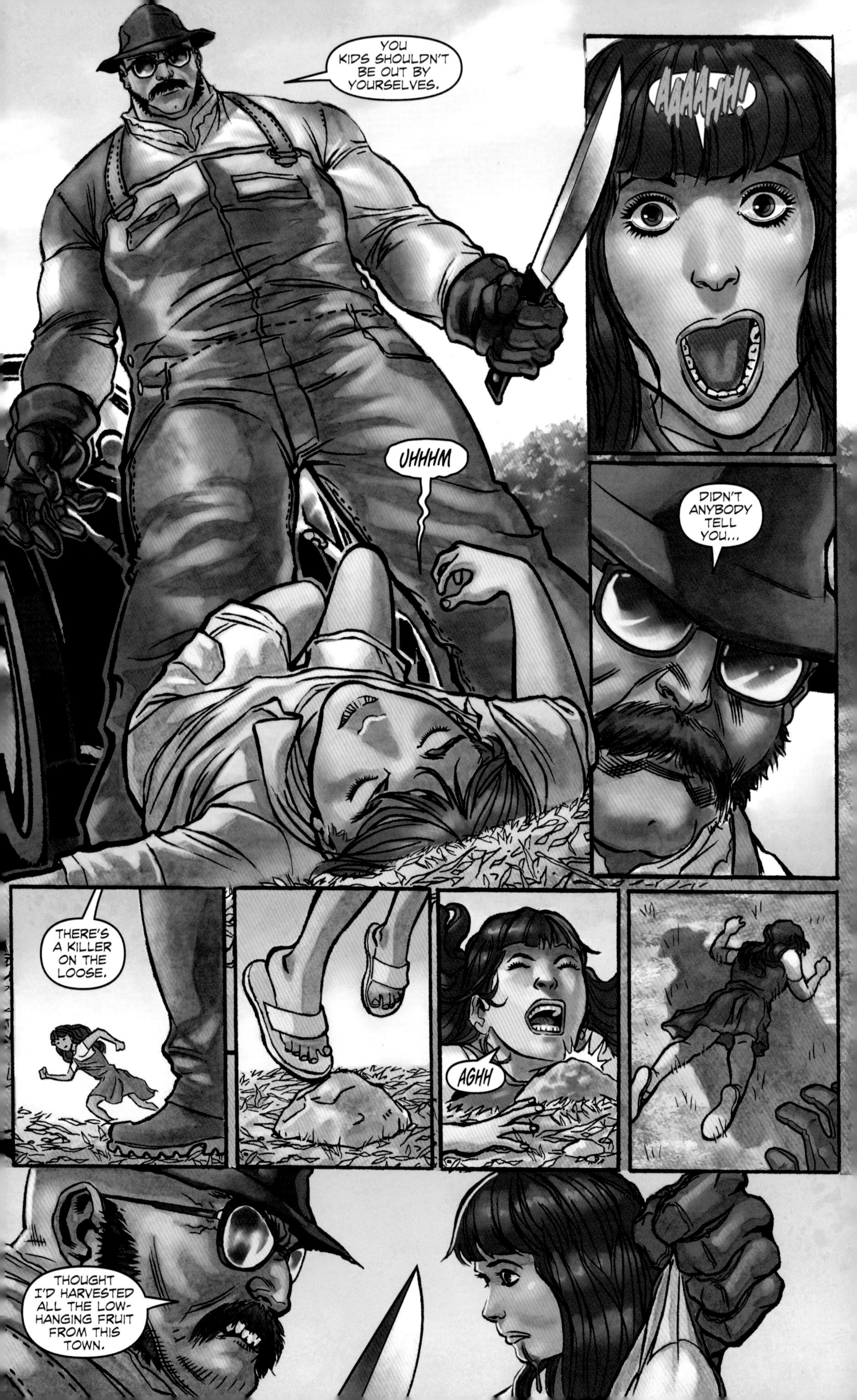
YOU KIDS SHOULDN'T BE OUT BY YOURSELVES.
AAAAHH!
UHHHM
DIDN'T ANYBODY TELL YOU...
THERE'S A KILLER ON THE LOOSE.
AGHH
THOUGHT I'D HARVESTED ALL THE LOW-HANGING FRUIT FROM THIS TOWN.

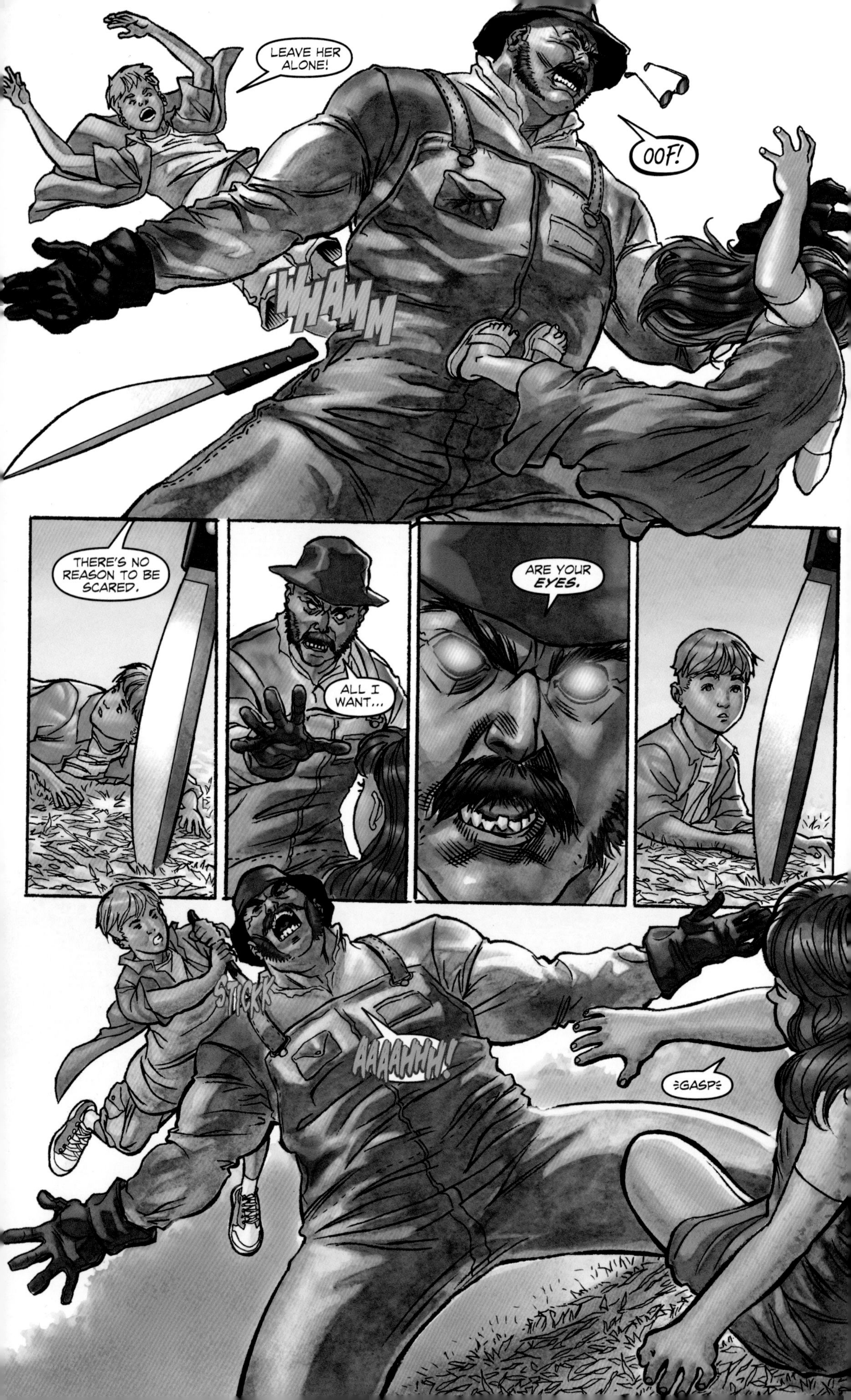
LEAVE HER ALONE!
OOF!
WHAMM
THERE'S NO REASON TO BE SCARED.
ALL I WANT...
ARE YOUR EYES.
STICKK
AAAAHHH!
GASP

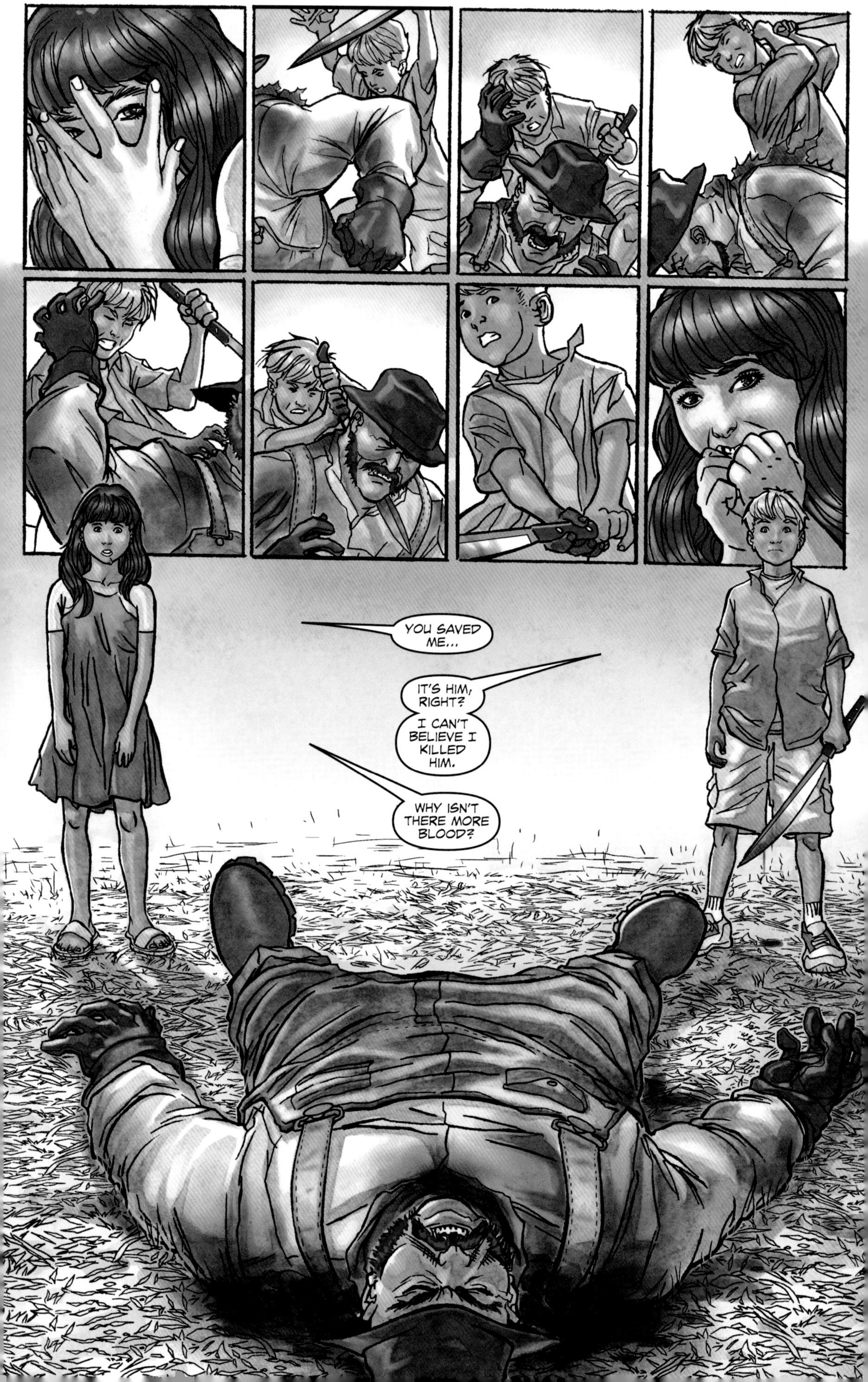
YOU SAVED ME...
IT'S HIM, RIGHT?
I CAN'T BELIEVE I KILLED HIM.
WHY ISN'T THERE MORE BLOOD?

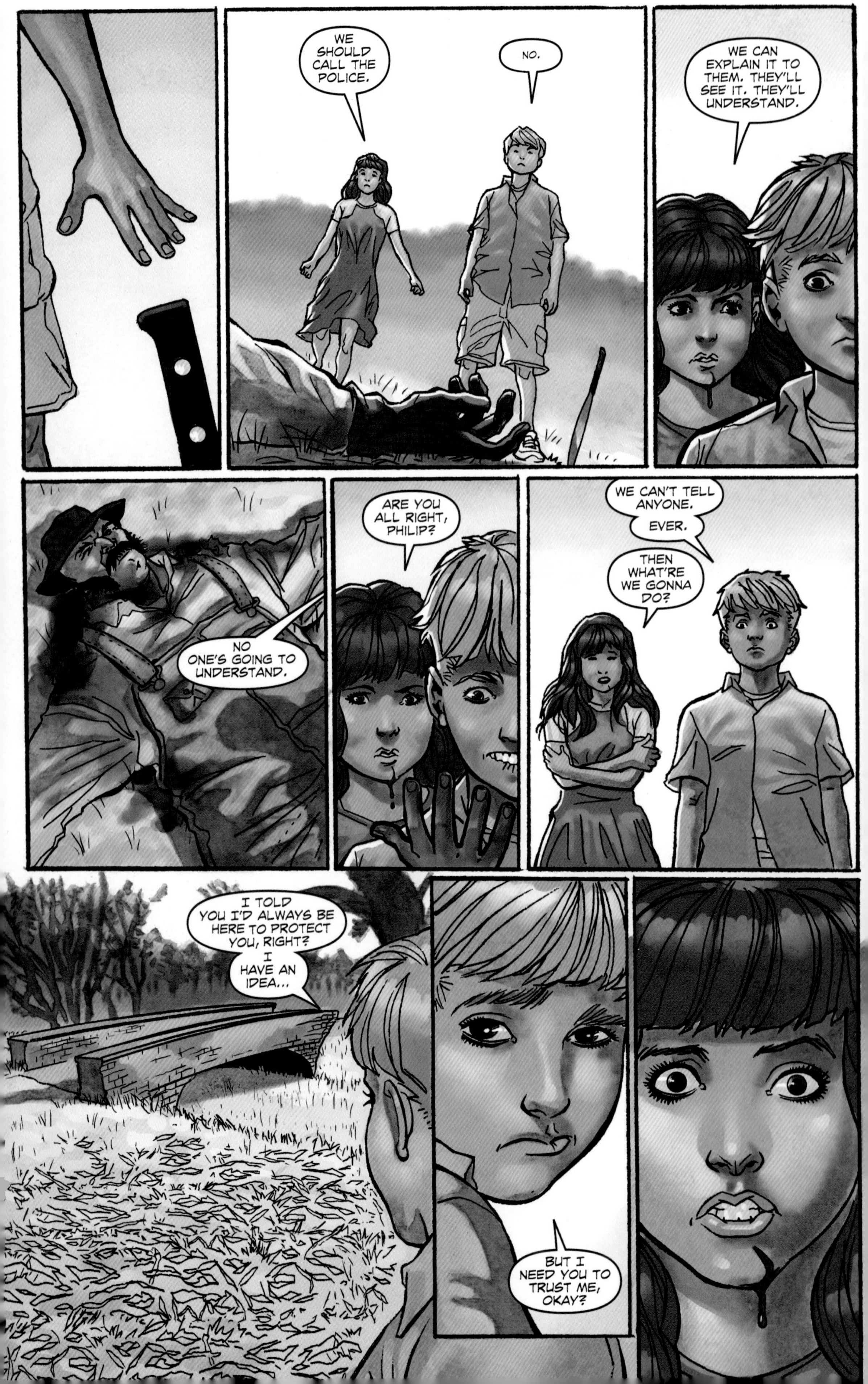
WE SHOULD CALL THE POLICE.
NO.
WE CAN EXPLAIN IT TO THEM. THEY'LL SEE IT. THEY'LL UNDERSTAND.
NO ONE'S GOING TO UNDERSTAND.
ARE YOU ALL RIGHT, PHILIP?
WE CAN'T TELL ANYONE.
EVER.
THEN WHAT'RE WE GONNA DO?
I TOLD YOU I'D ALWAYS BE HERE TO PROTECT YOU, RIGHT?
I HAVE AN IDEA...
BUT I NEED YOU TO TRUST ME, OKAY?

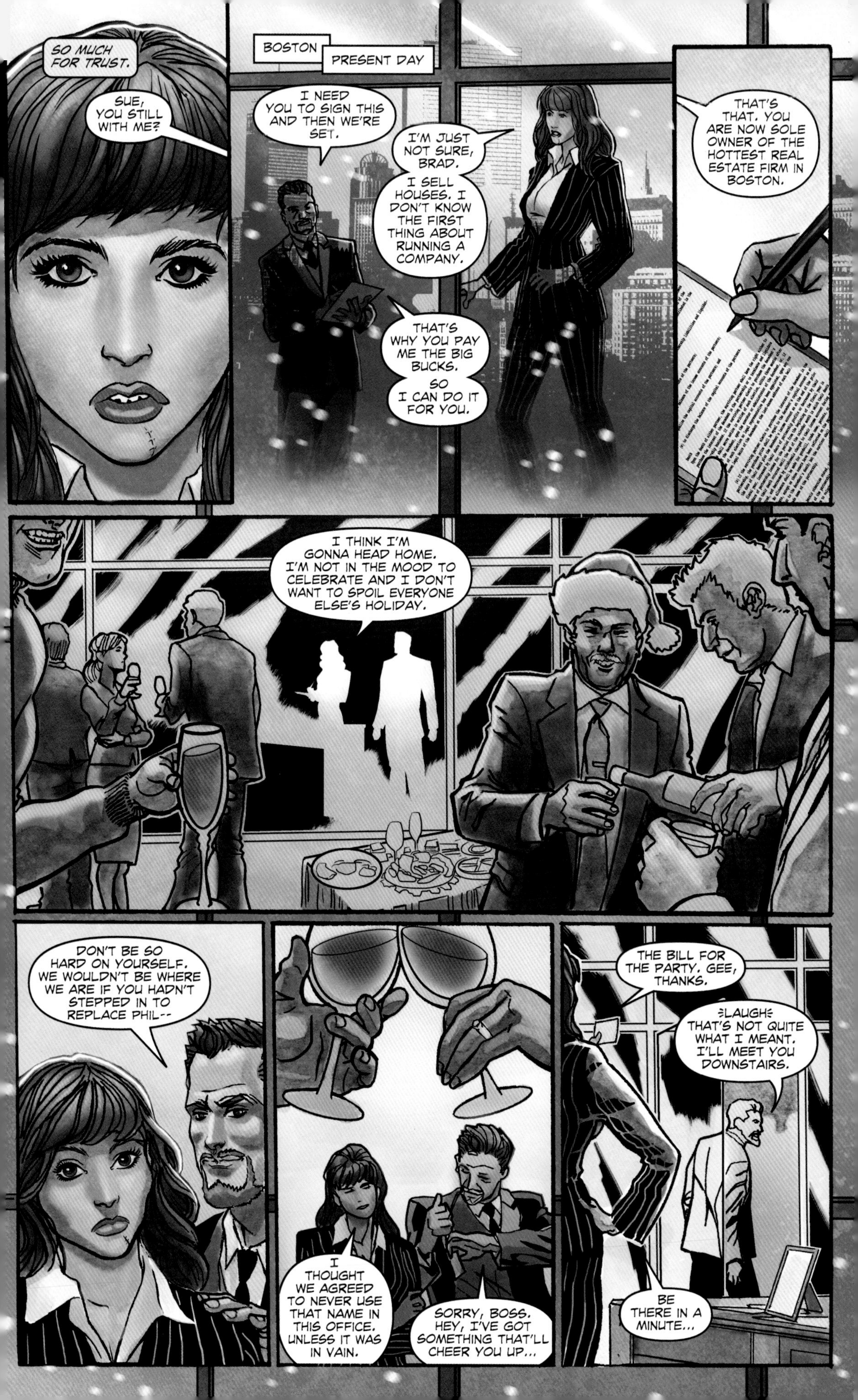
SO MUCH FOR TRUST.
SUE, YOU STILL WITH ME?
BOSTON
PRESENT DAY
I NEED YOU TO SIGN THIS AND THEN WE'RE SET.
I'M JUST NOT SURE, BRAD.
I SELL HOUSES. I DON'T KNOW THE FIRST THING ABOUT RUNNING A COMPANY.
THAT'S WHY YOU PAY ME THE BIG BUCKS.
SO I CAN DO IT FOR YOU.
THAT'S THAT. YOU ARE NOW SOLE OWNER OF THE HOTTEST REAL ESTATE FIRM IN BOSTON.
I THINK I'M GONNA HEAD HOME. I'M NOT IN THE MOOD TO CELEBRATE AND I DON'T WANT TO SPOIL EVERYONE ELSE'S HOLIDAY.
DON'T BE SO HARD ON YOURSELF. WE WOULDN'T BE WHERE WE ARE IF YOU HADN'T STEPPED IN TO REPLACE PHIL--
I THOUGHT WE AGREED TO NEVER USE THAT NAME IN THIS OFFICE. UNLESS IT WAS IN VAIN.
SORRY, BOSS. HEY, I'VE GOT SOMETHING THAT'LL CHEER YOU UP...
THE BILL FOR THE PARTY. GEE, THANKS.
=LAUGH= THAT'S NOT QUITE WHAT I MEANT. I'LL MEET YOU DOWNSTAIRS.
BE THERE IN A MINUTE...

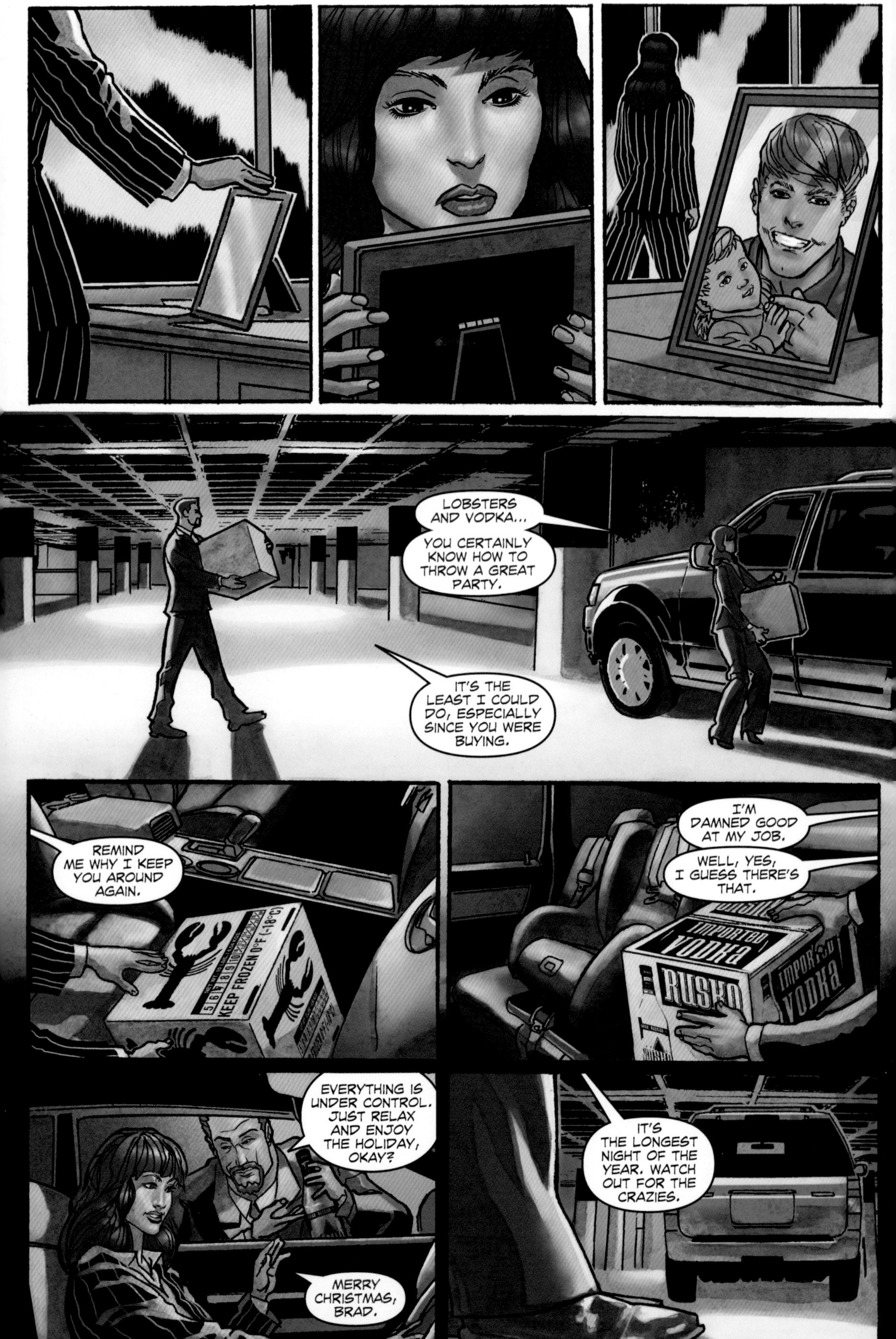
LOBSTERS AND VODKA...
YOU CERTAINLY KNOW HOW TO THROW A GREAT PARTY.
IT'S THE LEAST I COULD DO, ESPECIALLY SINCE YOU WERE BUYING.
REMIND ME WHY I KEEP YOU AROUND AGAIN.
KEEP FROZEN 0°F (-18°C)
I'M DAMNED GOOD AT MY JOB.
WELL, YES, I GUESS THERE'S THAT.
IMPORTED VODKA
RUSKO
EVERYTHING IS UNDER CONTROL. JUST RELAX AND ENJOY THE HOLIDAY, OKAY?
MERRY CHRISTMAS, BRAD.
IT'S THE LONGEST NIGHT OF THE YEAR. WATCH OUT FOR THE CRAZIES.

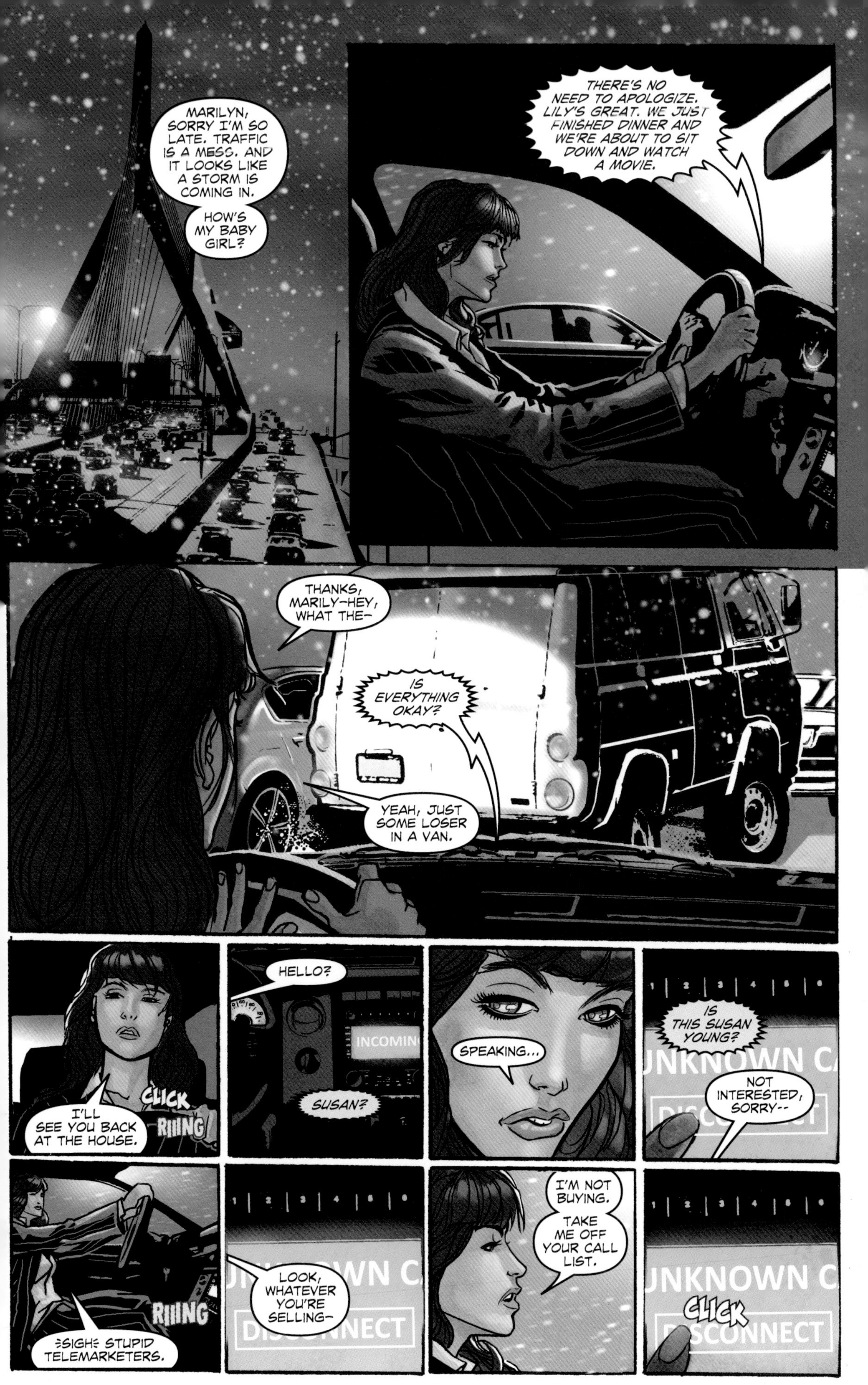
MARILYN, SORRY I'M SO LATE. TRAFFIC IS A MESS. AND IT LOOKS LIKE A STORM IS COMING IN.
HOW'S MY BABY GIRL?
THERE'S NO NEED TO APOLOGIZE. LILY'S GREAT. WE JUST FINISHED DINNER AND WE'RE ABOUT TO SIT DOWN AND WATCH A MOVIE.
THANKS, MARILY-HEY, WHAT THE-
IS EVERYTHING OKAY?
YEAH, JUST SOME LOSER IN A VAN.
I'LL SEE YOU BACK AT THE HOUSE.
CLICK
RIIING
HELLO?
INCOMING
SUSAN?
SPEAKING...
IS THIS SUSAN YOUNG?
UNKNOWN CA
NOT INTERESTED, SORRY--
RIIING
ƎSIGHƐ STUPID TELEMARKETERS.
LOOK, WHATEVER YOU'RE SELLING-
DISCONNECT
I'M NOT BUYING.
TAKE ME OFF YOUR CALL LIST.
UNKNOWN CA
CLICK
DISCONNECT

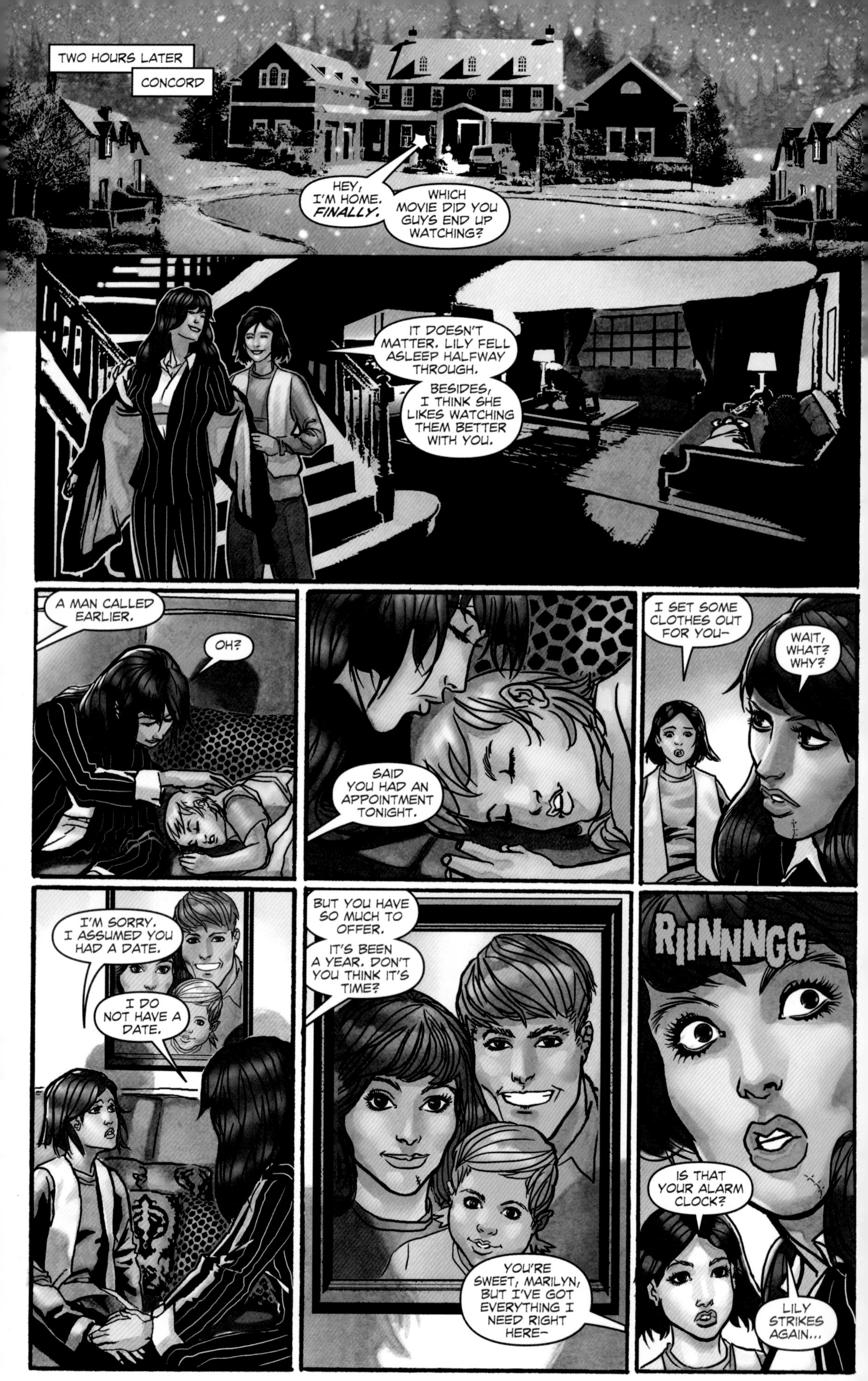
TWO HOURS LATER
CONCORD
HEY, I'M HOME. *FINALLY.*
WHICH MOVIE DID YOU GUYS END UP WATCHING?
IT DOESN'T MATTER. LILY FELL ASLEEP HALFWAY THROUGH.
BESIDES, I THINK SHE LIKES WATCHING THEM BETTER WITH YOU.
A MAN CALLED EARLIER.
OH?
SAID YOU HAD AN APPOINTMENT TONIGHT.
I SET SOME CLOTHES OUT FOR YOU-
WAIT, WHAT? WHY?
I'M SORRY. I ASSUMED YOU HAD A DATE.
I DO NOT HAVE A DATE.
BUT YOU HAVE SO MUCH TO OFFER.
IT'S BEEN A YEAR. DON'T YOU THINK IT'S TIME?
YOU'RE SWEET, MARILYN, BUT I'VE GOT EVERYTHING I NEED RIGHT HERE-
RIINNNGG
IS THAT YOUR ALARM CLOCK?
LILY STRIKES AGAIN...

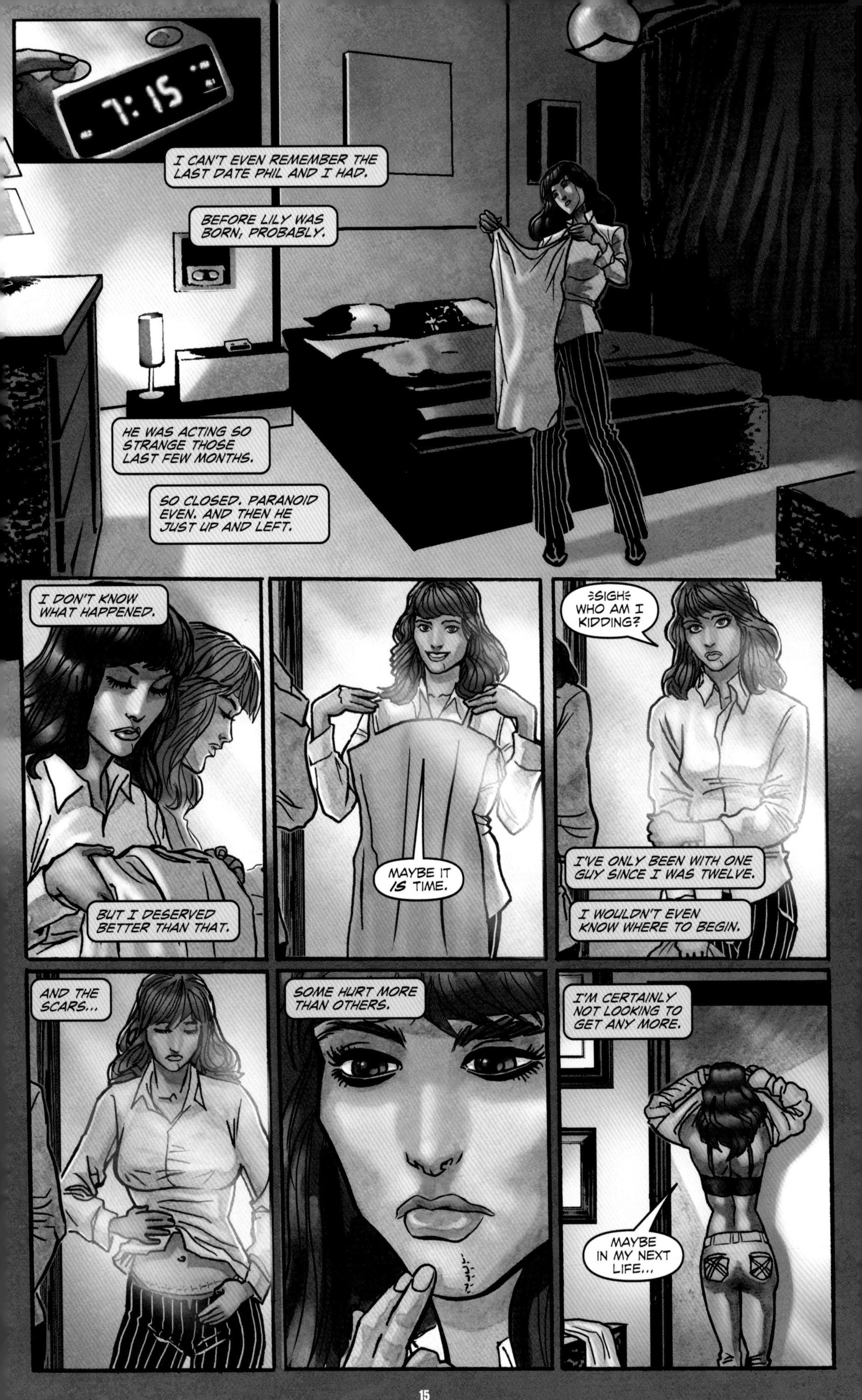
7:15
I CAN'T EVEN REMEMBER THE LAST DATE PHIL AND I HAD.
BEFORE LILY WAS BORN, PROBABLY.
HE WAS ACTING SO STRANGE THOSE LAST FEW MONTHS.
SO CLOSED. PARANOID EVEN. AND THEN HE JUST UP AND LEFT.
I DON'T KNOW WHAT HAPPENED.
BUT I DESERVED BETTER THAN THAT.
MAYBE IT *IS* TIME.
=SIGH= WHO AM I KIDDING?
I'VE ONLY BEEN WITH ONE GUY SINCE I WAS TWELVE.
I WOULDN'T EVEN KNOW WHERE TO BEGIN.
AND THE SCARS...
SOME HURT MORE THAN OTHERS.
I'M CERTAINLY NOT LOOKING TO GET ANY MORE.
MAYBE IN MY NEXT LIFE...

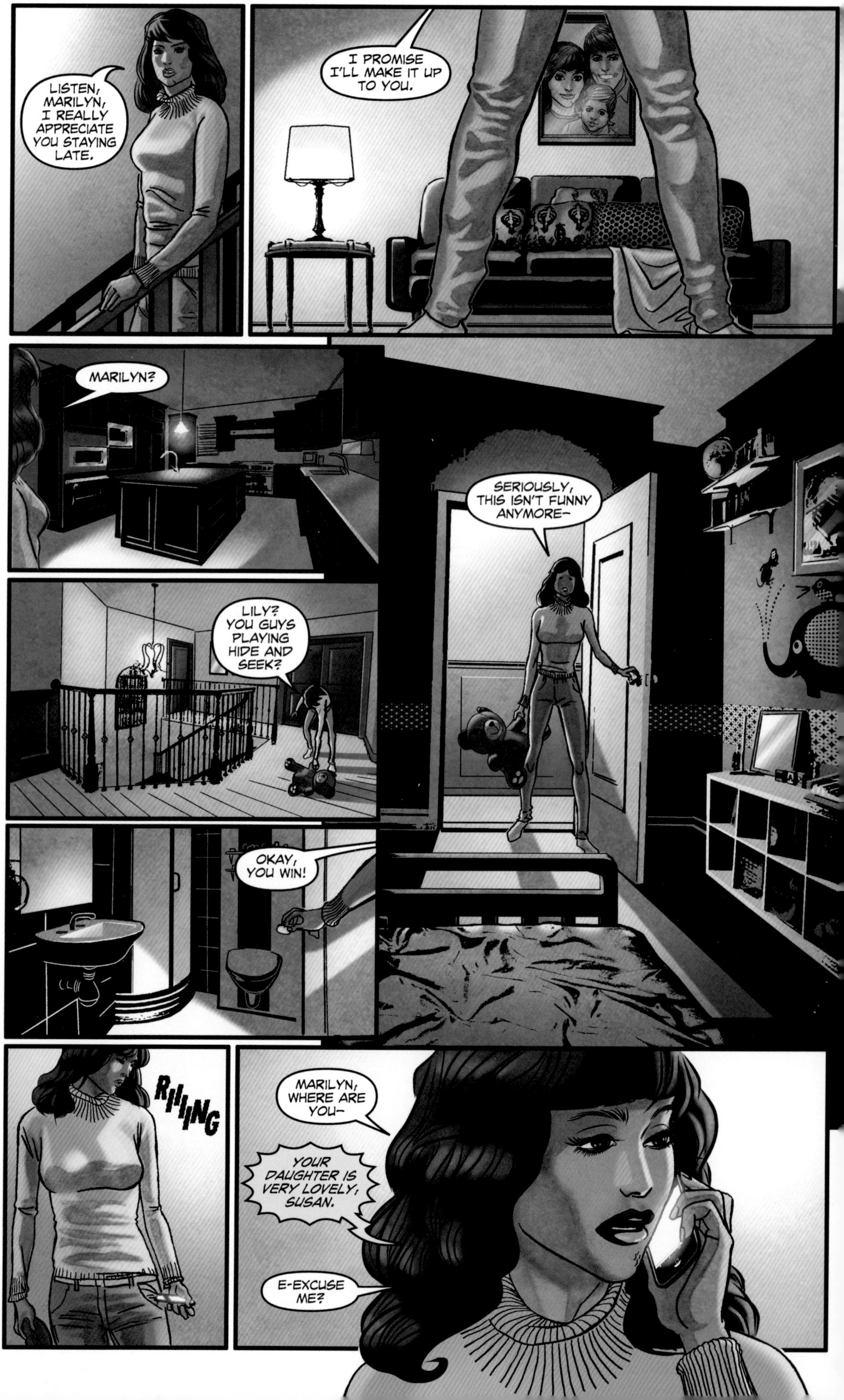

LISTEN, MARILYN, I REALLY APPRECIATE YOU STAYING LATE.
I PROMISE I'LL MAKE IT UP TO YOU.
MARILYN?
LILY? YOU GUYS PLAYING HIDE AND SEEK?
OKAY, YOU WIN!
SERIOUSLY, THIS ISN'T FUNNY ANYMORE-
RIIING
MARILYN, WHERE ARE YOU-
YOUR DAUGHTER IS VERY LOVELY, SUSAN.
E-EXCUSE ME?

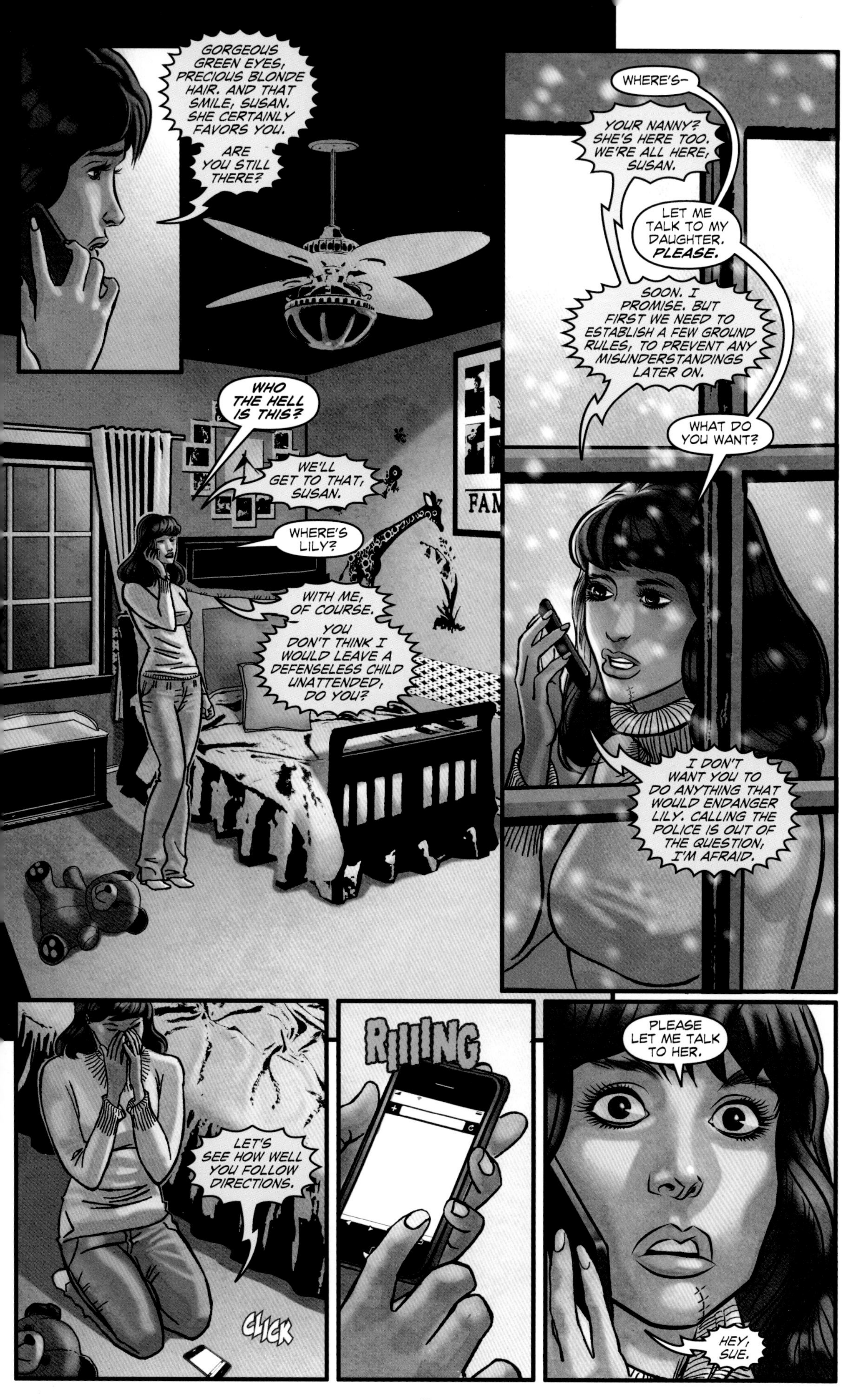
GORGEOUS GREEN EYES, PRECIOUS BLONDE HAIR. AND THAT SMILE, SUSAN. SHE CERTAINLY FAVORS YOU.
ARE YOU STILL THERE?
WHO THE HELL IS THIS?
WE'LL GET TO THAT, SUSAN.
WHERE'S LILY?
WITH ME, OF COURSE.
YOU DON'T THINK I WOULD LEAVE A DEFENSELESS CHILD UNATTENDED, DO YOU?
FAM
WHERE'S—
YOUR NANNY? SHE'S HERE TOO. WE'RE ALL HERE, SUSAN.
LET ME TALK TO MY DAUGHTER. PLEASE.
SOON. I PROMISE. BUT FIRST WE NEED TO ESTABLISH A FEW GROUND RULES, TO PREVENT ANY MISUNDERSTANDINGS LATER ON.
WHAT DO YOU WANT?
I DON'T WANT YOU TO DO ANYTHING THAT WOULD ENDANGER LILY. CALLING THE POLICE IS OUT OF THE QUESTION, I'M AFRAID.
LET'S SEE HOW WELL YOU FOLLOW DIRECTIONS.
CLICK
RIIIING
PLEASE LET ME TALK TO HER.
HEY, SUE.

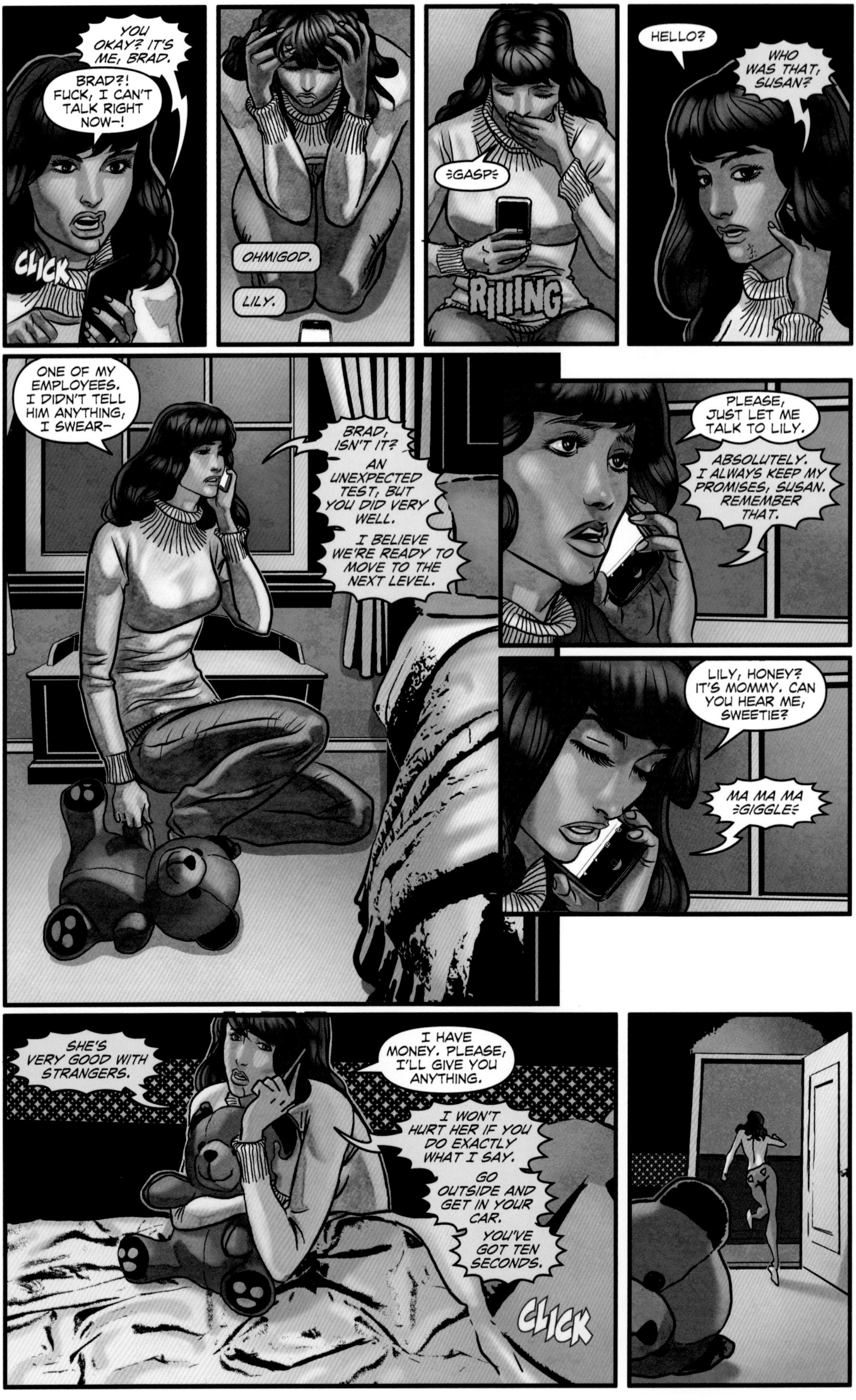

YOU OKAY? IT'S ME, BRAD.
BRAD?! FUCK, I CAN'T TALK RIGHT NOW-!
CLICK
OHMIGOD.
LILY.
GASP
RIIIING
HELLO?
WHO WAS THAT, SUSAN?
ONE OF MY EMPLOYEES. I DIDN'T TELL HIM ANYTHING, I SWEAR-
BRAD, ISN'T IT?
AN UNEXPECTED TEST, BUT YOU DID VERY WELL.
I BELIEVE WE'RE READY TO MOVE TO THE NEXT LEVEL.
PLEASE, JUST LET ME TALK TO LILY.
ABSOLUTELY. I ALWAYS KEEP MY PROMISES, SUSAN. REMEMBER THAT.
LILY, HONEY? IT'S MOMMY. CAN YOU HEAR ME, SWEETIE?
MA MA MA GIGGLE
SHE'S VERY GOOD WITH STRANGERS.
I HAVE MONEY. PLEASE, I'LL GIVE YOU ANYTHING.
I WON'T HURT HER IF YOU DO EXACTLY WHAT I SAY.
GO OUTSIDE AND GET IN YOUR CAR.
YOU'VE GOT TEN SECONDS.
CLICK

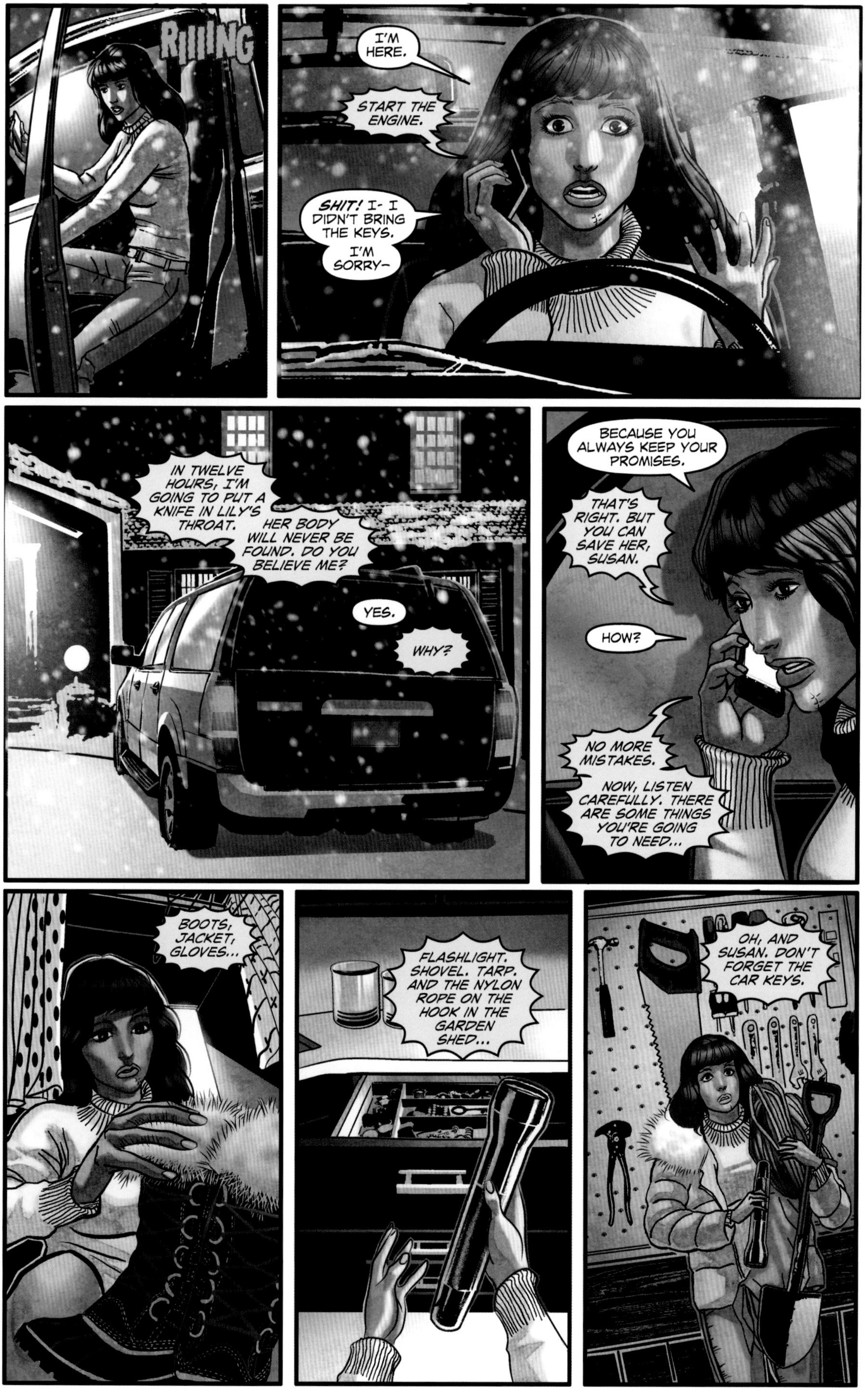
RIIIING
I'M HERE.
START THE ENGINE.
SHIT! I- I DIDN'T BRING THE KEYS.
I'M SORRY-
IN TWELVE HOURS, I'M GOING TO PUT A KNIFE IN LILY'S THROAT.
HER BODY WILL NEVER BE FOUND. DO YOU BELIEVE ME?
YES.
WHY?
BECAUSE YOU ALWAYS KEEP YOUR PROMISES.
THAT'S RIGHT. BUT YOU CAN SAVE HER, SUSAN.
HOW?
NO MORE MISTAKES.
NOW, LISTEN CAREFULLY. THERE ARE SOME THINGS YOU'RE GOING TO NEED...
BOOTS, JACKET, GLOVES...
FLASHLIGHT. SHOVEL. TARP. AND THE NYLON ROPE ON THE HOOK IN THE GARDEN SHED...
OH, AND SUSAN. DON'T FORGET THE CAR KEYS.

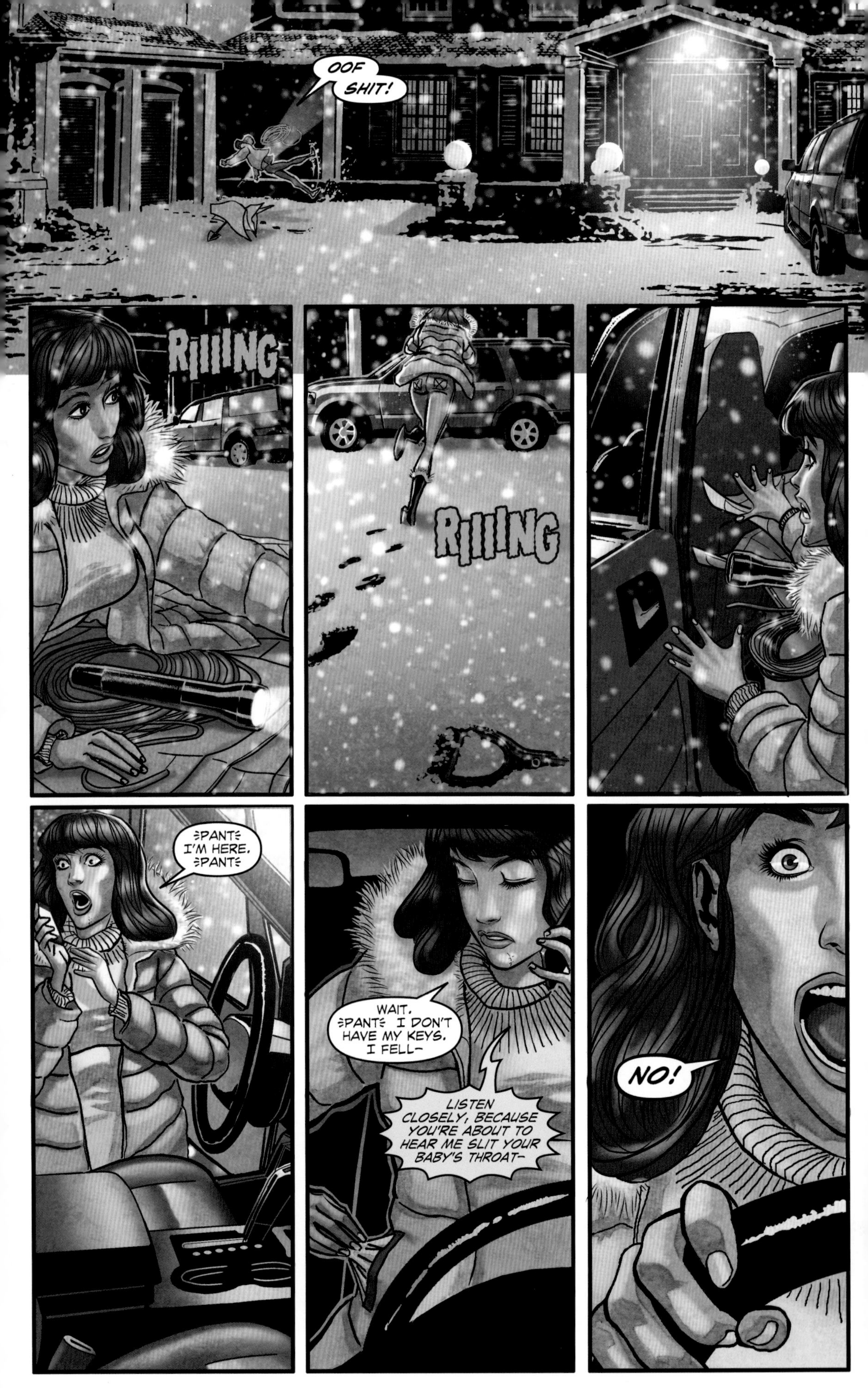
OOF SHIT!
RIIIING
RIIIING
PANT I'M HERE. PANT
WAIT. PANT I DON'T HAVE MY KEYS. I FELL-
LISTEN CLOSELY, BECAUSE YOU'RE ABOUT TO HEAR ME SLIT YOUR BABY'S THROAT-
NO!

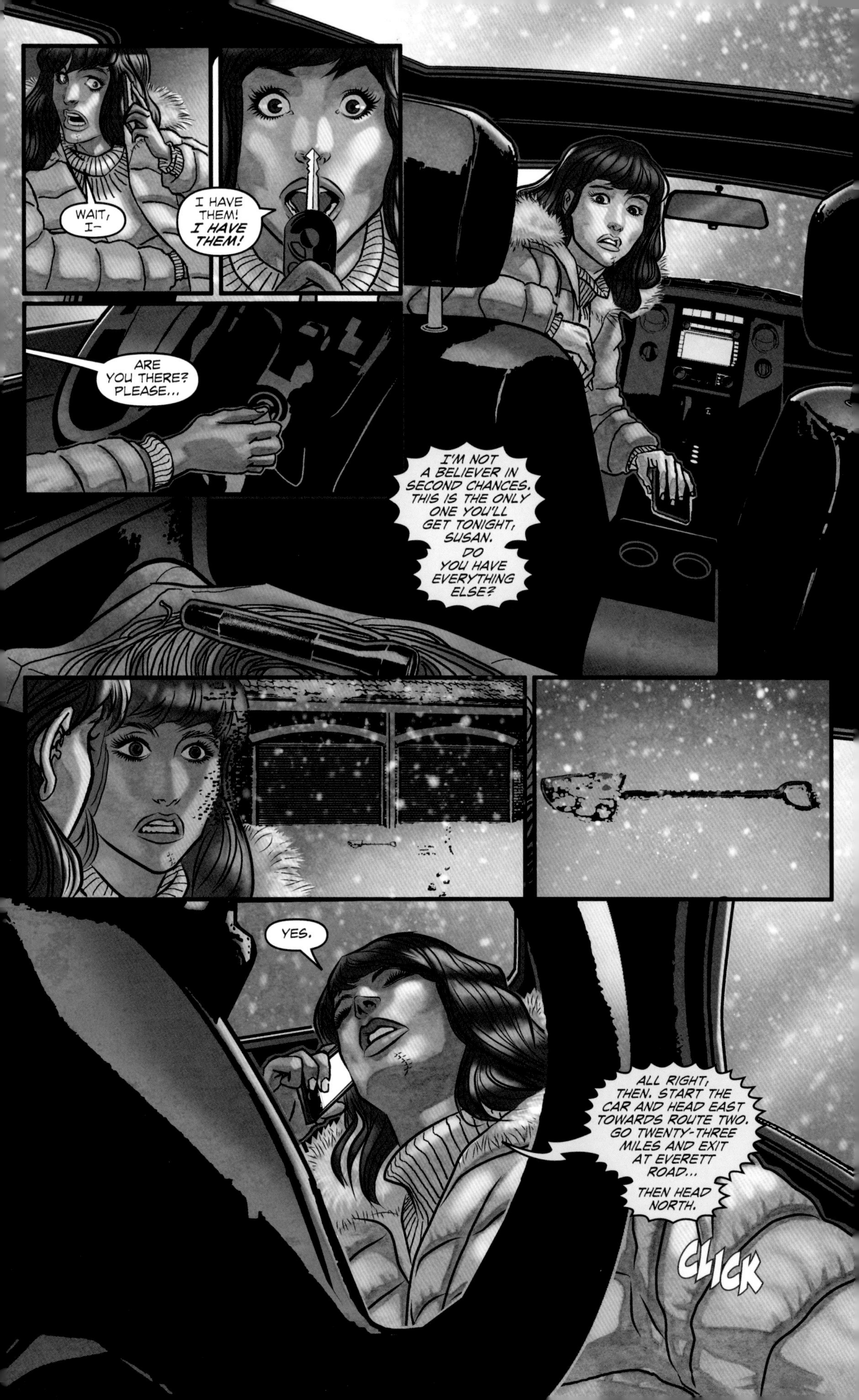
WAIT, I–
I HAVE THEM! I HAVE THEM!
ARE YOU THERE? PLEASE...
I'M NOT A BELIEVER IN SECOND CHANCES. THIS IS THE ONLY ONE YOU'LL GET TONIGHT, SUSAN.
DO YOU HAVE EVERYTHING ELSE?
YES.
ALL RIGHT, THEN. START THE CAR AND HEAD EAST TOWARDS ROUTE TWO. GO TWENTY-THREE MILES AND EXIT AT EVERETT ROAD...
THEN HEAD NORTH.
CLICK

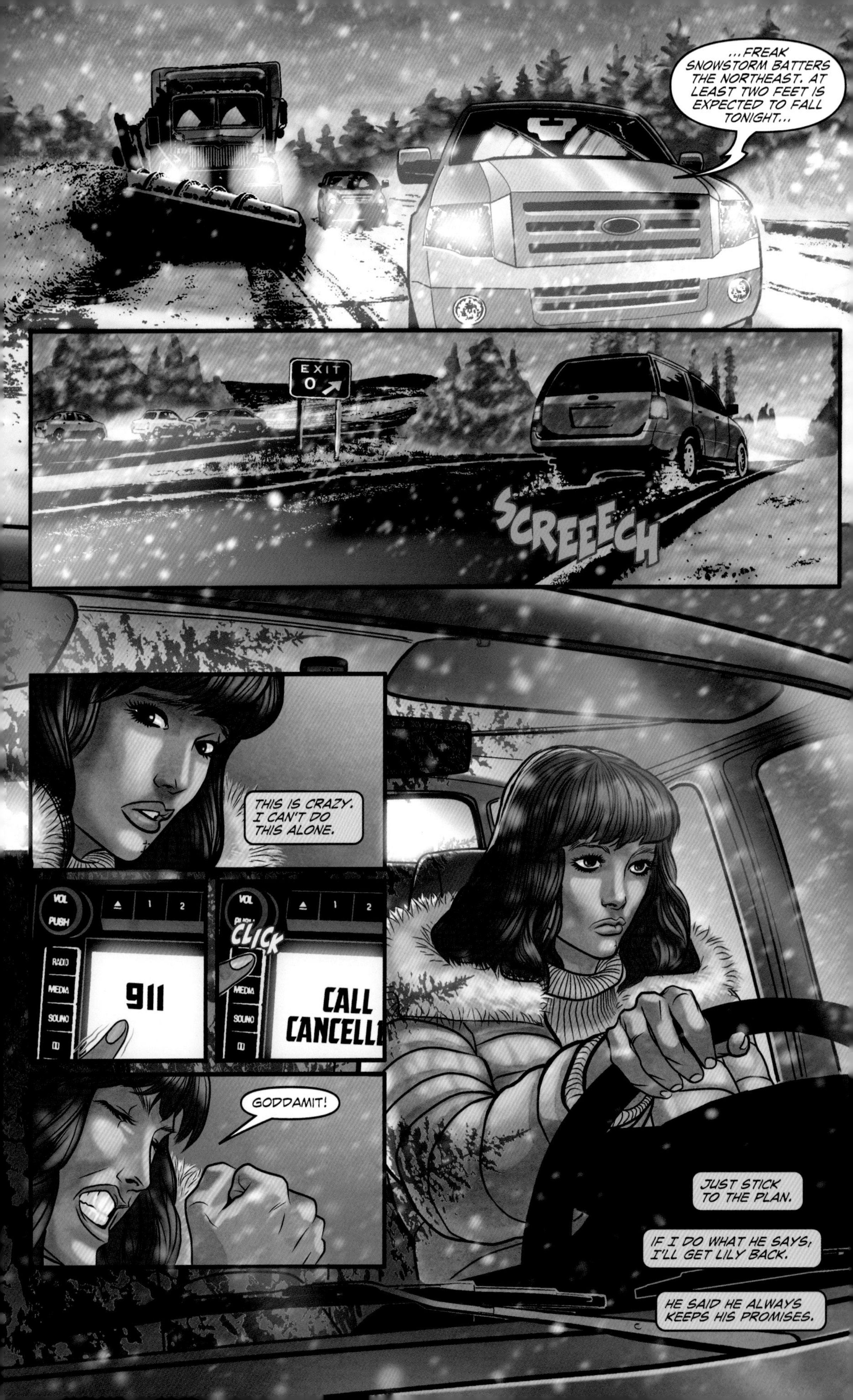
...FREAK SNOWSTORM BATTERS THE NORTHEAST. AT LEAST TWO FEET IS EXPECTED TO FALL TONIGHT...
EXIT
0
SCREEECH
THIS IS CRAZY. I CAN'T DO THIS ALONE.
VOL
PUSH
1
2
RADIO
MEDIA
SOUND
911
CLICK
CALL
CANCELL
GODDAMIT!
JUST STICK TO THE PLAN.
IF I DO WHAT HE SAYS, I'LL GET LILY BACK.
HE SAID HE ALWAYS KEEPS HIS PROMISES.

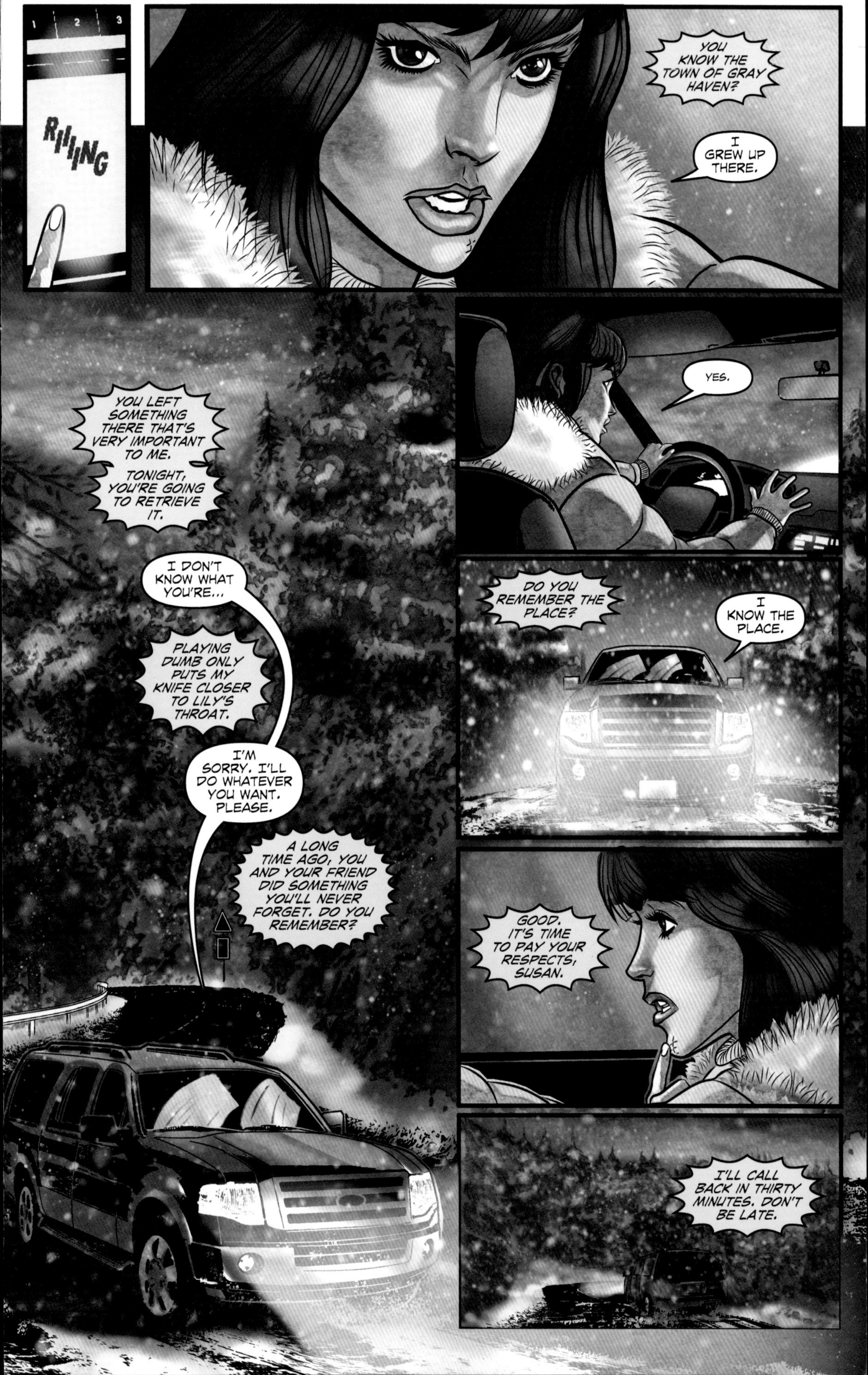
1 2 3
RIIING
YOU KNOW THE TOWN OF GRAY HAVEN?
I GREW UP THERE.
YES.
YOU LEFT SOMETHING THERE THAT'S VERY IMPORTANT TO ME.
TONIGHT, YOU'RE GOING TO RETRIEVE IT.
I DON'T KNOW WHAT YOU'RE...
PLAYING DUMB ONLY PUTS MY KNIFE CLOSER TO LILY'S THROAT.
I'M SORRY. I'LL DO WHATEVER YOU WANT. PLEASE.
A LONG TIME AGO, YOU AND YOUR FRIEND DID SOMETHING YOU'LL NEVER FORGET. DO YOU REMEMBER?
DO YOU REMEMBER THE PLACE?
I KNOW THE PLACE.
GOOD. IT'S TIME TO PAY YOUR RESPECTS, SUSAN.
I'LL CALL BACK IN THIRTY MINUTES. DON'T BE LATE.

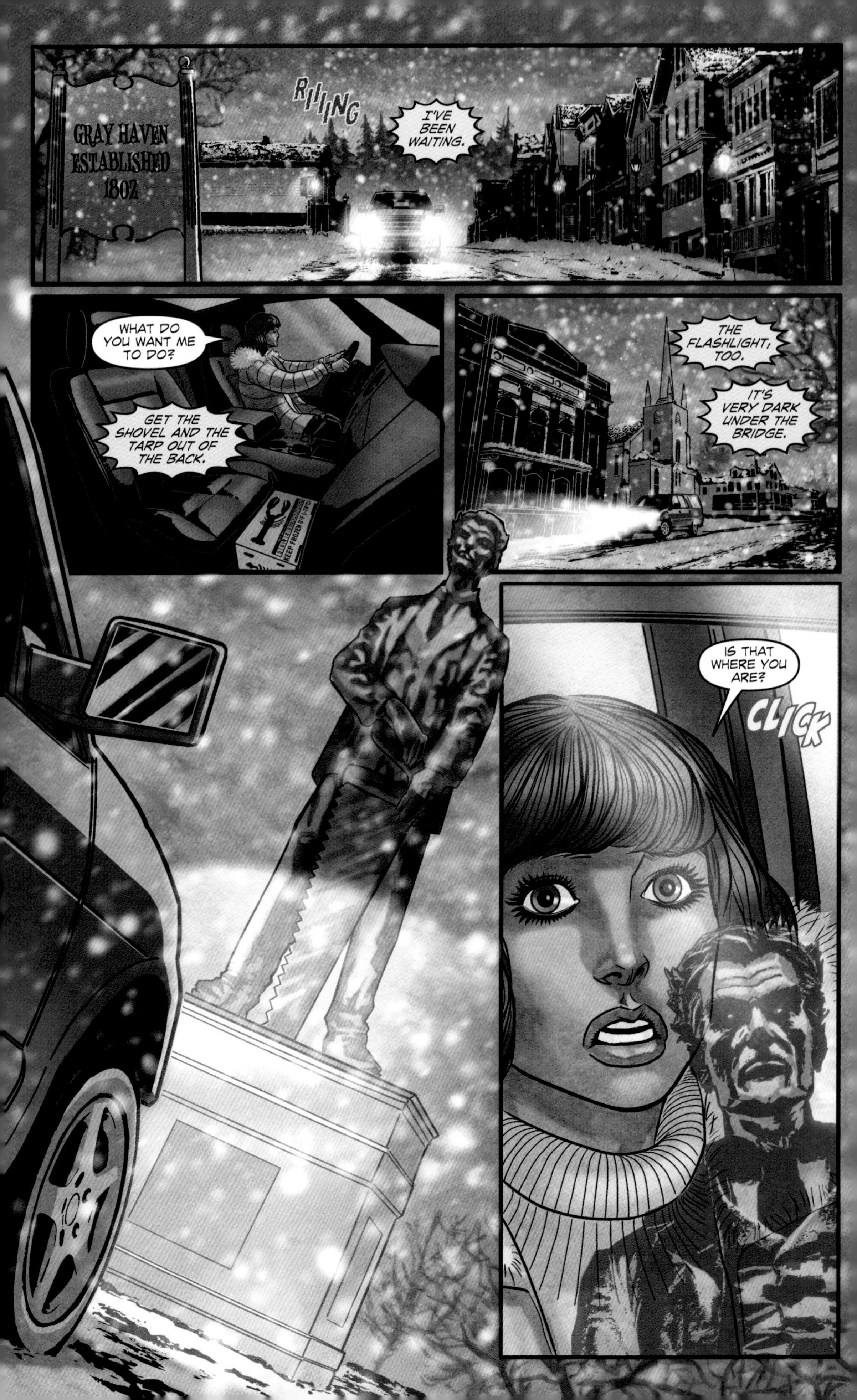
GRAY HAVEN
ESTABLISHED
1802
RIIIING
I'VE BEEN WAITING.
WHAT DO YOU WANT ME TO DO?
GET THE SHOVEL AND THE TARP OUT OF THE BACK.
KEEP FROZEN
THE FLASHLIGHT, TOO.
IT'S VERY DARK UNDER THE BRIDGE.
IS THAT WHERE YOU ARE?
CLICK

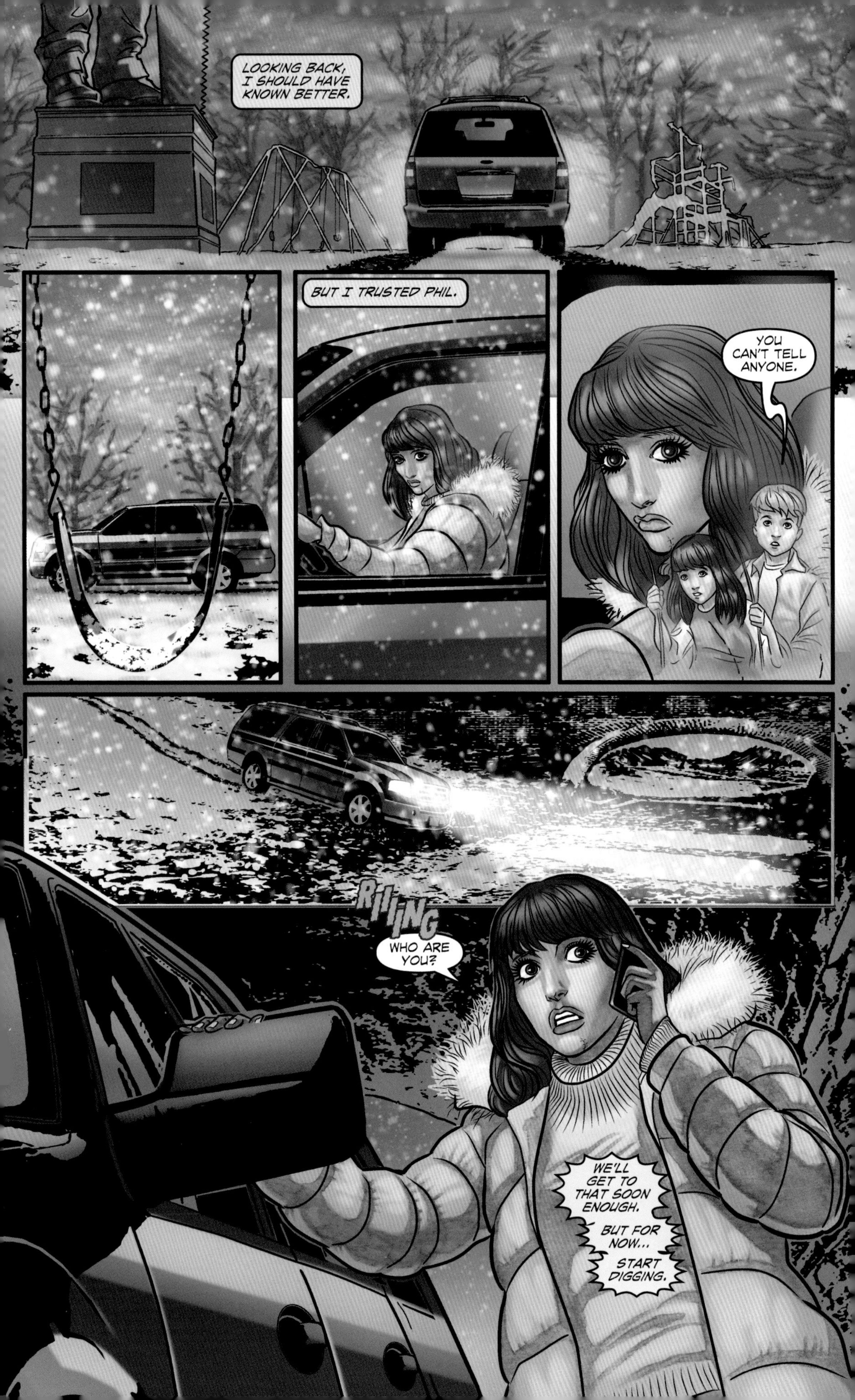

LOOKING BACK, I SHOULD HAVE KNOWN BETTER.
BUT I TRUSTED PHIL.
YOU CAN'T TELL ANYONE.
RIIIING
WHO ARE YOU?
WE'LL GET TO THAT SOON ENOUGH.
BUT FOR NOW...
START DIGGING.

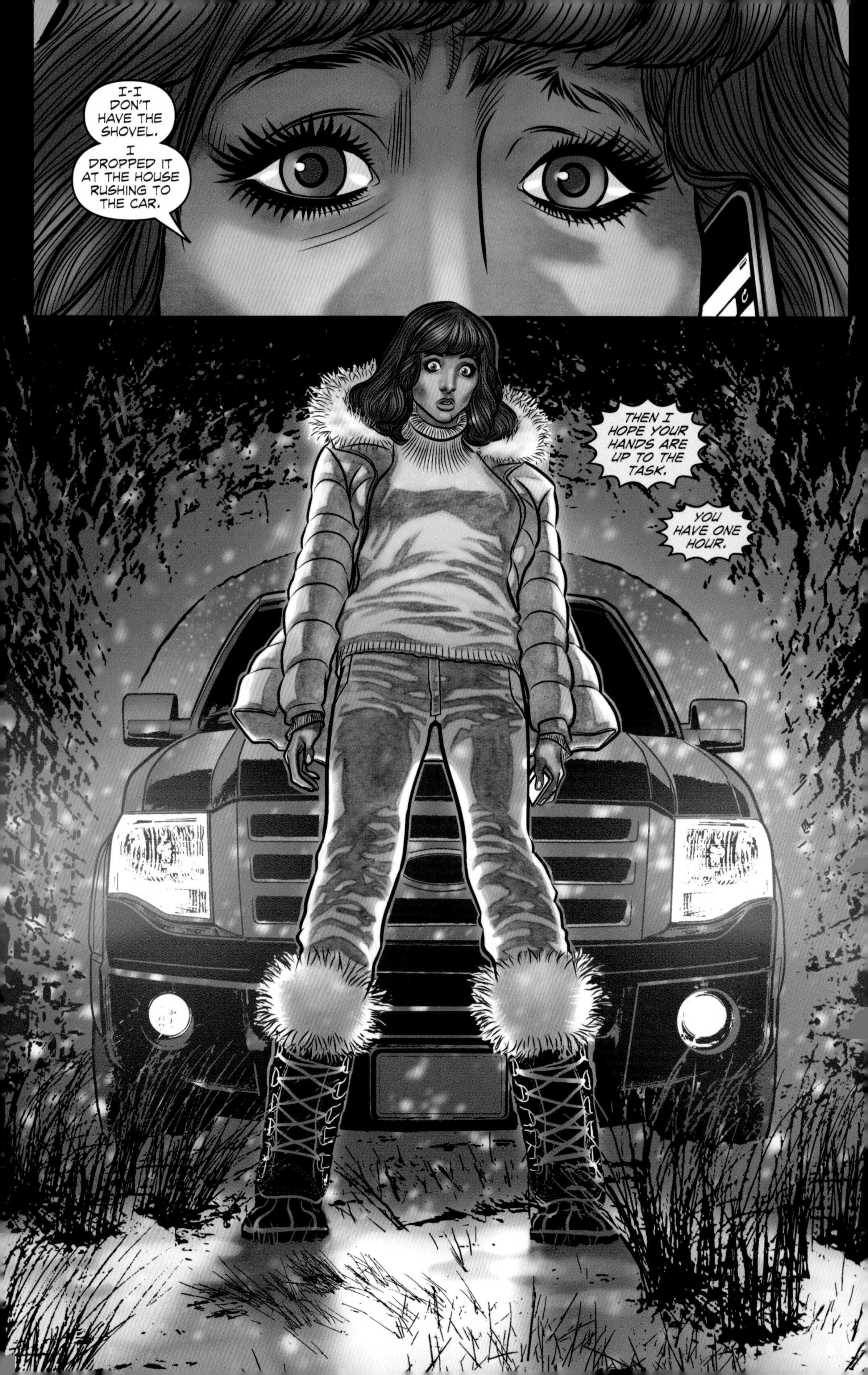
I-I DON'T HAVE THE SHOVEL.
I DROPPED IT AT THE HOUSE RUSHING TO THE CAR.
THEN I HOPE YOUR HANDS ARE UP TO THE TASK.
YOU HAVE ONE HOUR.

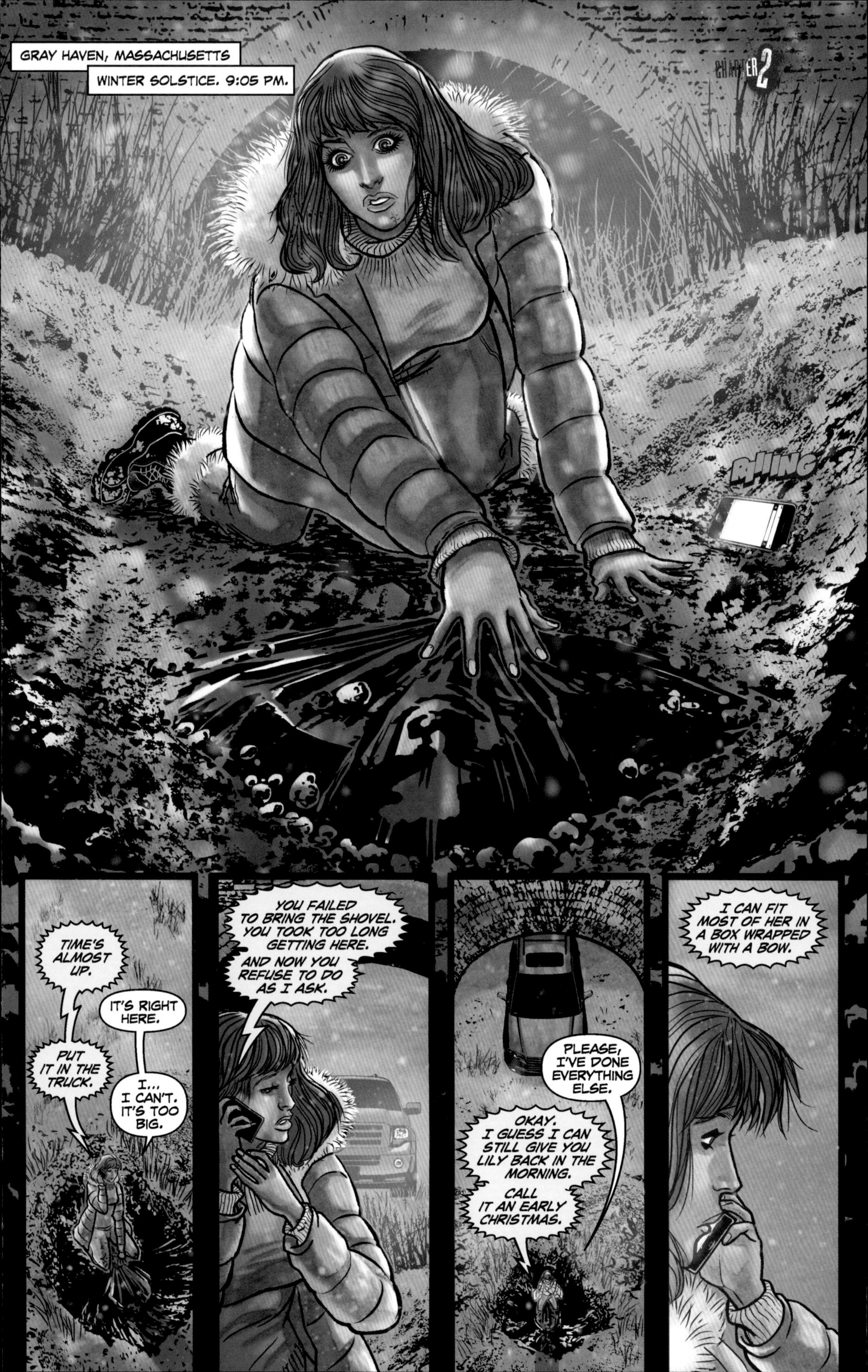
GRAY HAVEN, MASSACHUSETTS
WINTER SOLSTICE. 9:05 PM.
CHAPTER 2
RIIING
TIME'S ALMOST UP.
IT'S RIGHT HERE.
PUT IT IN THE TRUCK.
I... I CAN'T. IT'S TOO BIG.
YOU FAILED TO BRING THE SHOVEL. YOU TOOK TOO LONG GETTING HERE.
AND NOW YOU REFUSE TO DO AS I ASK.
PLEASE, I'VE DONE EVERYTHING ELSE.
OKAY. I GUESS I CAN STILL GIVE YOU LILY BACK IN THE MORNING.
CALL IT AN EARLY CHRISTMAS.
I CAN FIT MOST OF HER IN A BOX WRAPPED WITH A BOW.

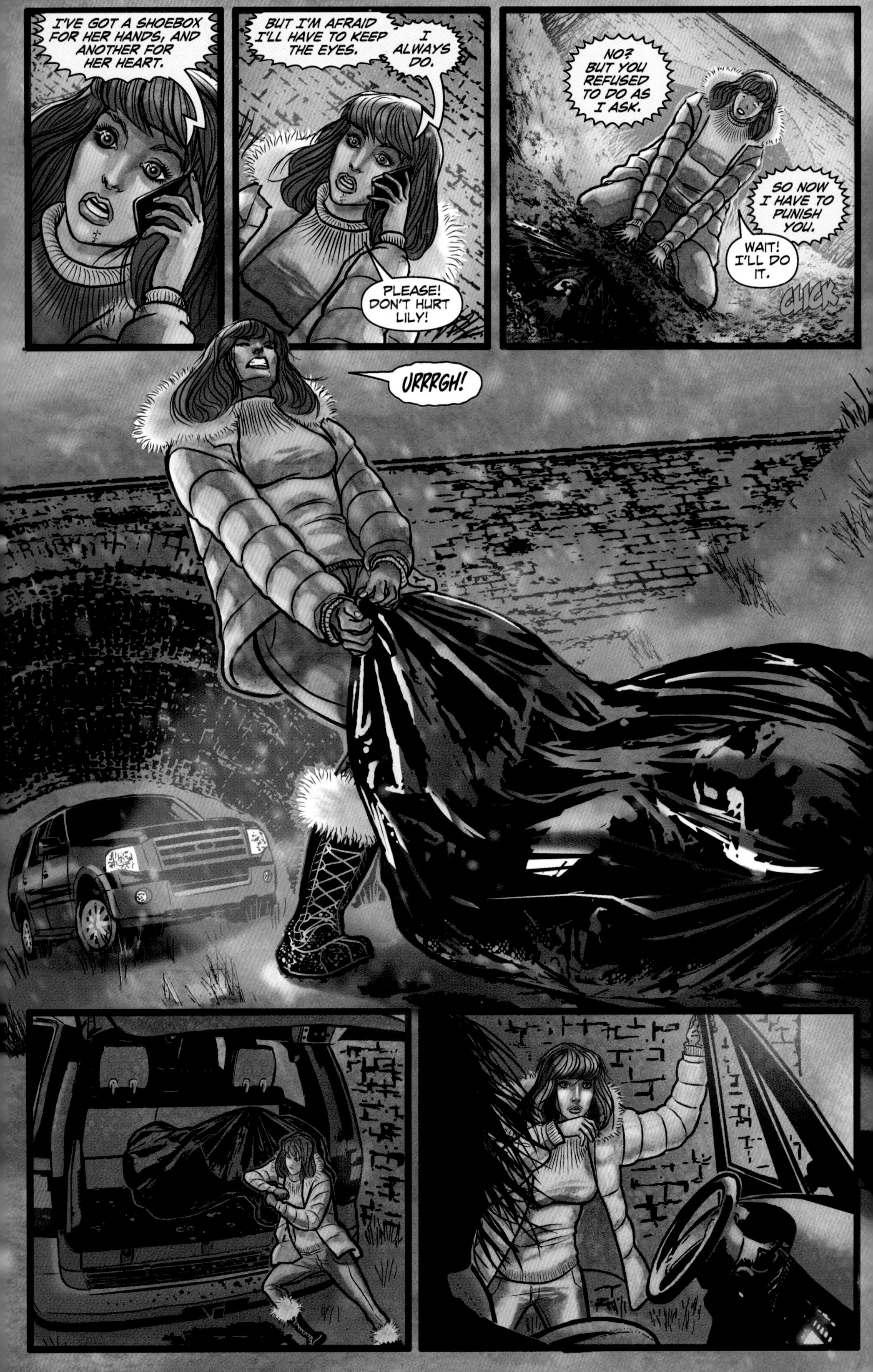
I'VE GOT A SHOEBOX FOR HER HANDS, AND ANOTHER FOR HER HEART.
BUT I'M AFRAID I'LL HAVE TO KEEP THE EYES.
I ALWAYS DO.
PLEASE! DON'T HURT LILY!
NO? BUT YOU REFUSED TO DO AS I ASK.
SO NOW I HAVE TO PUNISH YOU.
WAIT! I'LL DO IT.
CLICK
URRRGH!

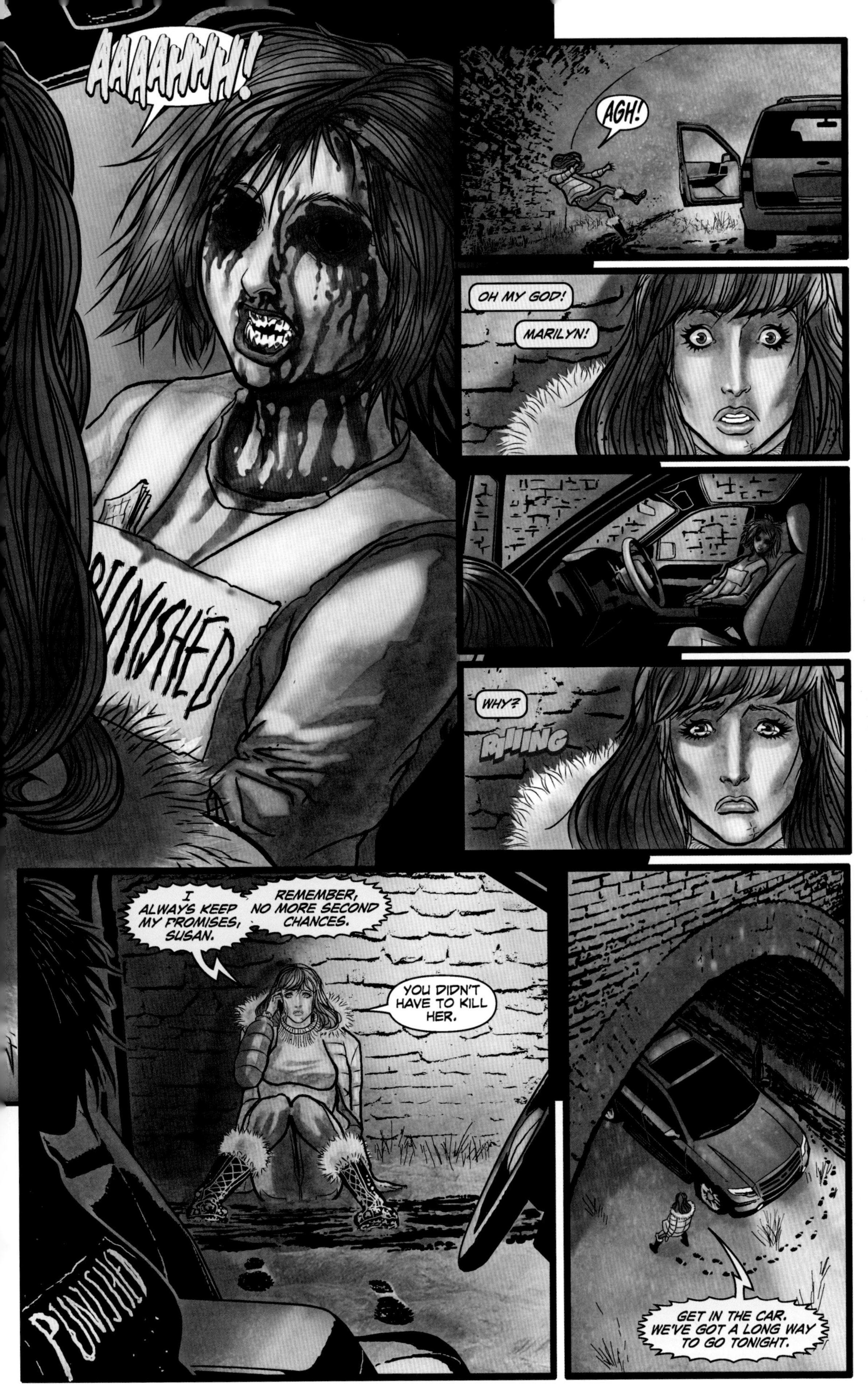
AAAAHHH!
PUNISHED
AGH!
OH MY GOD!
MARILYN!
WHY?
RIIIING
PUNISHED
I ALWAYS KEEP MY PROMISES, SUSAN.
REMEMBER, NO MORE SECOND CHANCES.
YOU DIDN'T HAVE TO KILL HER.
GET IN THE CAR. WE'VE GOT A LONG WAY TO GO TONIGHT.

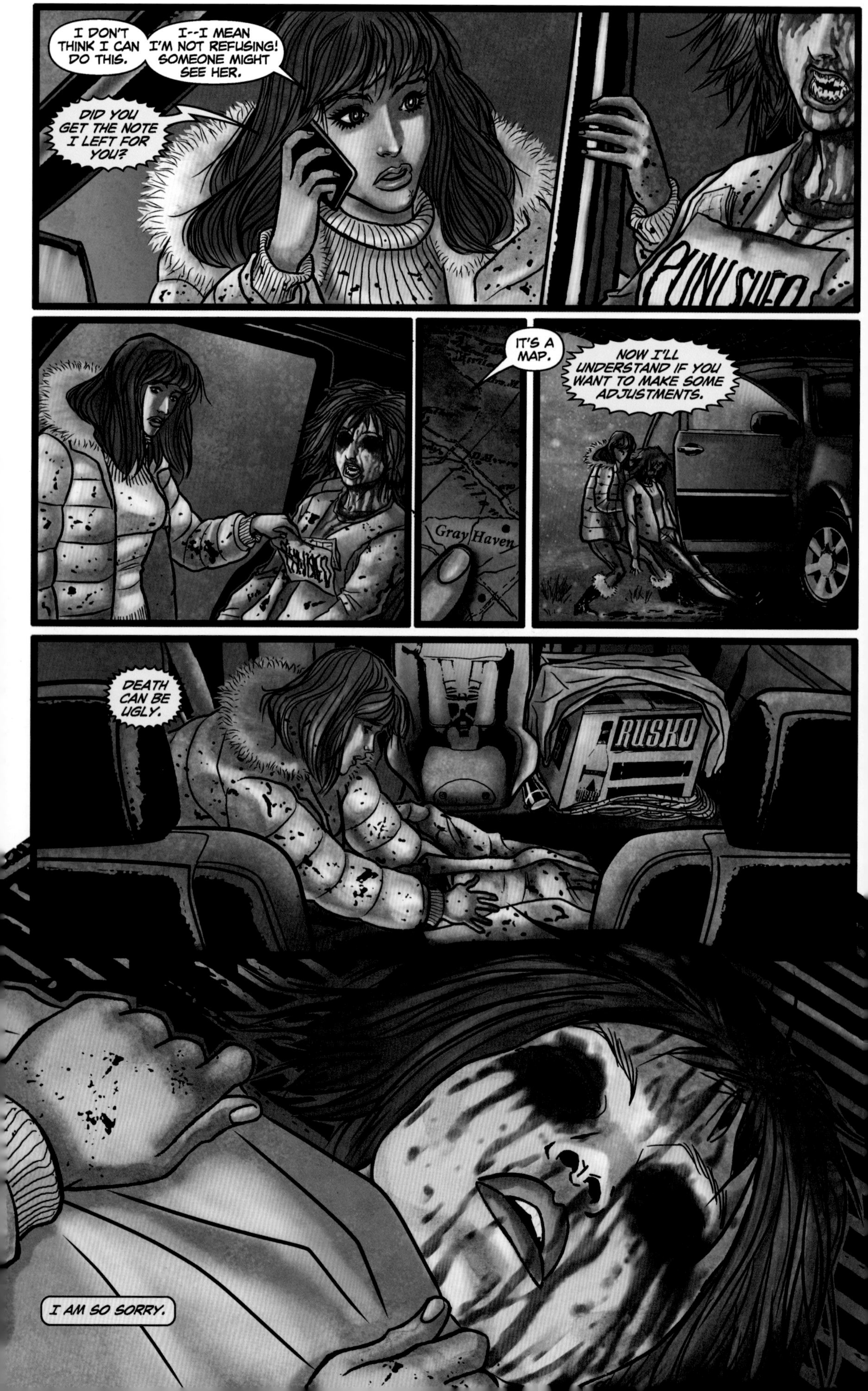
I DON'T THINK I CAN DO THIS.
I--I MEAN I'M NOT REFUSING! SOMEONE MIGHT SEE HER.
DID YOU GET THE NOTE I LEFT FOR YOU?
IT'S A MAP.
Gray Haven
NOW I'LL UNDERSTAND IF YOU WANT TO MAKE SOME ADJUSTMENTS.
DEATH CAN BE UGLY.
RUSKO
I AM SO SORRY.

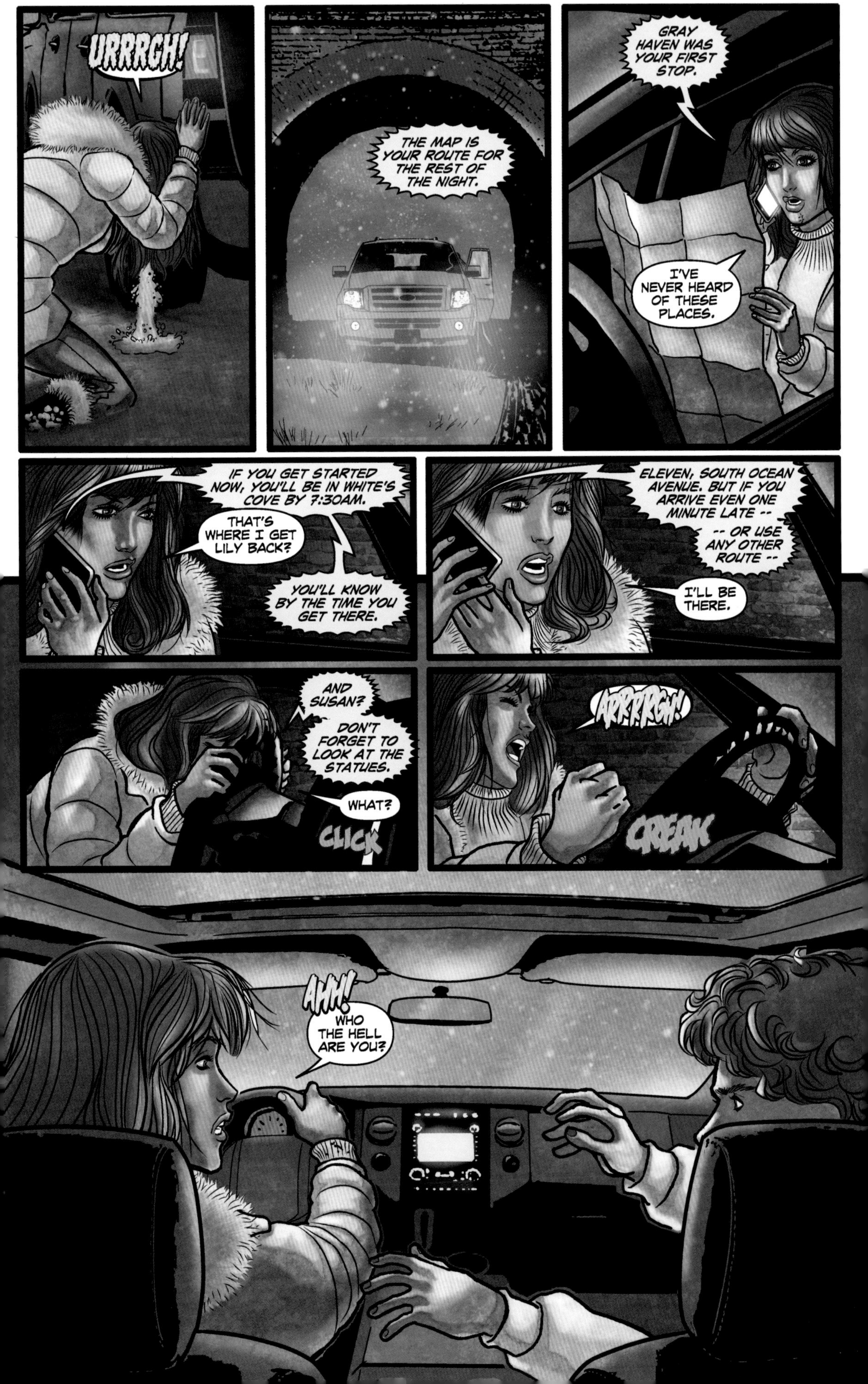
URRRGH!
THE MAP IS YOUR ROUTE FOR THE REST OF THE NIGHT.
GRAY HAVEN WAS YOUR FIRST STOP.
I'VE NEVER HEARD OF THESE PLACES.
IF YOU GET STARTED NOW, YOU'LL BE IN WHITE'S COVE BY 7:30AM.
THAT'S WHERE I GET LILY BACK?
YOU'LL KNOW BY THE TIME YOU GET THERE.
ELEVEN, SOUTH OCEAN AVENUE. BUT IF YOU ARRIVE EVEN ONE MINUTE LATE --
-- OR USE ANY OTHER ROUTE --
I'LL BE THERE.
AND SUSAN?
DON'T FORGET TO LOOK AT THE STATUES.
WHAT?
CLICK
ARRRRGH!
CREAK
AHH!
WHO THE HELL ARE YOU?

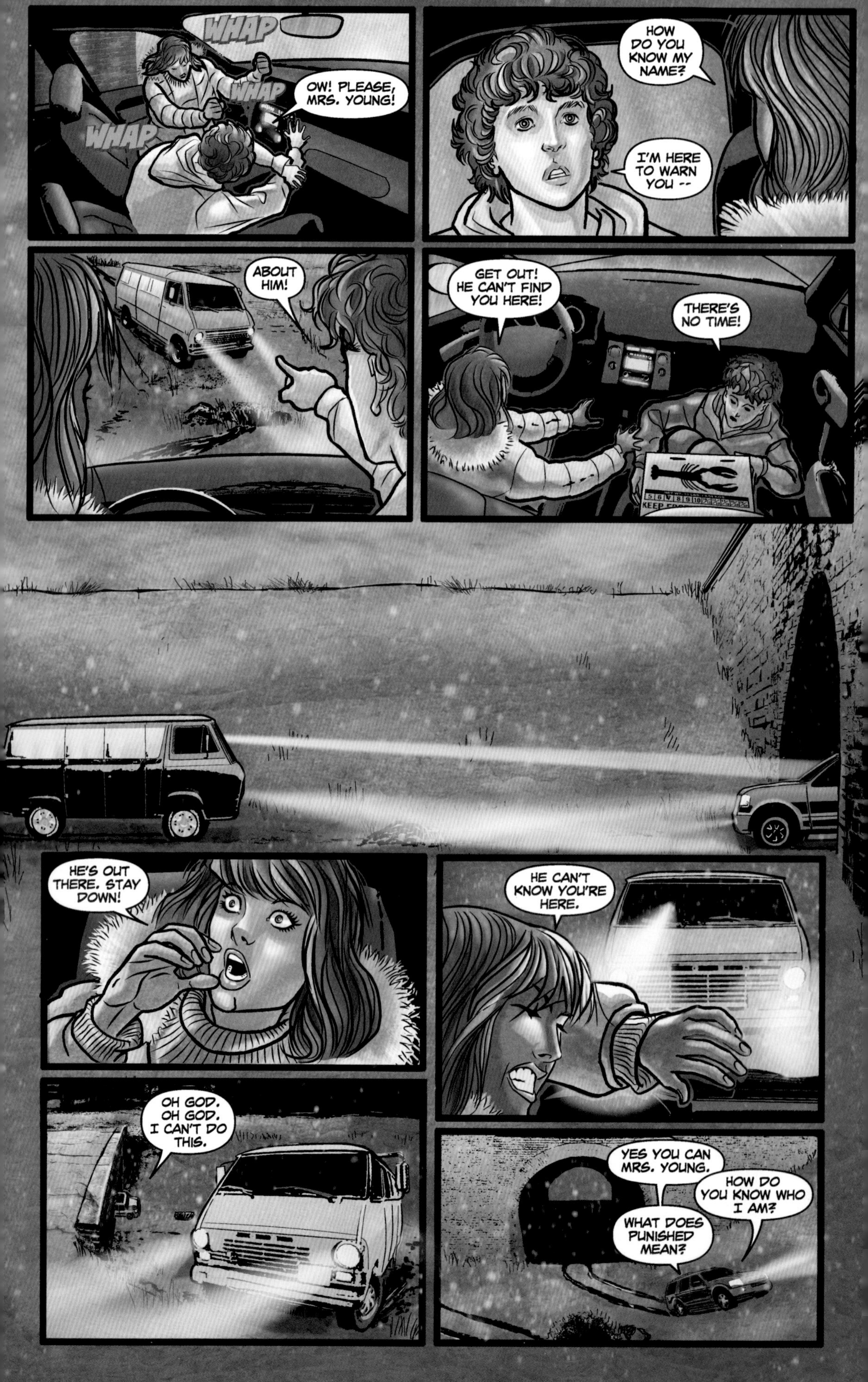
WHAP
WHAP
WHAP
OW! PLEASE, MRS. YOUNG!
HOW DO YOU KNOW MY NAME?
I'M HERE TO WARN YOU --
ABOUT HIM!
GET OUT! HE CAN'T FIND YOU HERE!
THERE'S NO TIME!
HE'S OUT THERE. STAY DOWN!
HE CAN'T KNOW YOU'RE HERE.
OH GOD. OH GOD. I CAN'T DO THIS.
YES YOU CAN MRS. YOUNG.
HOW DO YOU KNOW WHO I AM?
WHAT DOES PUNISHED MEAN?

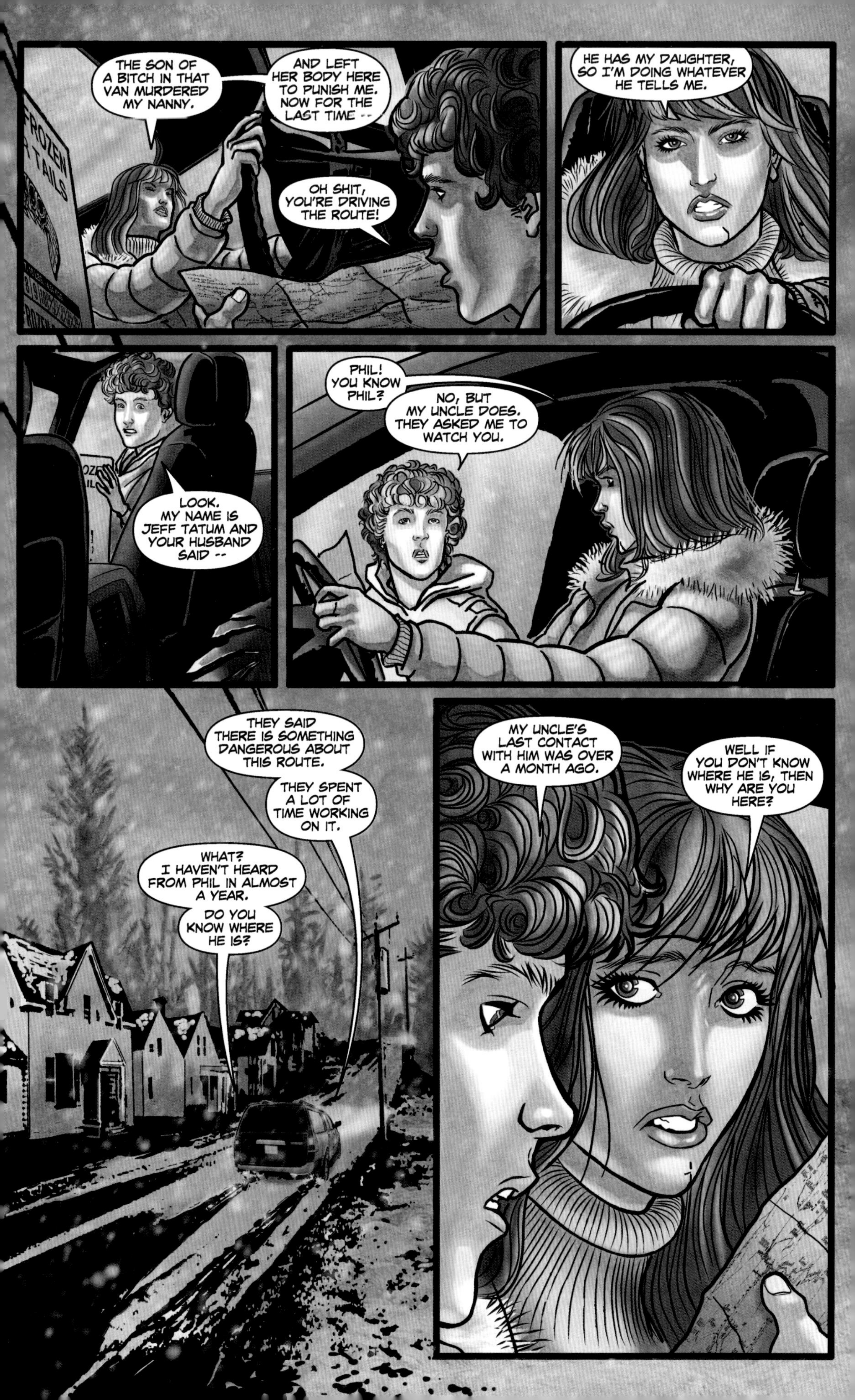
THE SON OF A BITCH IN THAT VAN MURDERED MY NANNY.
AND LEFT HER BODY HERE TO PUNISH ME. NOW FOR THE LAST TIME --
OH SHIT, YOU'RE DRIVING THE ROUTE!
FROZEN TAILS
HE HAS MY DAUGHTER, SO I'M DOING WHATEVER HE TELLS ME.
LOOK. MY NAME IS JEFF TATUM AND YOUR HUSBAND SAID --
PHIL! YOU KNOW PHIL?
NO, BUT MY UNCLE DOES. THEY ASKED ME TO WATCH YOU.
THEY SAID THERE IS SOMETHING DANGEROUS ABOUT THIS ROUTE.
THEY SPENT A LOT OF TIME WORKING ON IT.
WHAT? I HAVEN'T HEARD FROM PHIL IN ALMOST A YEAR.
DO YOU KNOW WHERE HE IS?
MY UNCLE'S LAST CONTACT WITH HIM WAS OVER A MONTH AGO.
WELL IF YOU DON'T KNOW WHERE HE IS, THEN WHY ARE YOU HERE?

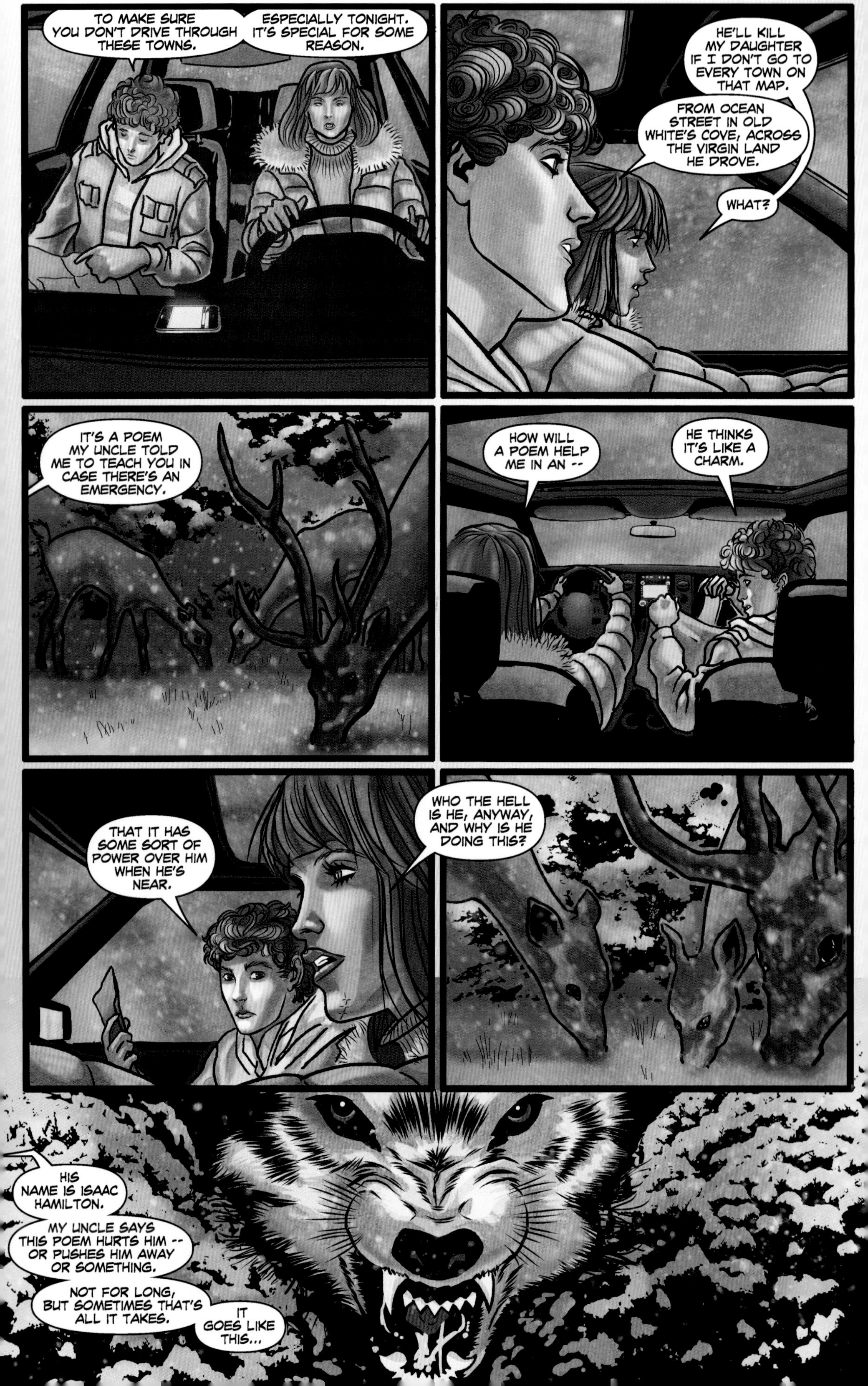
TO MAKE SURE YOU DON'T DRIVE THROUGH THESE TOWNS.
ESPECIALLY TONIGHT. IT'S SPECIAL FOR SOME REASON.
HE'LL KILL MY DAUGHTER IF I DON'T GO TO EVERY TOWN ON THAT MAP.
FROM OCEAN STREET IN OLD WHITE'S COVE, ACROSS THE VIRGIN LAND HE DROVE.
WHAT?
IT'S A POEM MY UNCLE TOLD ME TO TEACH YOU IN CASE THERE'S AN EMERGENCY.
HOW WILL A POEM HELP ME IN AN --
HE THINKS IT'S LIKE A CHARM.
THAT IT HAS SOME SORT OF POWER OVER HIM WHEN HE'S NEAR.
WHO THE HELL IS HE, ANYWAY, AND WHY IS HE DOING THIS?
HIS NAME IS ISAAC HAMILTON.
MY UNCLE SAYS THIS POEM HURTS HIM -- OR PUSHES HIM AWAY OR SOMETHING.
NOT FOR LONG, BUT SOMETIMES THAT'S ALL IT TAKES.
IT GOES LIKE THIS...

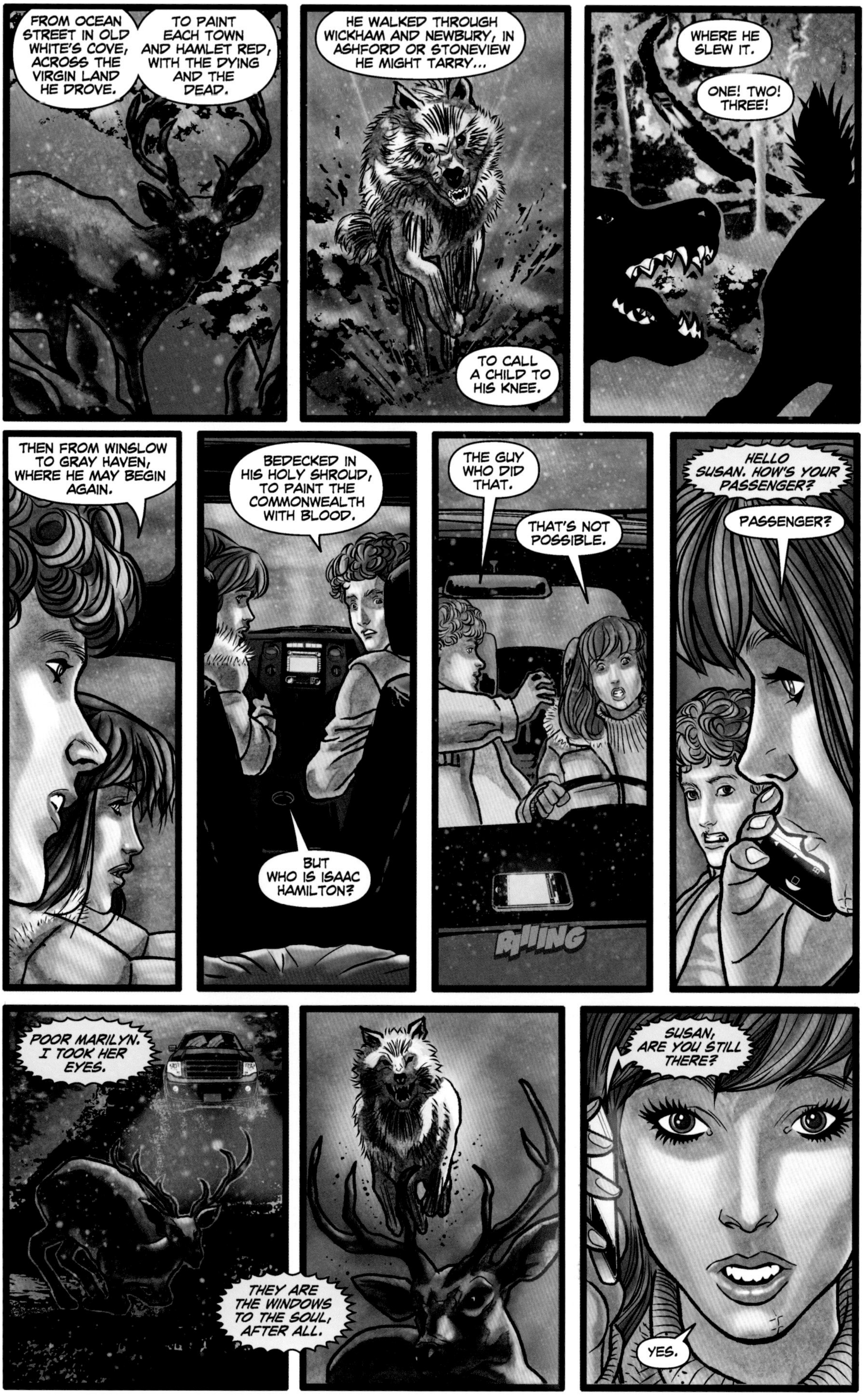
FROM OCEAN STREET IN OLD WHITE'S COVE, ACROSS THE VIRGIN LAND HE DROVE.
TO PAINT EACH TOWN AND HAMLET RED, WITH THE DYING AND THE DEAD.
HE WALKED THROUGH WICKHAM AND NEWBURY, IN ASHFORD OR STONEVIEW HE MIGHT TARRY...
TO CALL A CHILD TO HIS KNEE.
WHERE HE SLEW IT.
ONE! TWO! THREE!
THEN FROM WINSLOW TO GRAY HAVEN, WHERE HE MAY BEGIN AGAIN.
BEDECKED IN HIS HOLY SHROUD, TO PAINT THE COMMONWEALTH WITH BLOOD.
BUT WHO IS ISAAC HAMILTON?
THE GUY WHO DID THAT.
THAT'S NOT POSSIBLE.
RIIIING
HELLO SUSAN. HOW'S YOUR PASSENGER?
PASSENGER?
POOR MARILYN. I TOOK HER EYES.
THEY ARE THE WINDOWS TO THE SOUL, AFTER ALL.
SUSAN, ARE YOU STILL THERE?
YES.

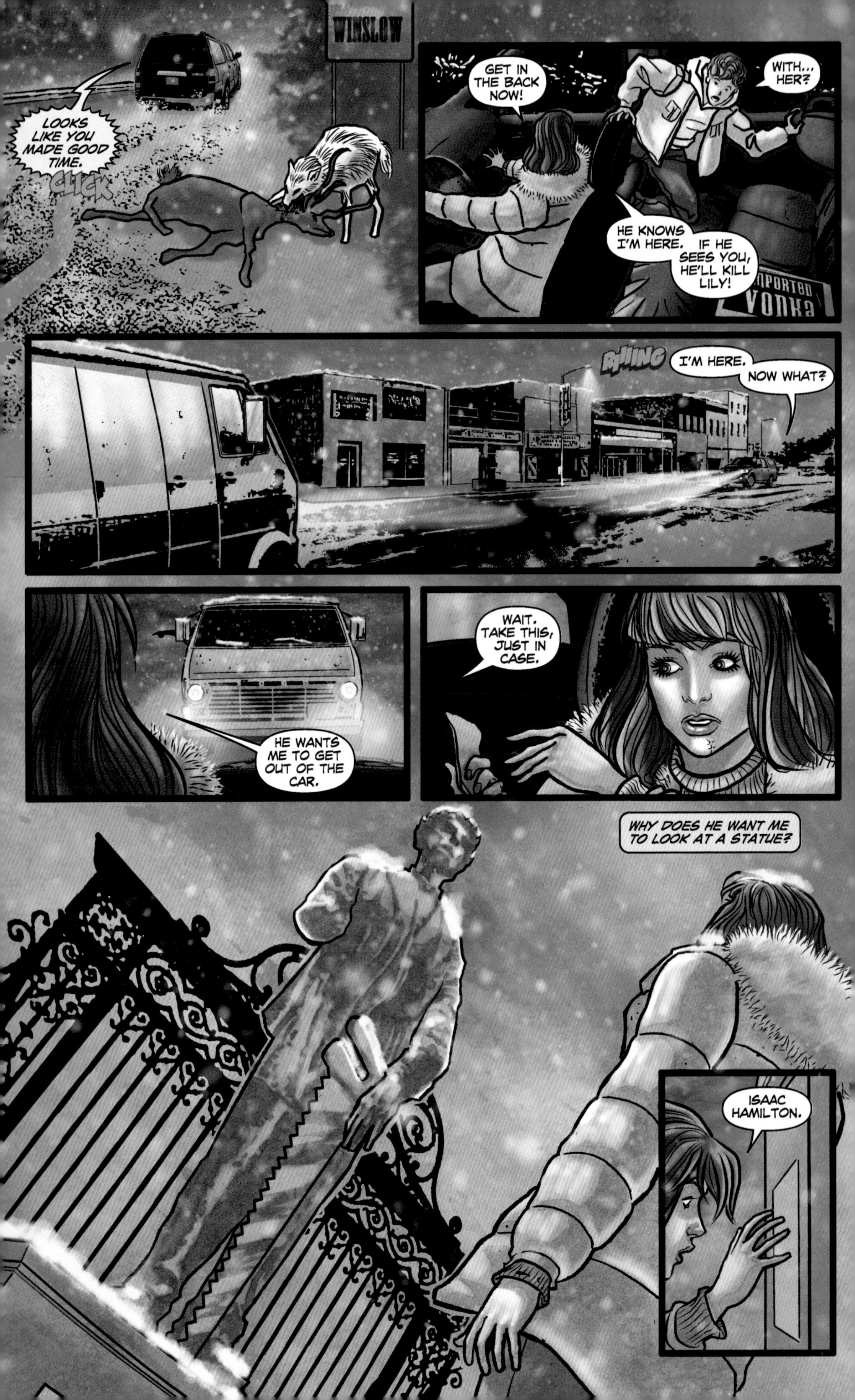
WINSLOW
LOOKS LIKE YOU MADE GOOD TIME.
CLICK
GET IN THE BACK NOW!
WITH... HER?
HE KNOWS I'M HERE.
IF HE SEES YOU, HE'LL KILL LILY!
IMPORTED VODKA
RIIING
I'M HERE.
NOW WHAT?
HE WANTS ME TO GET OUT OF THE CAR.
WAIT. TAKE THIS, JUST IN CASE.
WHY DOES HE WANT ME TO LOOK AT A STATUE?
ISAAC HAMILTON.

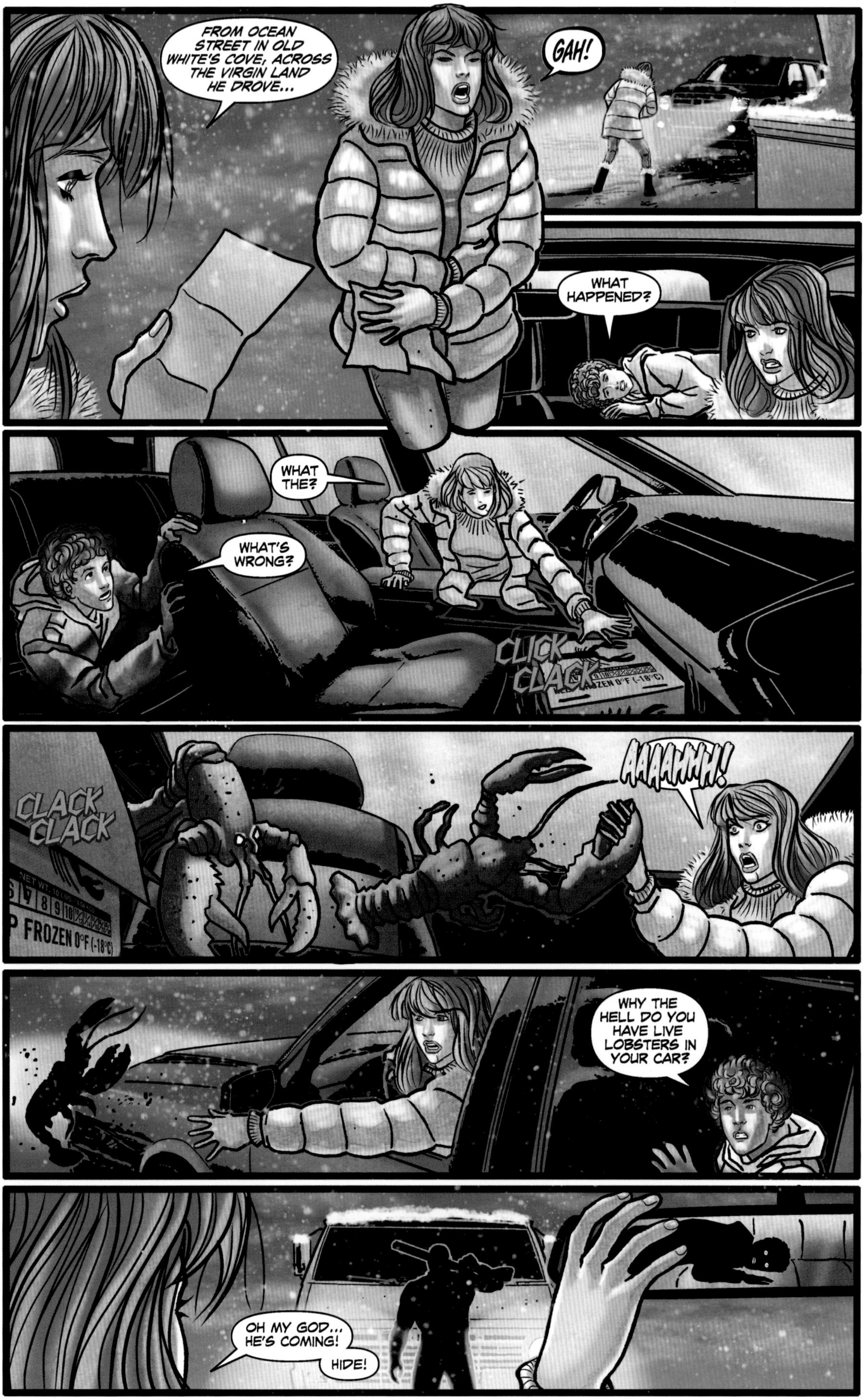
FROM OCEAN STREET IN OLD WHITE'S COVE, ACROSS THE VIRGIN LAND HE DROVE...
GAH!
WHAT HAPPENED?
WHAT THE?
WHAT'S WRONG?
CLICK CLACK
FROZEN 0°F (-18°C)
CLACK CLACK
AAAAHHH!
P FROZEN 0°F (-18°C)
WHY THE HELL DO YOU HAVE LIVE LOBSTERS IN YOUR CAR?
OH MY GOD... HE'S COMING!
HIDE!

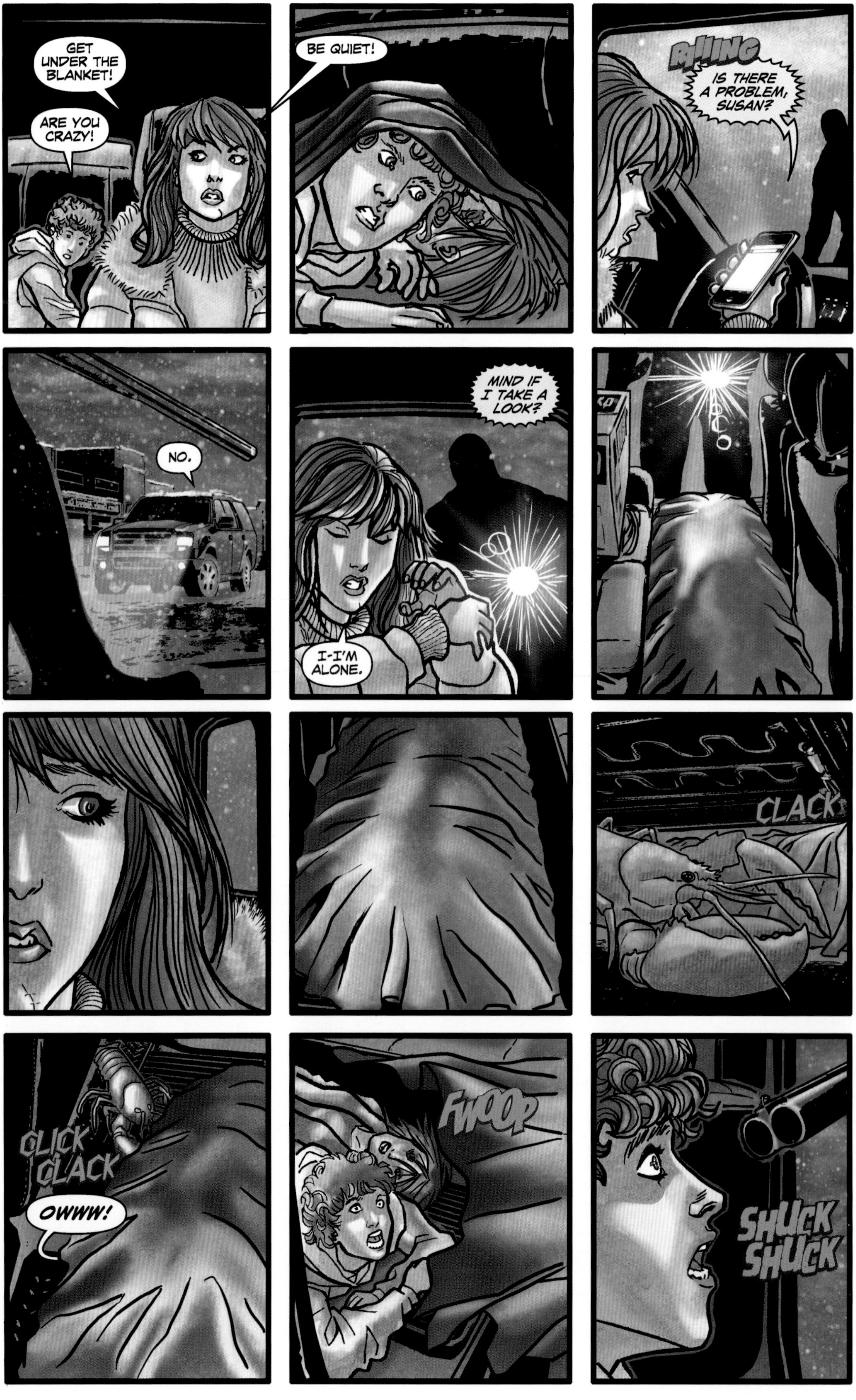
GET UNDER THE BLANKET!
ARE YOU CRAZY!
BE QUIET!
RIIIING
IS THERE A PROBLEM, SUSAN?
NO.
MIND IF I TAKE A LOOK?
I-I'M ALONE.
CLACK
CLICK CLACK
OWWW!
FWOOP
SHUCK SHUCK

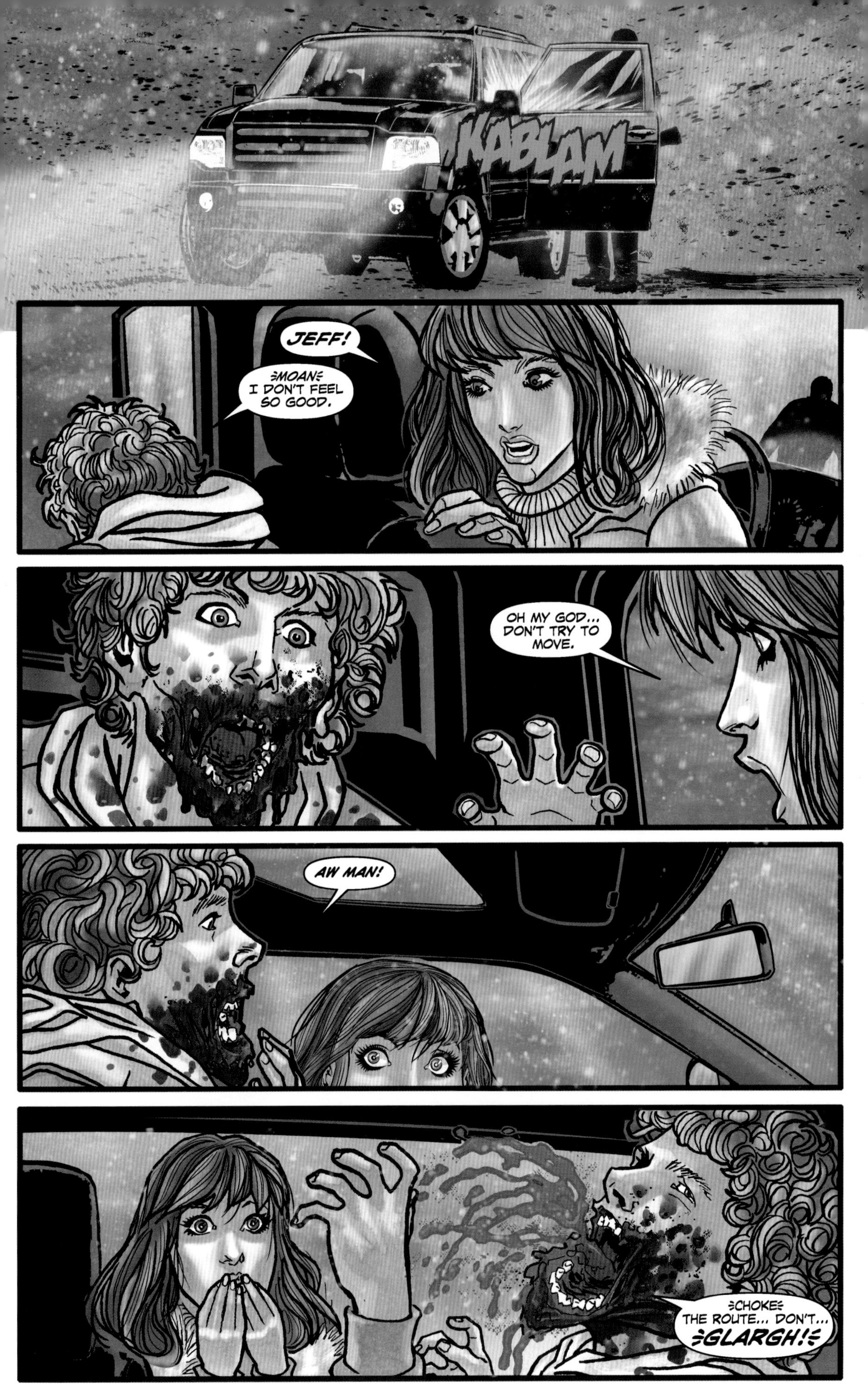
KABLAM
JEFF!
MOAN
I DON'T FEEL SO GOOD.
OH MY GOD... DON'T TRY TO MOVE.
AW MAN!
CHOKE
THE ROUTE... DON'T...
GLARGH!

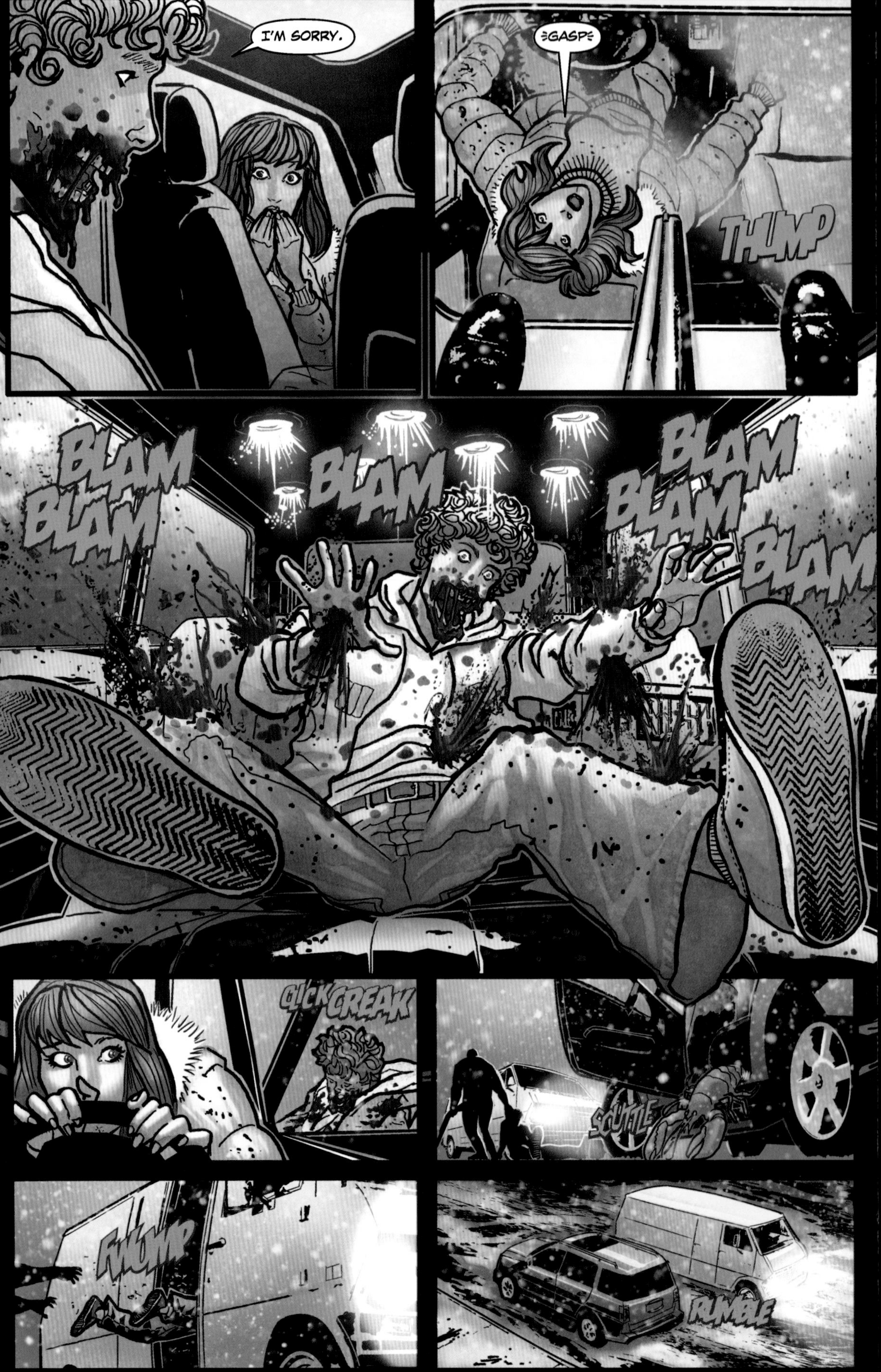
I'M SORRY.
GASP
THUMP
BLAM
BLAM
BLAM
BLAM
BLAM
BLAM
BLAM
BLAM
CLICK
CREAK
SCUTTLE
FWUMP
RUMBLE

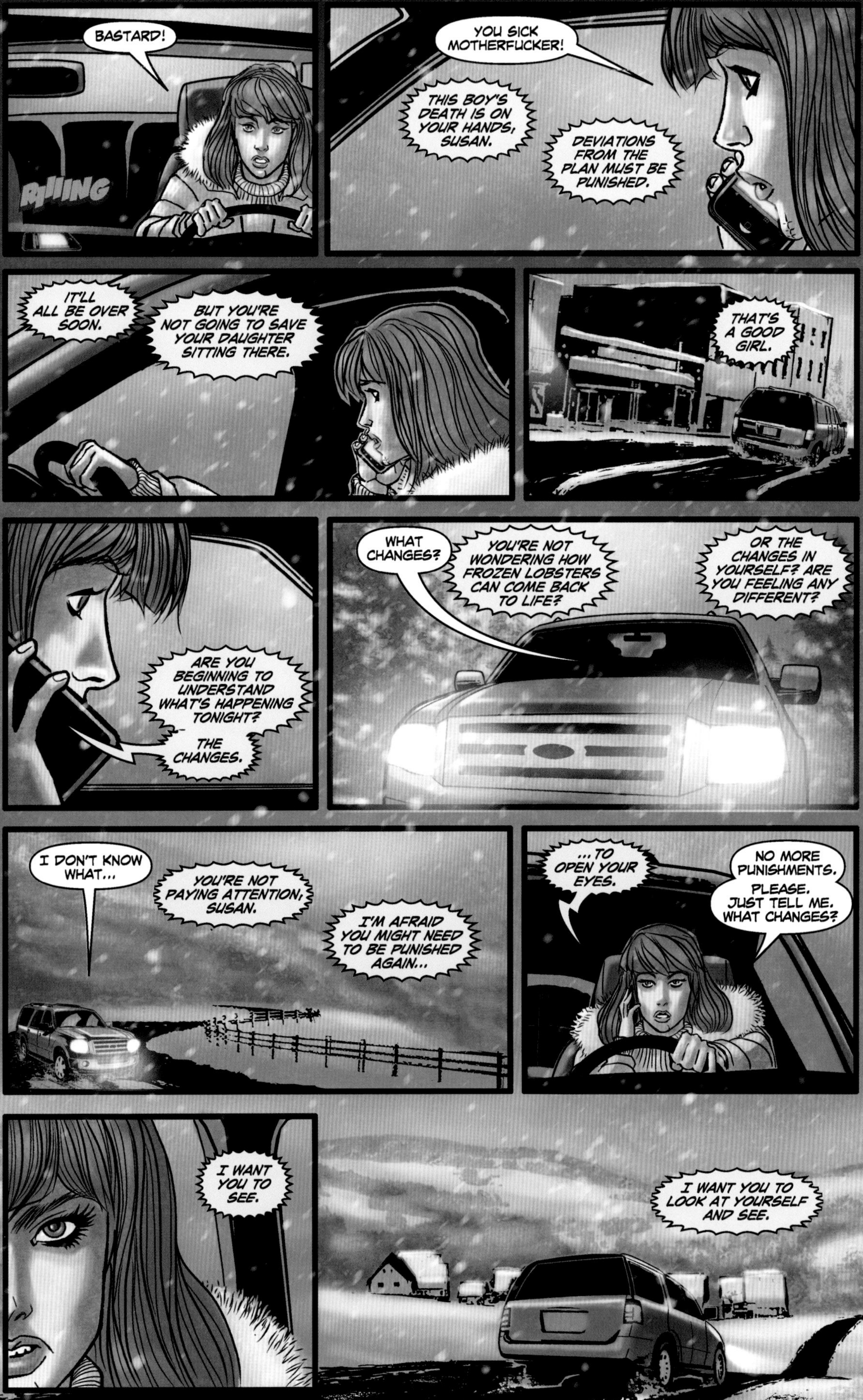
BASTARD!
RIIIING
YOU SICK MOTHERFUCKER!
THIS BOY'S DEATH IS ON YOUR HANDS, SUSAN.
DEVIATIONS FROM THE PLAN MUST BE PUNISHED.
IT'LL ALL BE OVER SOON.
BUT YOU'RE NOT GOING TO SAVE YOUR DAUGHTER SITTING THERE.
THAT'S A GOOD GIRL.
ARE YOU BEGINNING TO UNDERSTAND WHAT'S HAPPENING TONIGHT?
THE CHANGES.
WHAT CHANGES?
YOU'RE NOT WONDERING HOW FROZEN LOBSTERS CAN COME BACK TO LIFE?
OR THE CHANGES IN YOURSELF? ARE YOU FEELING ANY DIFFERENT?
I DON'T KNOW WHAT...
YOU'RE NOT PAYING ATTENTION, SUSAN.
I'M AFRAID YOU MIGHT NEED TO BE PUNISHED AGAIN...
...TO OPEN YOUR EYES.
NO MORE PUNISHMENTS. PLEASE. JUST TELL ME. WHAT CHANGES?
I WANT YOU TO SEE.
I WANT YOU TO LOOK AT YOURSELF AND SEE.

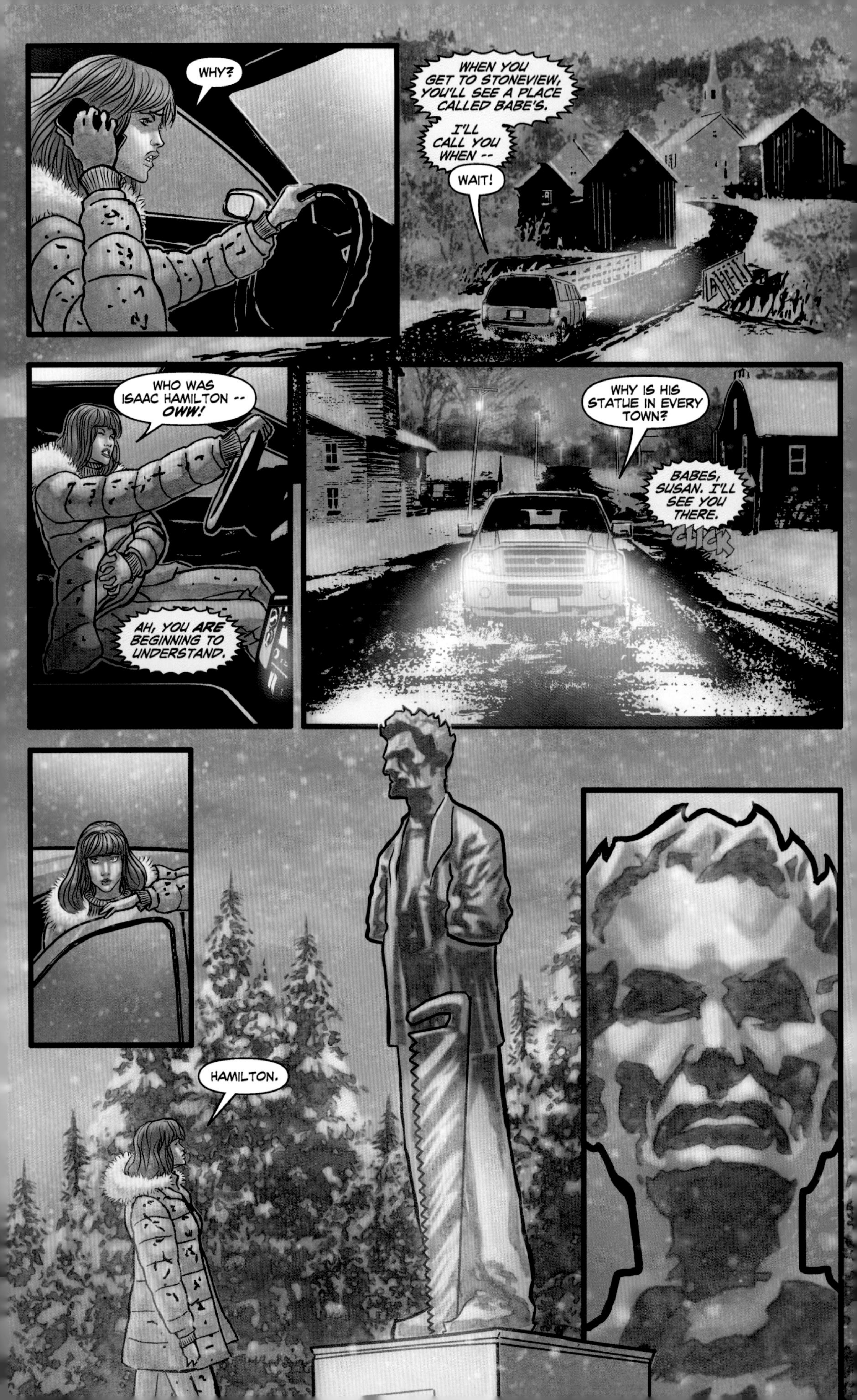
WHY?
WHEN YOU GET TO STONEVIEW, YOU'LL SEE A PLACE CALLED BABE'S.
I'LL CALL YOU WHEN --
WAIT!
WHO WAS ISAAC HAMILTON -- OWW!
AH, YOU ARE BEGINNING TO UNDERSTAND.
WHY IS HIS STATUE IN EVERY TOWN?
BABES, SUSAN. I'LL SEE YOU THERE.
CLICK
HAMILTON.

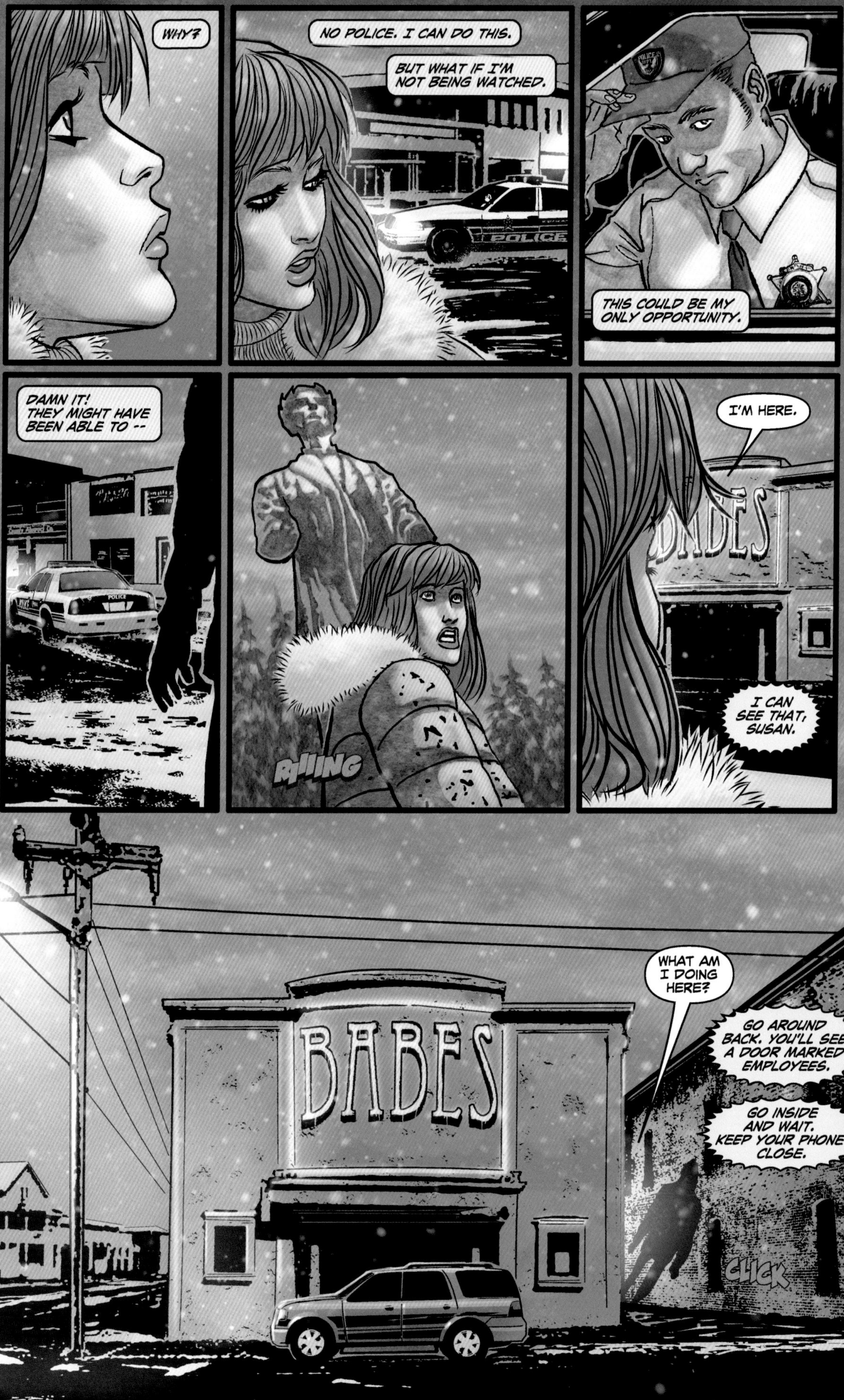
WHY?
NO POLICE. I CAN DO THIS.
BUT WHAT IF I'M NOT BEING WATCHED.
POLICE
THIS COULD BE MY ONLY OPPORTUNITY.
DAMN IT! THEY MIGHT HAVE BEEN ABLE TO --
POLICE
RIIIING
I'M HERE.
BABES
I CAN SEE THAT, SUSAN.
BABES
WHAT AM I DOING HERE?
GO AROUND BACK. YOU'LL SEE A DOOR MARKED EMPLOYEES.
GO INSIDE AND WAIT. KEEP YOUR PHONE CLOSE.
CLICK

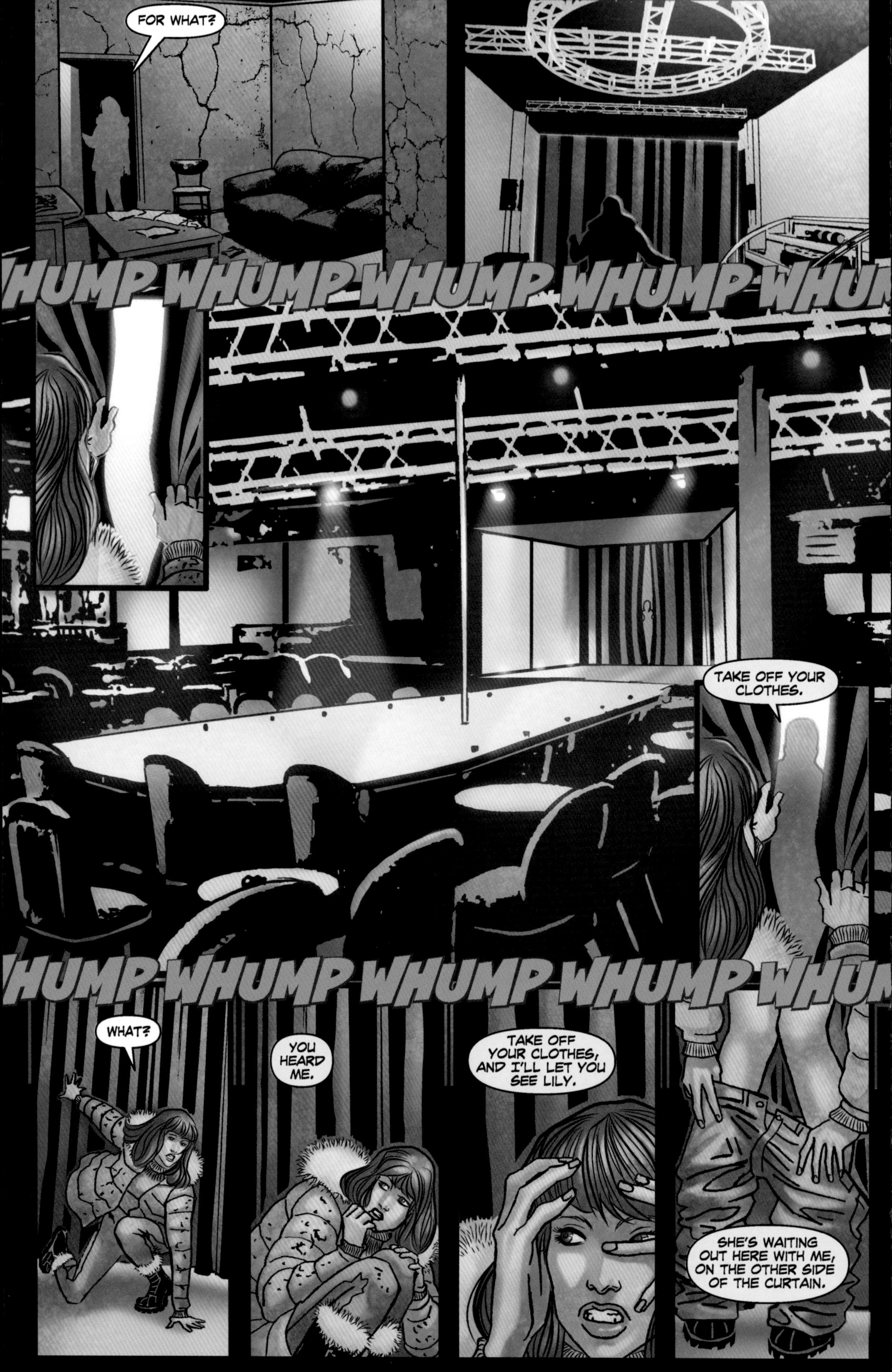

FOR WHAT?
WHUMP WHUMP WHUMP
TAKE OFF YOUR CLOTHES.
WHUMP WHUMP WHUMP
WHAT?
YOU HEARD ME.
TAKE OFF YOUR CLOTHES, AND I'LL LET YOU SEE LILY.
SHE'S WAITING OUT HERE WITH ME, ON THE OTHER SIDE OF THE CURTAIN.

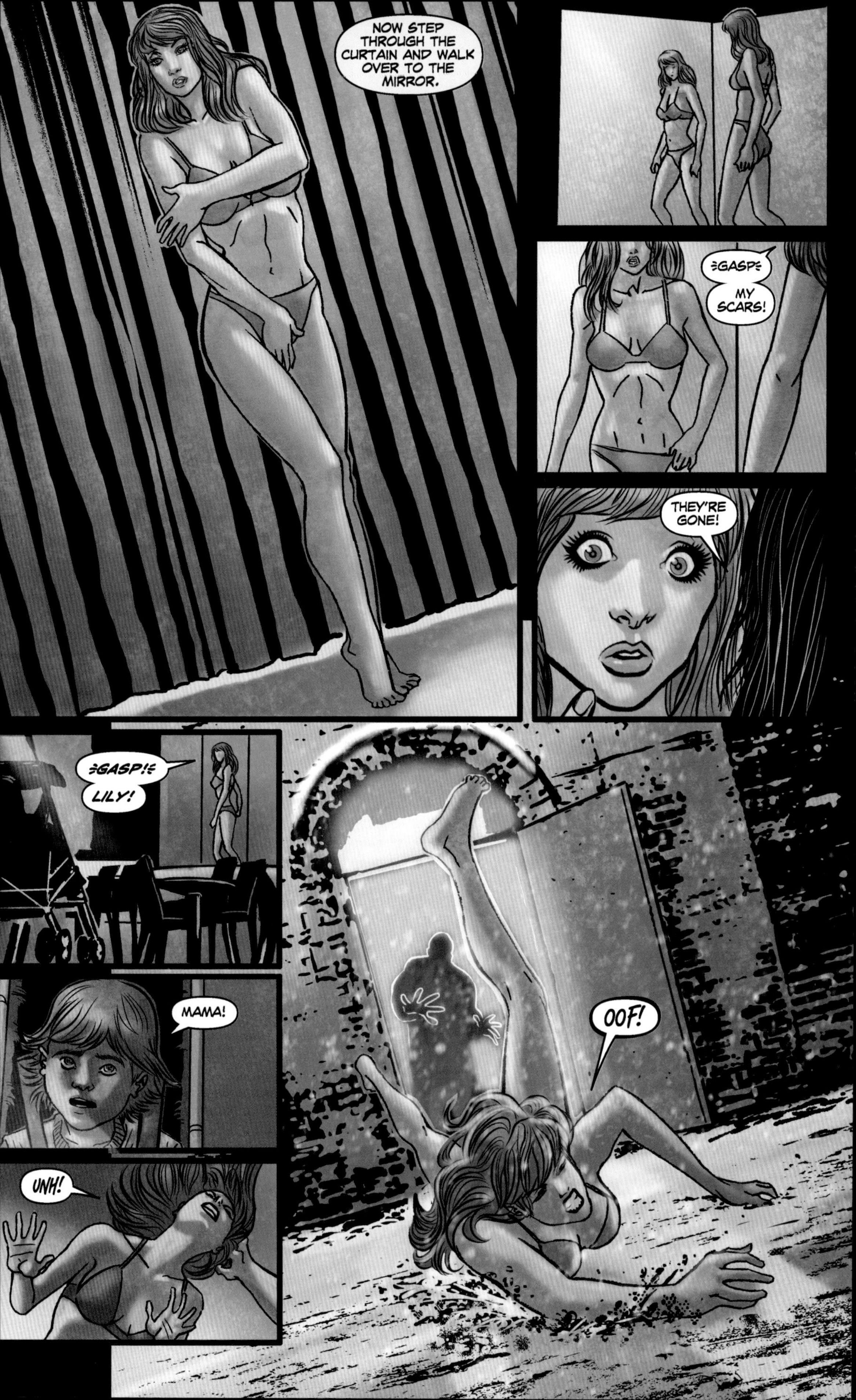
NOW STEP THROUGH THE CURTAIN AND WALK OVER TO THE MIRROR.
GASP
MY SCARS!
THEY'RE GONE!
GASP!
LILY!
MAMA!
UNH!
OOF!

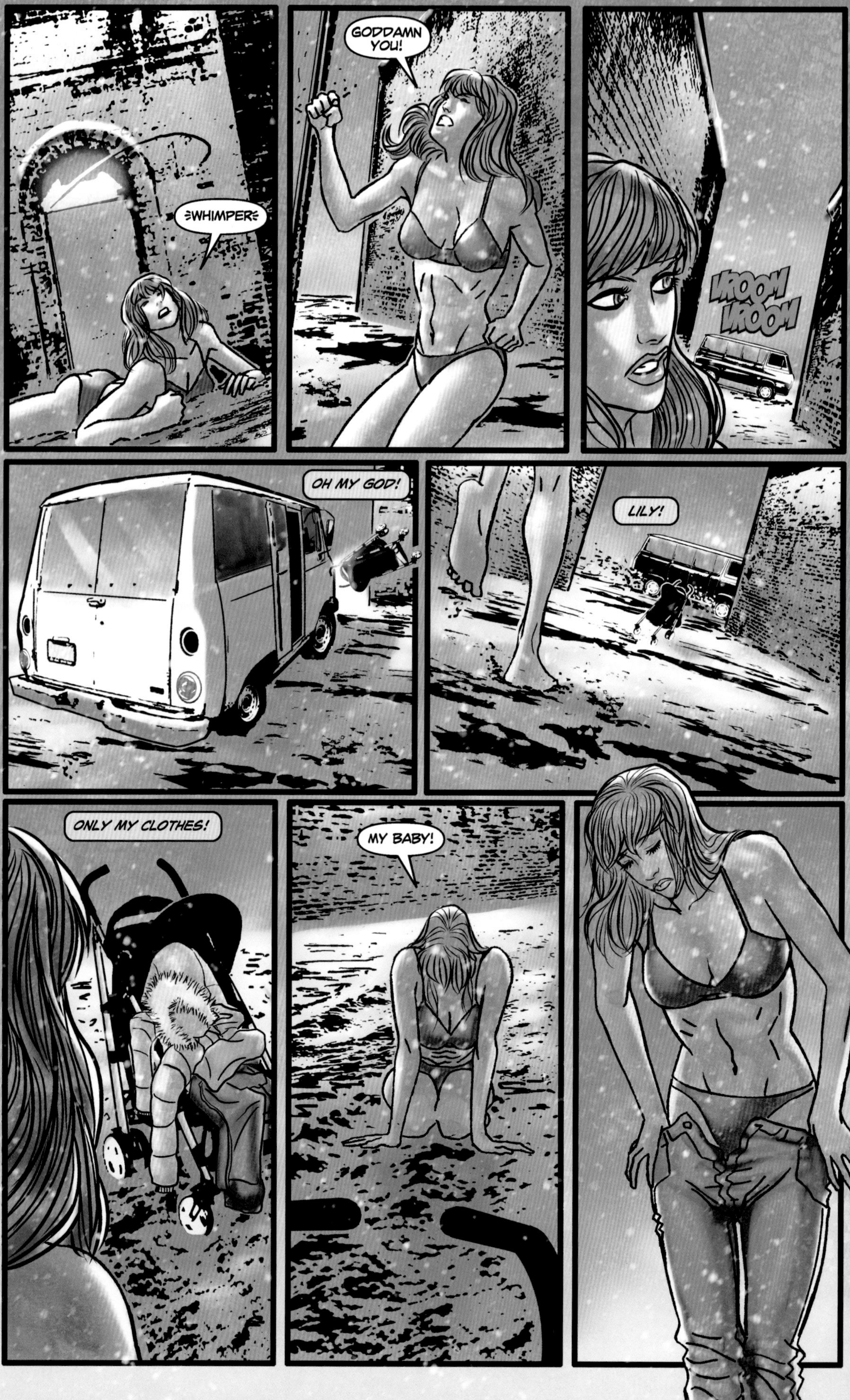
WHIMPER
GODDAMN YOU!
VROOM VROOM
OH MY GOD!
LILY!
ONLY MY CLOTHES!
MY BABY!

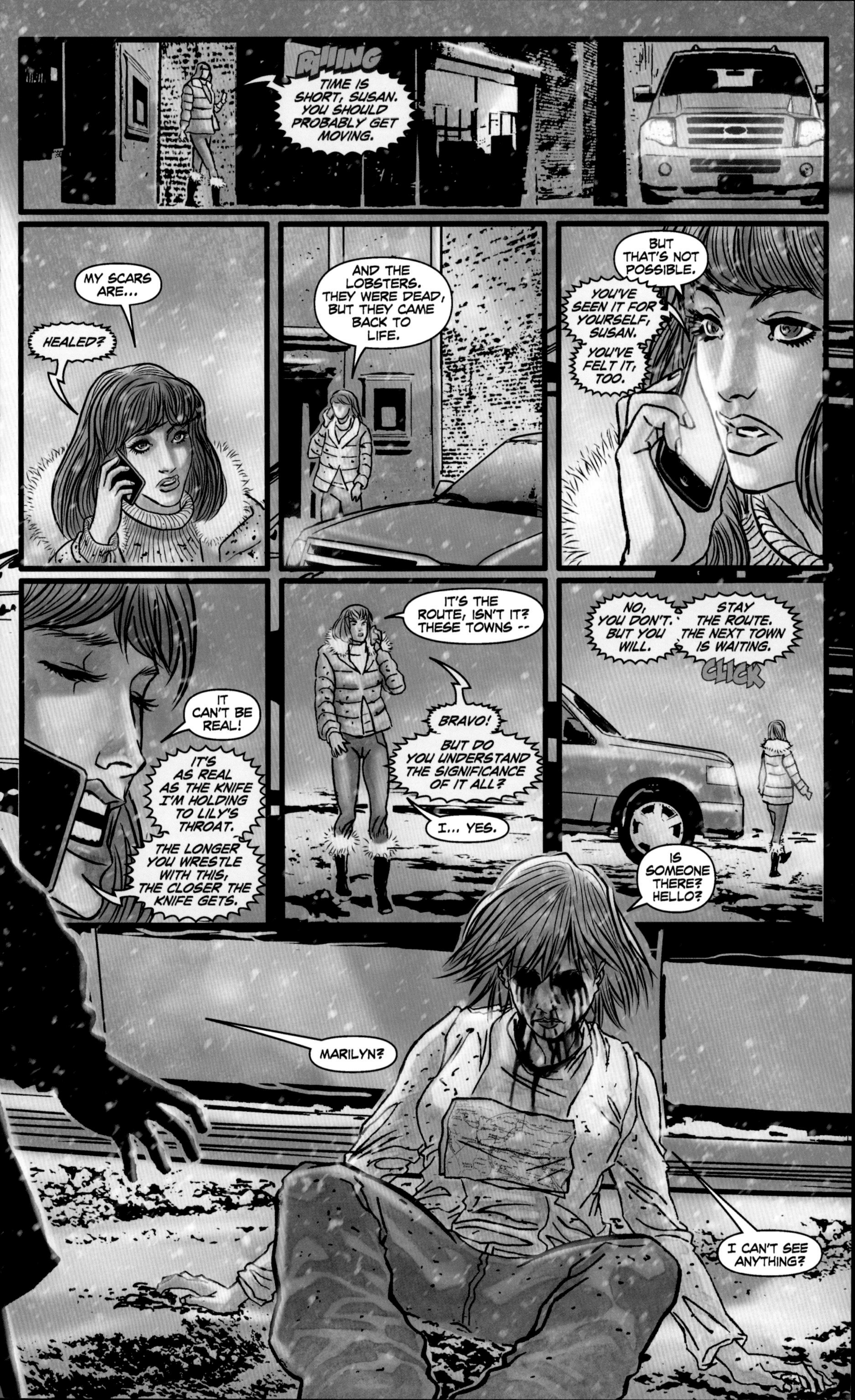

RRIIING
TIME IS SHORT, SUSAN. YOU SHOULD PROBABLY GET MOVING.
MY SCARS ARE...
HEALED?
AND THE LOBSTERS. THEY WERE DEAD, BUT THEY CAME BACK TO LIFE.
BUT THAT'S NOT POSSIBLE.
YOU'VE SEEN IT FOR YOURSELF, SUSAN.
YOU'VE FELT IT, TOO.
IT CAN'T BE REAL!
IT'S AS REAL AS THE KNIFE I'M HOLDING TO LILY'S THROAT.
THE LONGER YOU WRESTLE WITH THIS, THE CLOSER THE KNIFE GETS.
IT'S THE ROUTE, ISN'T IT? THESE TOWNS --
BRAVO!
BUT DO YOU UNDERSTAND THE SIGNIFICANCE OF IT ALL?
I... YES.
NO, YOU DON'T. BUT YOU WILL.
STAY THE ROUTE. THE NEXT TOWN IS WAITING.
CLICK
IS SOMEONE THERE? HELLO?
MARILYN?
I CAN'T SEE ANYTHING?

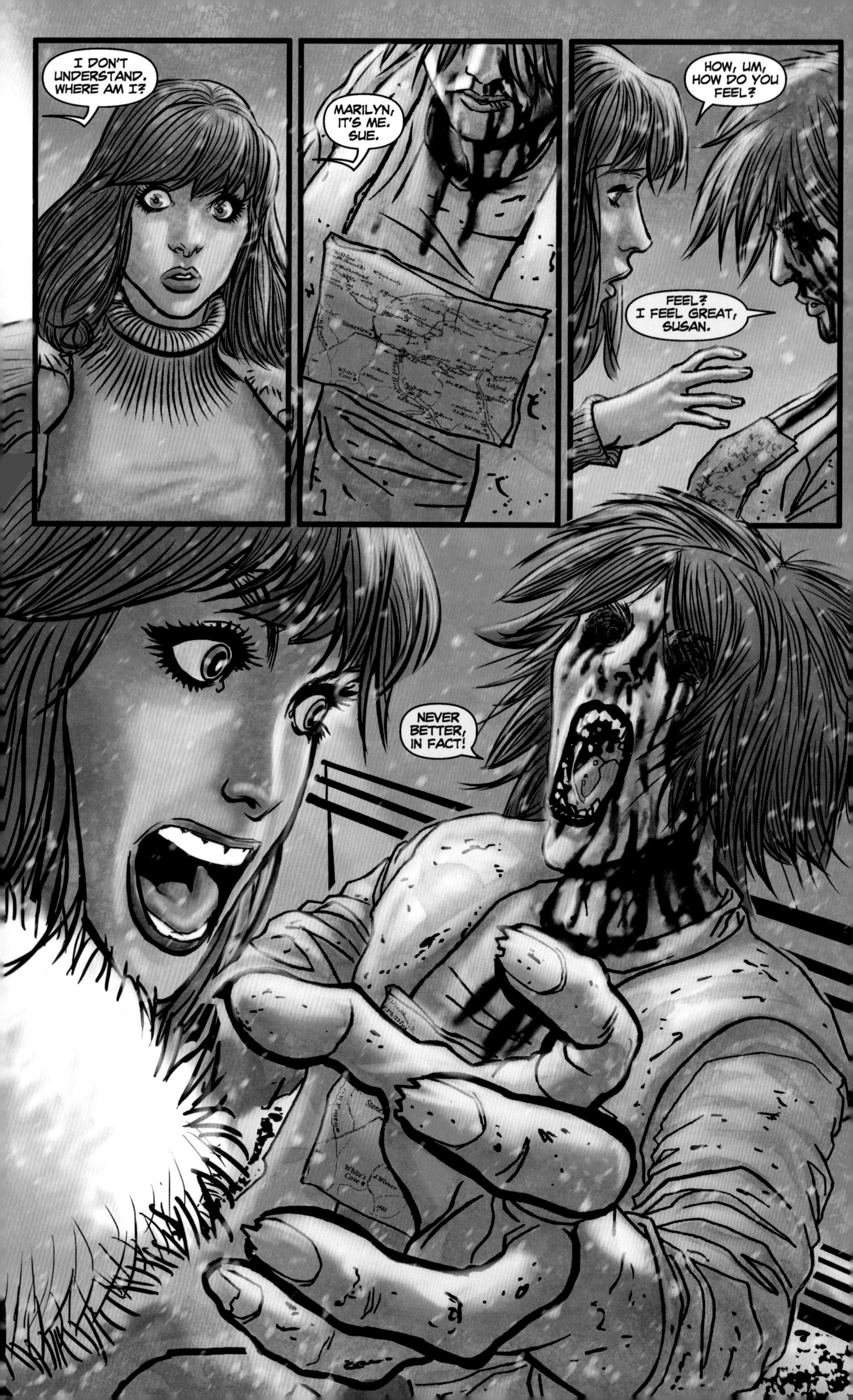
I DON'T UNDERSTAND. WHERE AM I?
MARILYN, IT'S ME. SUE.
HOW, UM, HOW DO YOU FEEL?
FEEL? I FEEL GREAT, SUSAN.
NEVER BETTER, IN FACT!

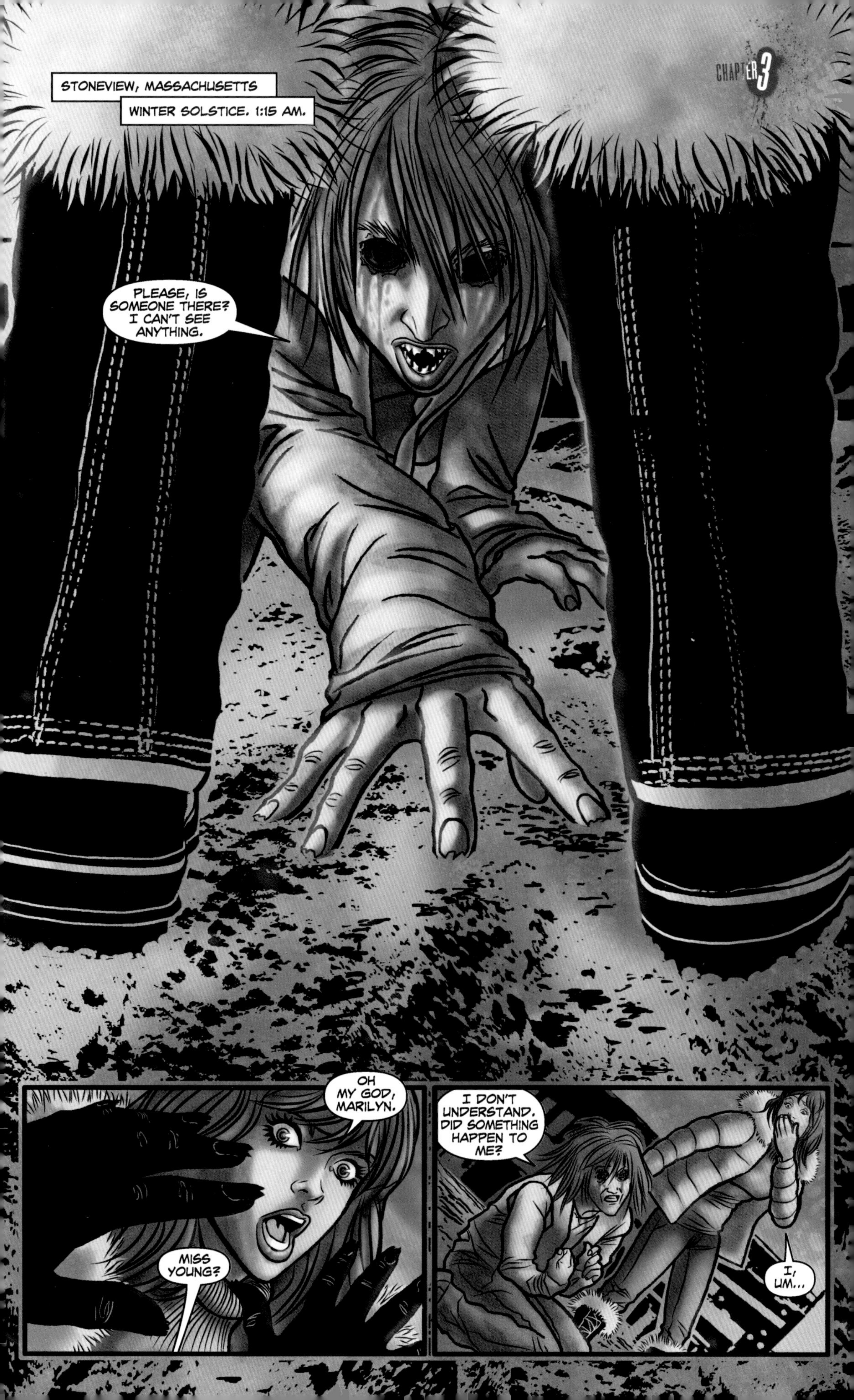
CHAPTER 3
STONEVIEW, MASSACHUSETTS
WINTER SOLSTICE. 1:15 AM.
PLEASE, IS SOMEONE THERE? I CAN'T SEE ANYTHING.
OH MY GOD, MARILYN.
MISS YOUNG?
I DON'T UNDERSTAND. DID SOMETHING HAPPEN TO ME?
I, UM...

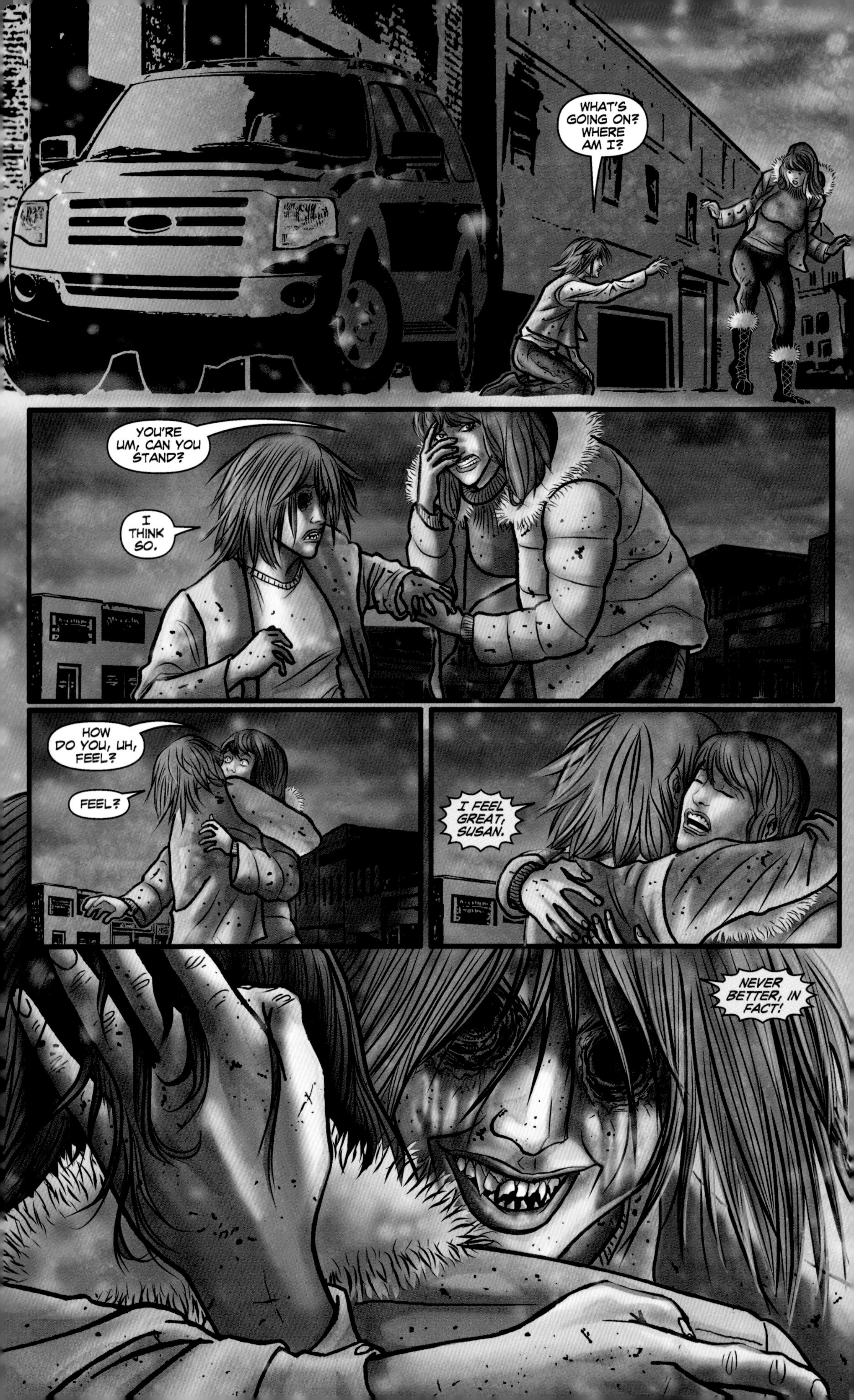
WHAT'S GOING ON? WHERE AM I?
YOU'RE UM, CAN YOU STAND?
I THINK SO.
HOW DO YOU, UH, FEEL?
FEEL?
I FEEL GREAT, SUSAN.
NEVER BETTER, IN FACT!

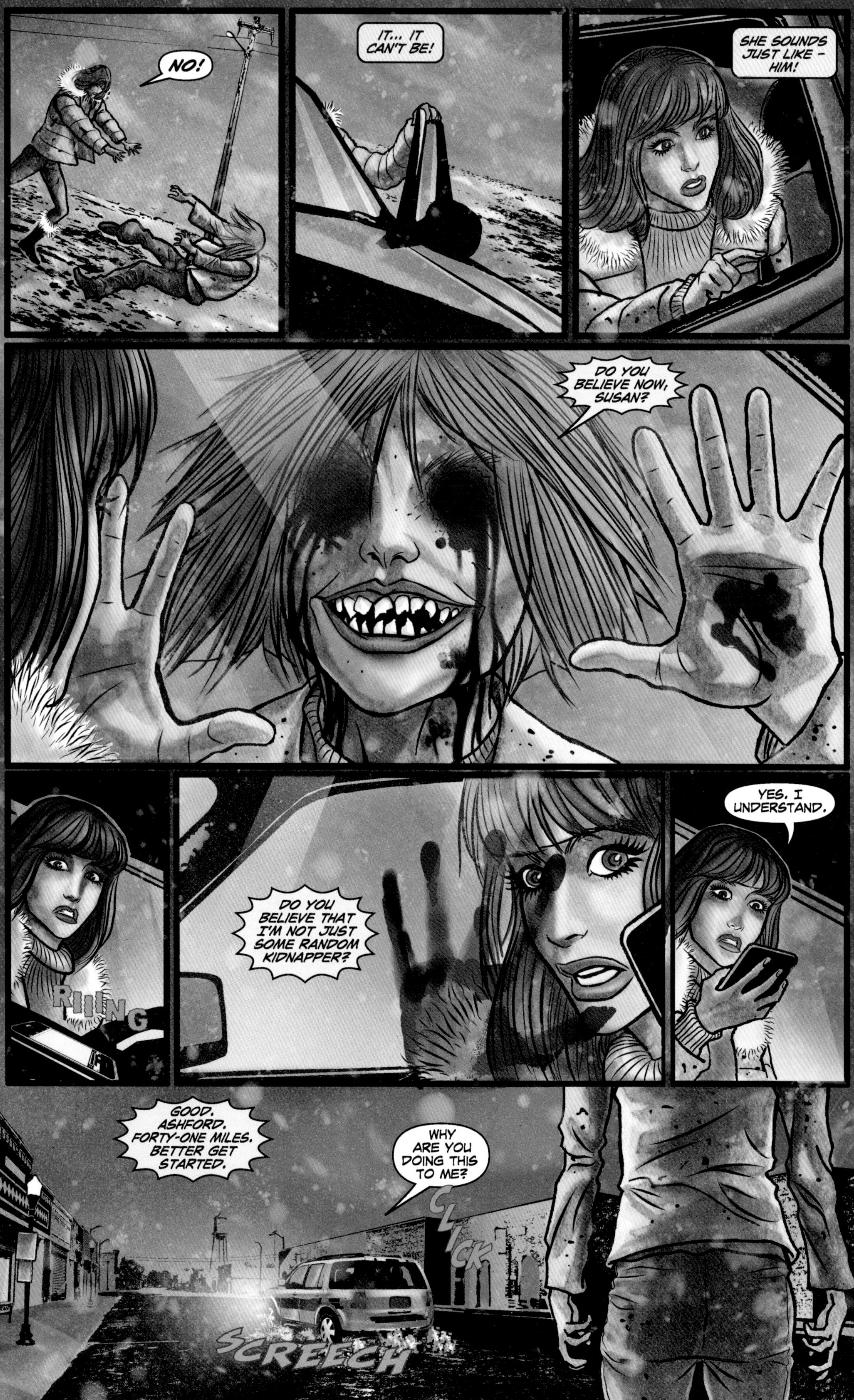
NO!
IT... IT CAN'T BE!
SHE SOUNDS JUST LIKE - HIM!
DO YOU BELIEVE NOW, SUSAN?
RIIING
DO YOU BELIEVE THAT I'M NOT JUST SOME RANDOM KIDNAPPER?
YES. I UNDERSTAND.
GOOD. ASHFORD. FORTY-ONE MILES. BETTER GET STARTED.
WHY ARE YOU DOING THIS TO ME?
CLICK
SCREECH

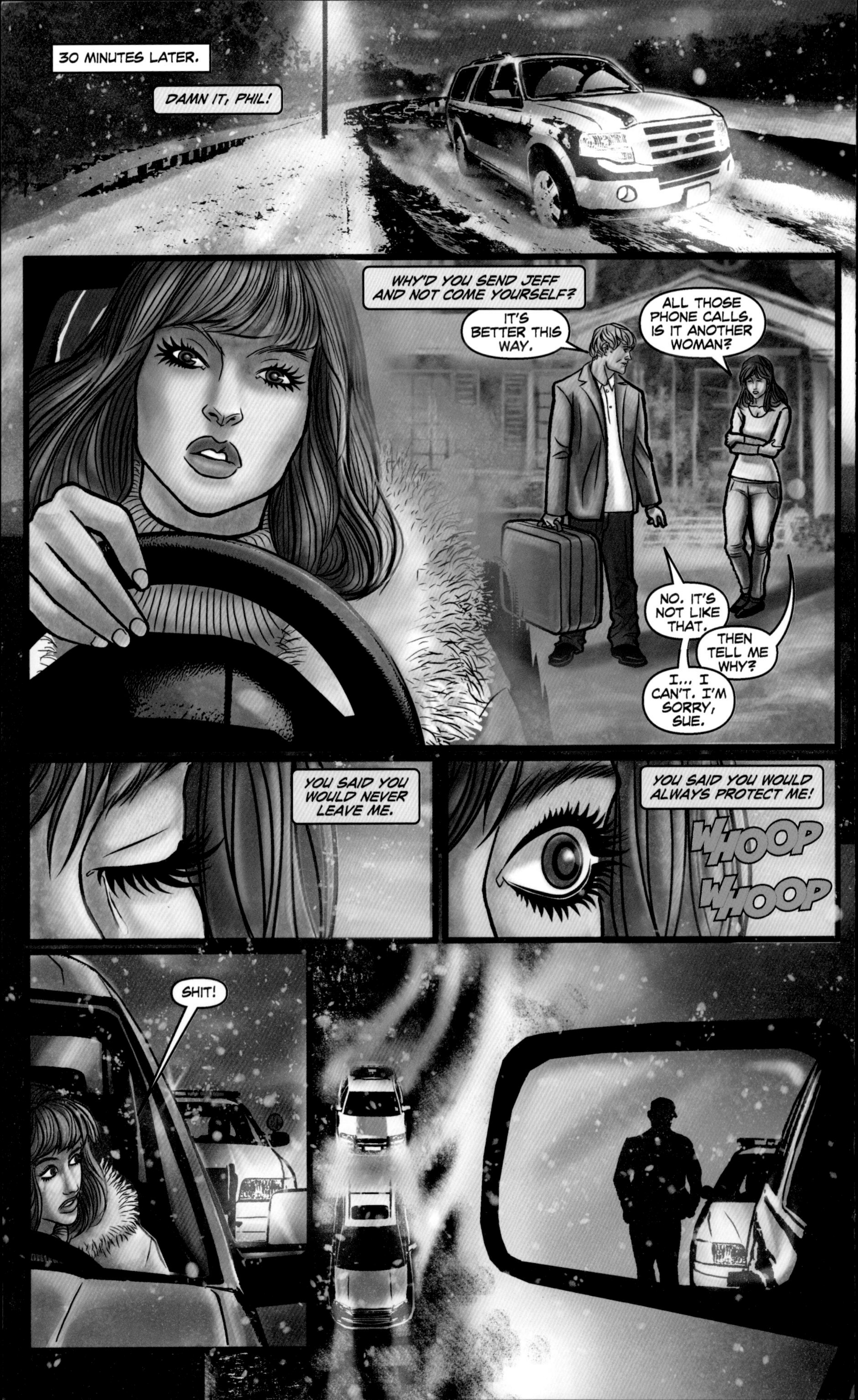
30 MINUTES LATER.
DAMN IT, PHIL!
WHY'D YOU SEND JEFF AND NOT COME YOURSELF?
IT'S BETTER THIS WAY.
ALL THOSE PHONE CALLS. IS IT ANOTHER WOMAN?
NO. IT'S NOT LIKE THAT.
THEN TELL ME WHY?
I... I CAN'T. I'M SORRY, SUE.
YOU SAID YOU WOULD NEVER LEAVE ME.
YOU SAID YOU WOULD ALWAYS PROTECT ME!
WHOOP
WHOOP
SHIT!

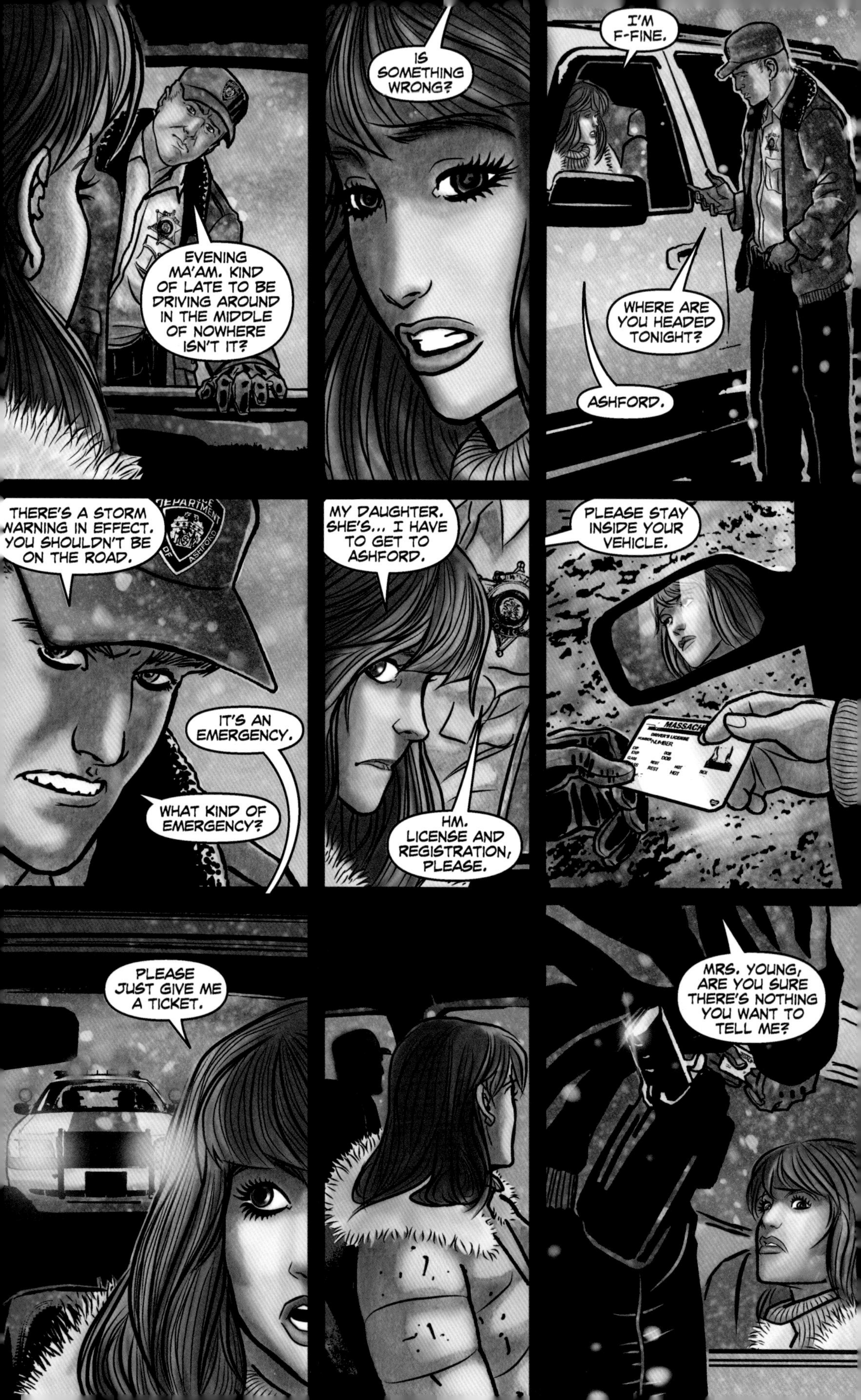
EVENING MA'AM. KIND OF LATE TO BE DRIVING AROUND IN THE MIDDLE OF NOWHERE ISN'T IT?
IS SOMETHING WRONG?
I'M F-FINE.
WHERE ARE YOU HEADED TONIGHT?
ASHFORD.
THERE'S A STORM WARNING IN EFFECT. YOU SHOULDN'T BE ON THE ROAD.
IT'S AN EMERGENCY.
WHAT KIND OF EMERGENCY?
MY DAUGHTER. SHE'S... I HAVE TO GET TO ASHFORD.
HM. LICENSE AND REGISTRATION, PLEASE.
PLEASE STAY INSIDE YOUR VEHICLE.
PLEASE JUST GIVE ME A TICKET.
MRS. YOUNG, ARE YOU SURE THERE'S NOTHING YOU WANT TO TELL ME?

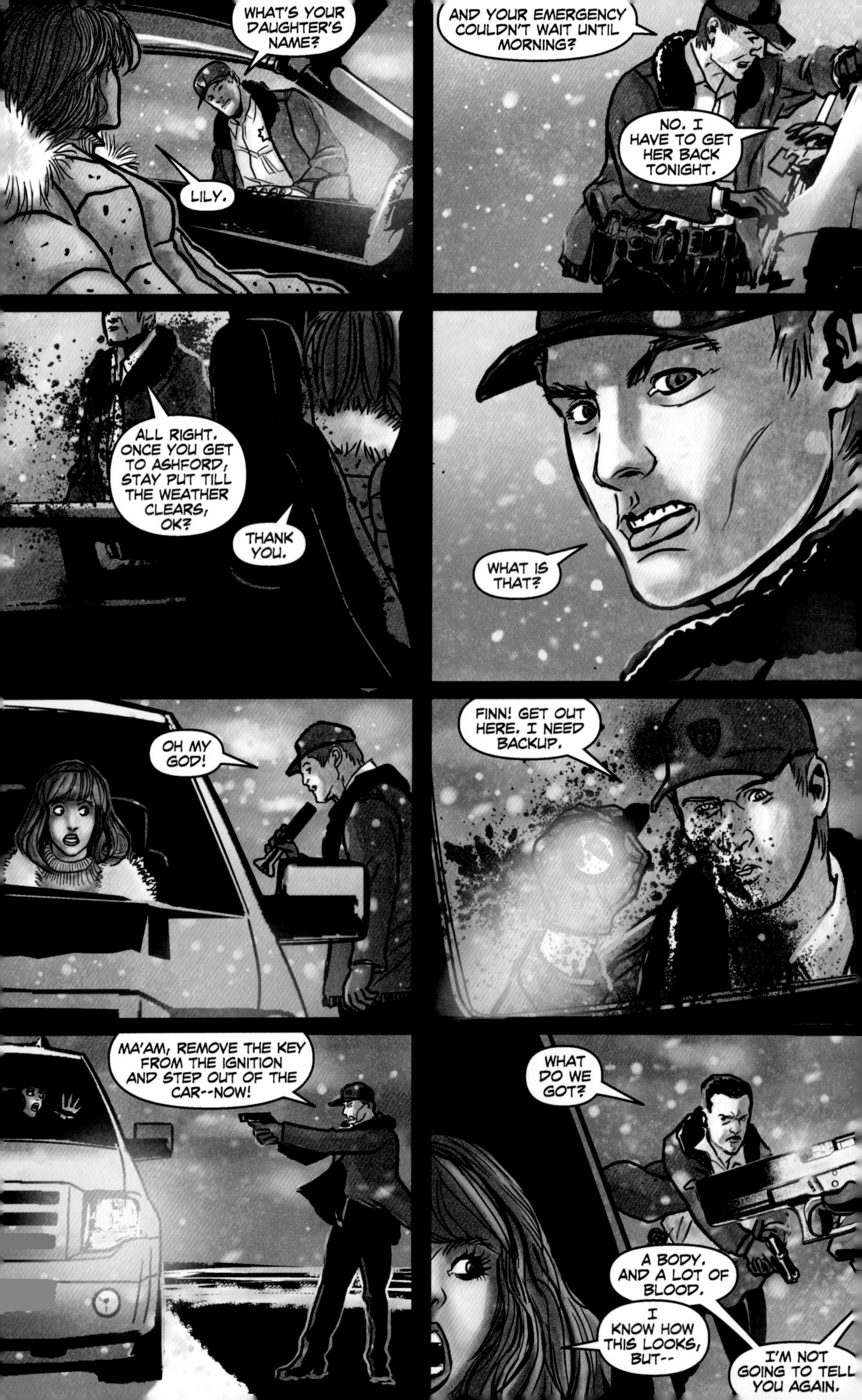
WHAT'S YOUR DAUGHTER'S NAME?
LILY.
AND YOUR EMERGENCY COULDN'T WAIT UNTIL MORNING?
NO. I HAVE TO GET HER BACK TONIGHT.
ALL RIGHT. ONCE YOU GET TO ASHFORD, STAY PUT TILL THE WEATHER CLEARS, OK?
THANK YOU.
WHAT IS THAT?
OH MY GOD!
FINN! GET OUT HERE. I NEED BACKUP.
MA'AM, REMOVE THE KEY FROM THE IGNITION AND STEP OUT OF THE CAR--NOW!
WHAT DO WE GOT?
A BODY. AND A LOT OF BLOOD.
I KNOW HOW THIS LOOKS, BUT--
I'M NOT GOING TO TELL YOU AGAIN.

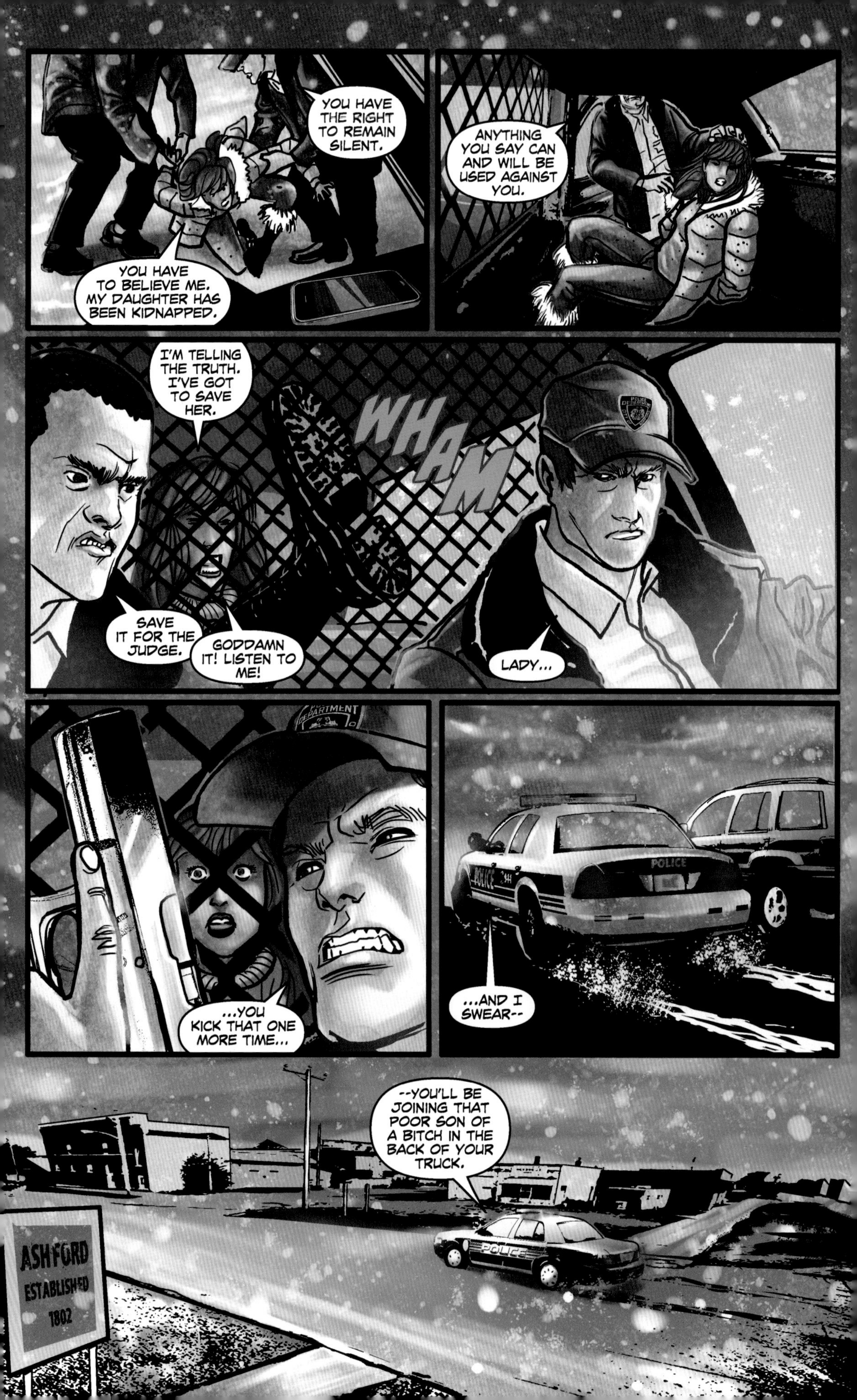
YOU HAVE THE RIGHT TO REMAIN SILENT.
YOU HAVE TO BELIEVE ME. MY DAUGHTER HAS BEEN KIDNAPPED.
ANYTHING YOU SAY CAN AND WILL BE USED AGAINST YOU.
I'M TELLING THE TRUTH. I'VE GOT TO SAVE HER.
WHAM
SAVE IT FOR THE JUDGE.
GODDAMN IT! LISTEN TO ME!
LADY...
...YOU KICK THAT ONE MORE TIME...
POLICE
...AND I SWEAR--
--YOU'LL BE JOINING THAT POOR SON OF A BITCH IN THE BACK OF YOUR TRUCK.
ASHFORD
ESTABLISHED
1802
POLICE

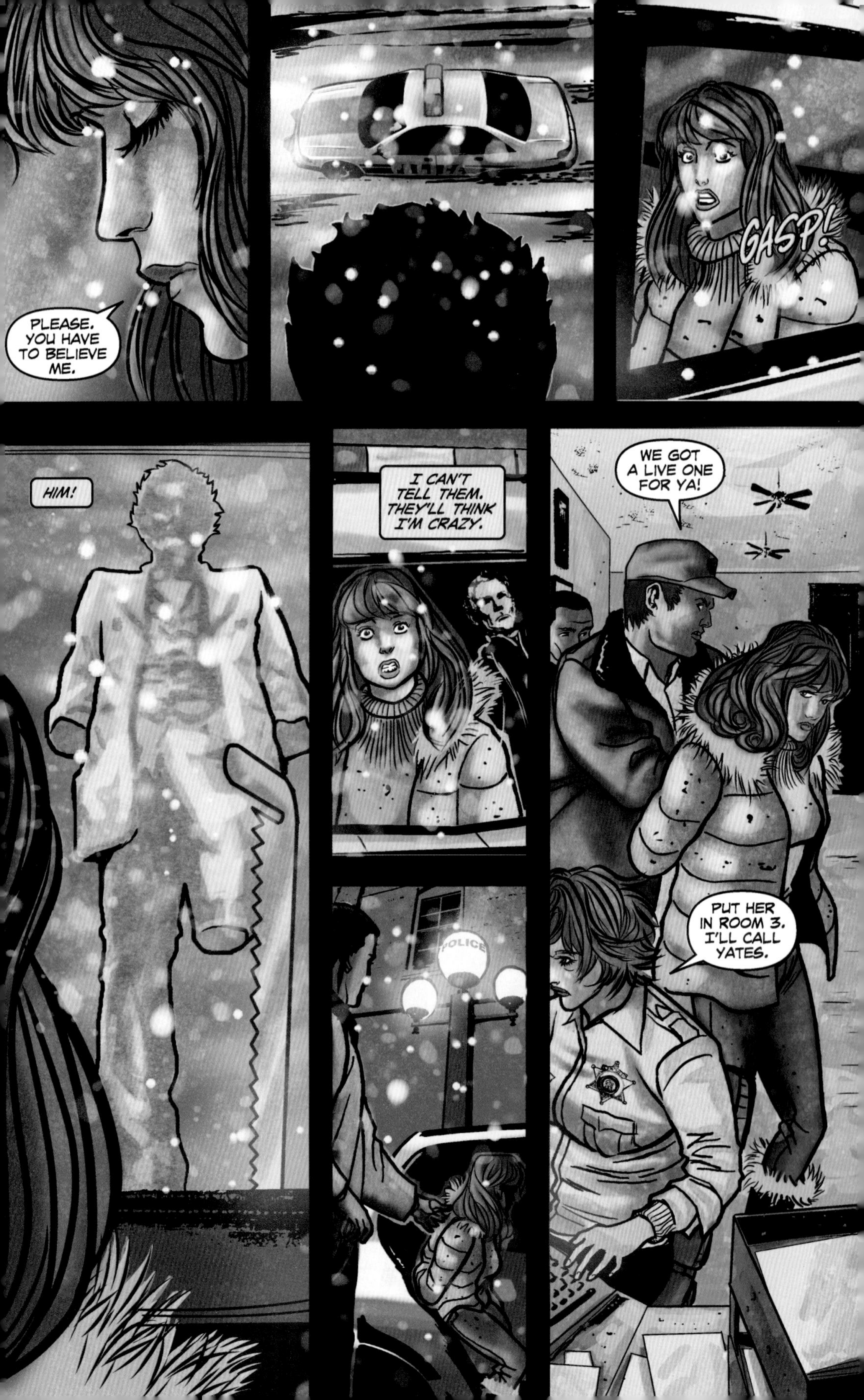
PLEASE. YOU HAVE TO BELIEVE ME.
GASP!
HIM!
I CAN'T TELL THEM. THEY'LL THINK I'M CRAZY.
POLICE
WE GOT A LIVE ONE FOR YA!
PUT HER IN ROOM 3. I'LL CALL YATES.

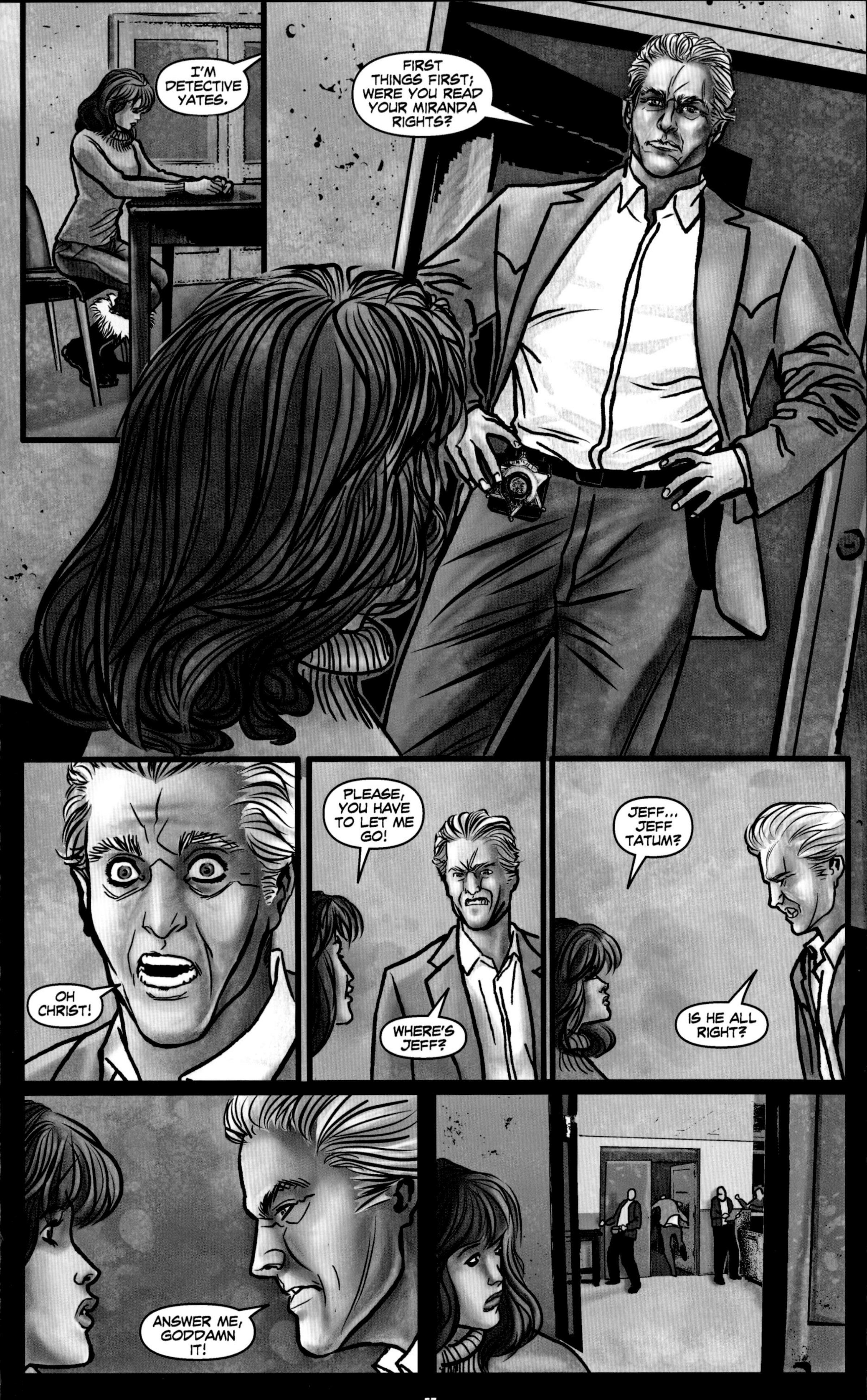
I'M DETECTIVE YATES.
FIRST THINGS FIRST; WERE YOU READ YOUR MIRANDA RIGHTS?
OH CHRIST!
PLEASE, YOU HAVE TO LET ME GO!
WHERE'S JEFF?
JEFF... JEFF TATUM?
IS HE ALL RIGHT?
ANSWER ME, GODDAMN IT!

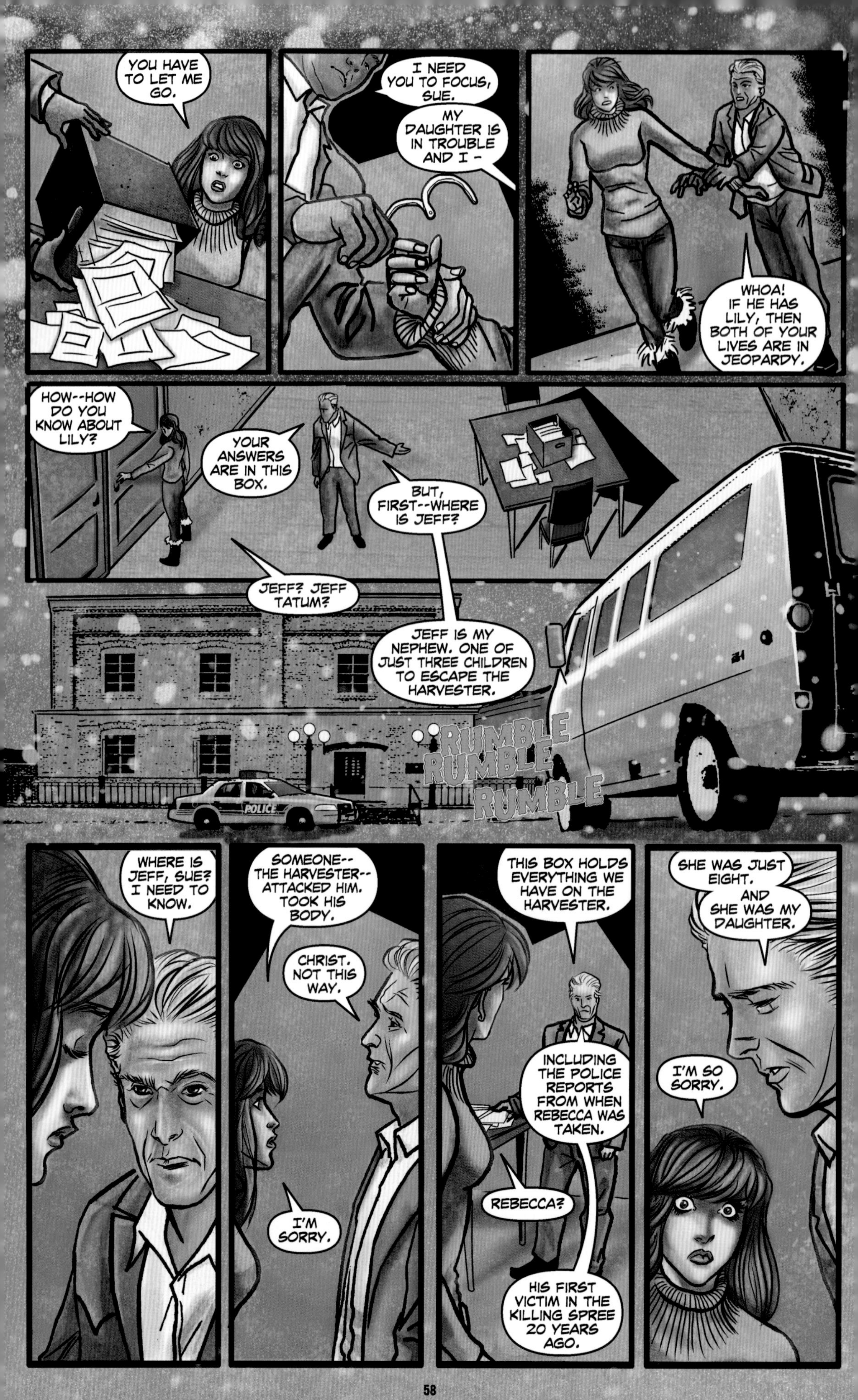
YOU HAVE TO LET ME GO.
I NEED YOU TO FOCUS, SUE.
MY DAUGHTER IS IN TROUBLE AND I -
WHOA! IF HE HAS LILY, THEN BOTH OF YOUR LIVES ARE IN JEOPARDY.
HOW--HOW DO YOU KNOW ABOUT LILY?
YOUR ANSWERS ARE IN THIS BOX.
BUT, FIRST--WHERE IS JEFF?
JEFF? JEFF TATUM?
JEFF IS MY NEPHEW. ONE OF JUST THREE CHILDREN TO ESCAPE THE HARVESTER.
RUMBLE RUMBLE RUMBLE
POLICE
WHERE IS JEFF, SUE? I NEED TO KNOW.
SOMEONE-- THE HARVESTER-- ATTACKED HIM. TOOK HIS BODY.
CHRIST. NOT THIS WAY.
I'M SORRY.
THIS BOX HOLDS EVERYTHING WE HAVE ON THE HARVESTER.
INCLUDING THE POLICE REPORTS FROM WHEN REBECCA WAS TAKEN.
REBECCA?
HIS FIRST VICTIM IN THE KILLING SPREE 20 YEARS AGO.
SHE WAS JUST EIGHT.
AND SHE WAS MY DAUGHTER.
I'M SO SORRY.

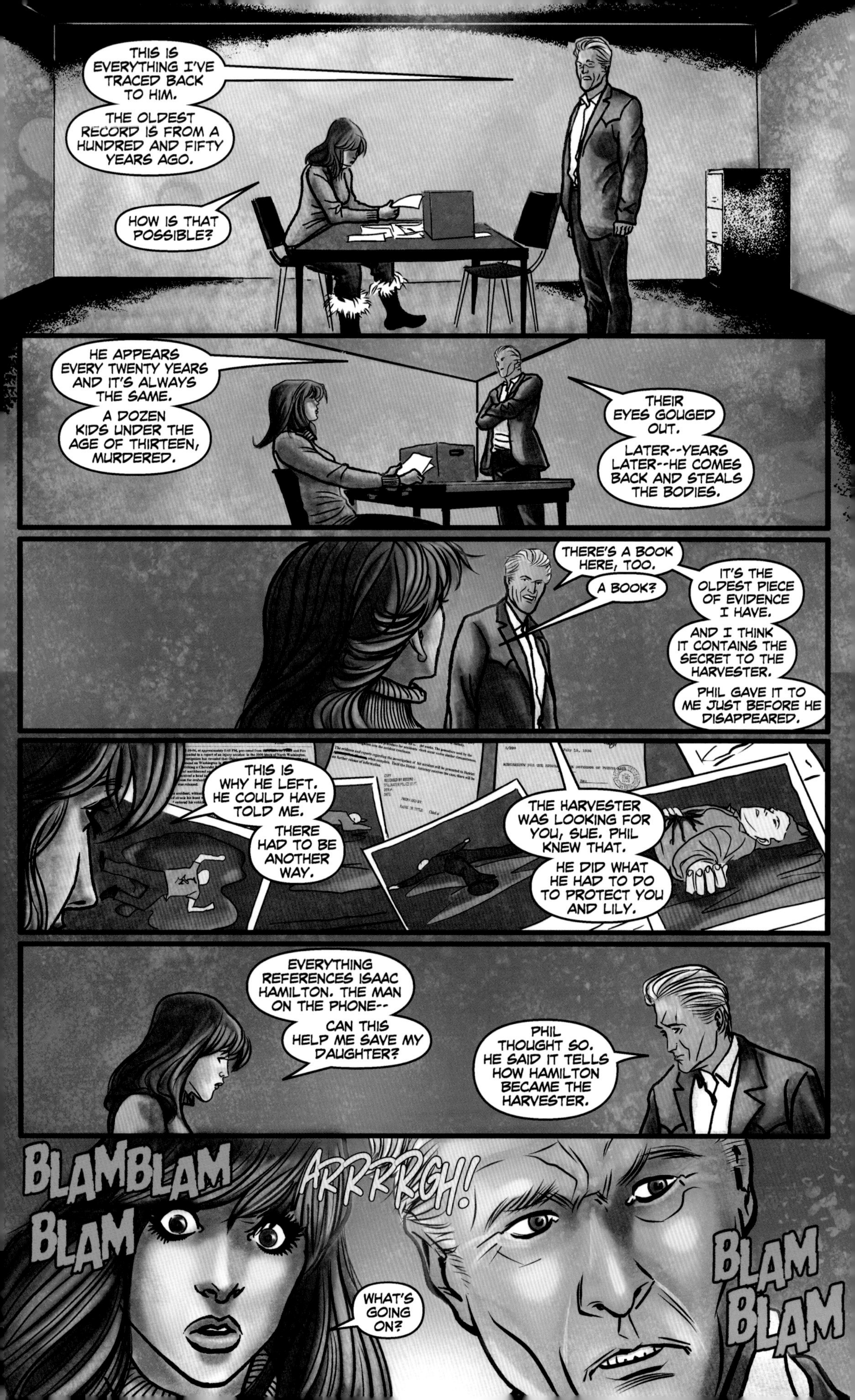
THIS IS EVERYTHING I'VE TRACED BACK TO HIM.
THE OLDEST RECORD IS FROM A HUNDRED AND FIFTY YEARS AGO.
HOW IS THAT POSSIBLE?
HE APPEARS EVERY TWENTY YEARS AND IT'S ALWAYS THE SAME.
A DOZEN KIDS UNDER THE AGE OF THIRTEEN, MURDERED.
THEIR EYES GOUGED OUT.
LATER--YEARS LATER--HE COMES BACK AND STEALS THE BODIES.
THERE'S A BOOK HERE, TOO.
A BOOK?
IT'S THE OLDEST PIECE OF EVIDENCE I HAVE.
AND I THINK IT CONTAINS THE SECRET TO THE HARVESTER.
PHIL GAVE IT TO ME JUST BEFORE HE DISAPPEARED.
THIS IS WHY HE LEFT. HE COULD HAVE TOLD ME.
THERE HAD TO BE ANOTHER WAY.
THE HARVESTER WAS LOOKING FOR YOU, SUE. PHIL KNEW THAT.
HE DID WHAT HE HAD TO DO TO PROTECT YOU AND LILY.
EVERYTHING REFERENCES ISAAC HAMILTON. THE MAN ON THE PHONE--
CAN THIS HELP ME SAVE MY DAUGHTER?
PHIL THOUGHT SO. HE SAID IT TELLS HOW HAMILTON BECAME THE HARVESTER.
BLAMBLAM BLAM
ARRRRGH!
BLAM BLAM
WHAT'S GOING ON?

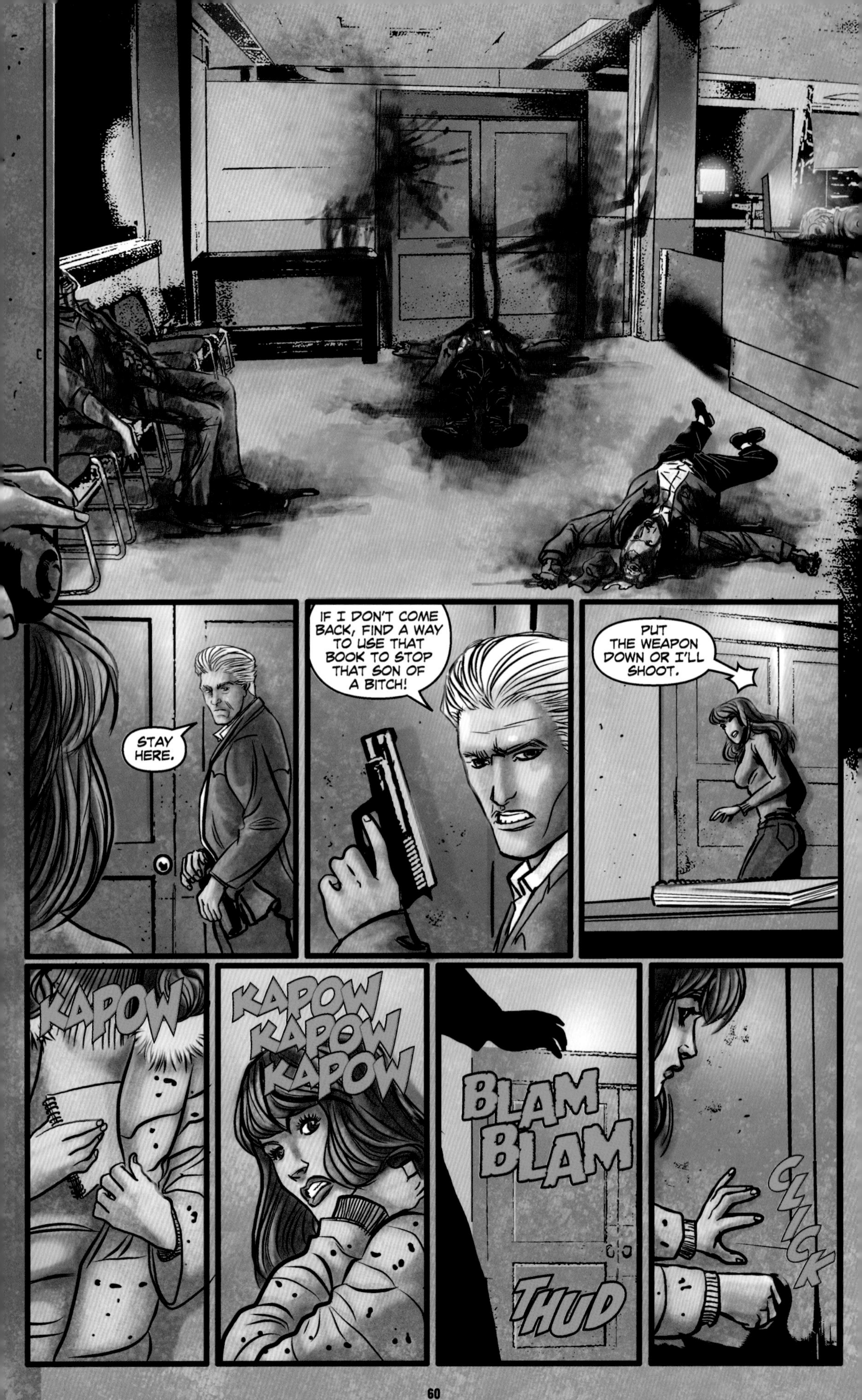
STAY HERE.
IF I DON'T COME BACK, FIND A WAY TO USE THAT BOOK TO STOP THAT SON OF A BITCH!
PUT THE WEAPON DOWN OR I'LL SHOOT.
KAPOW
KAPOW KAPOW KAPOW
BLAM BLAM
THUD
CLICK

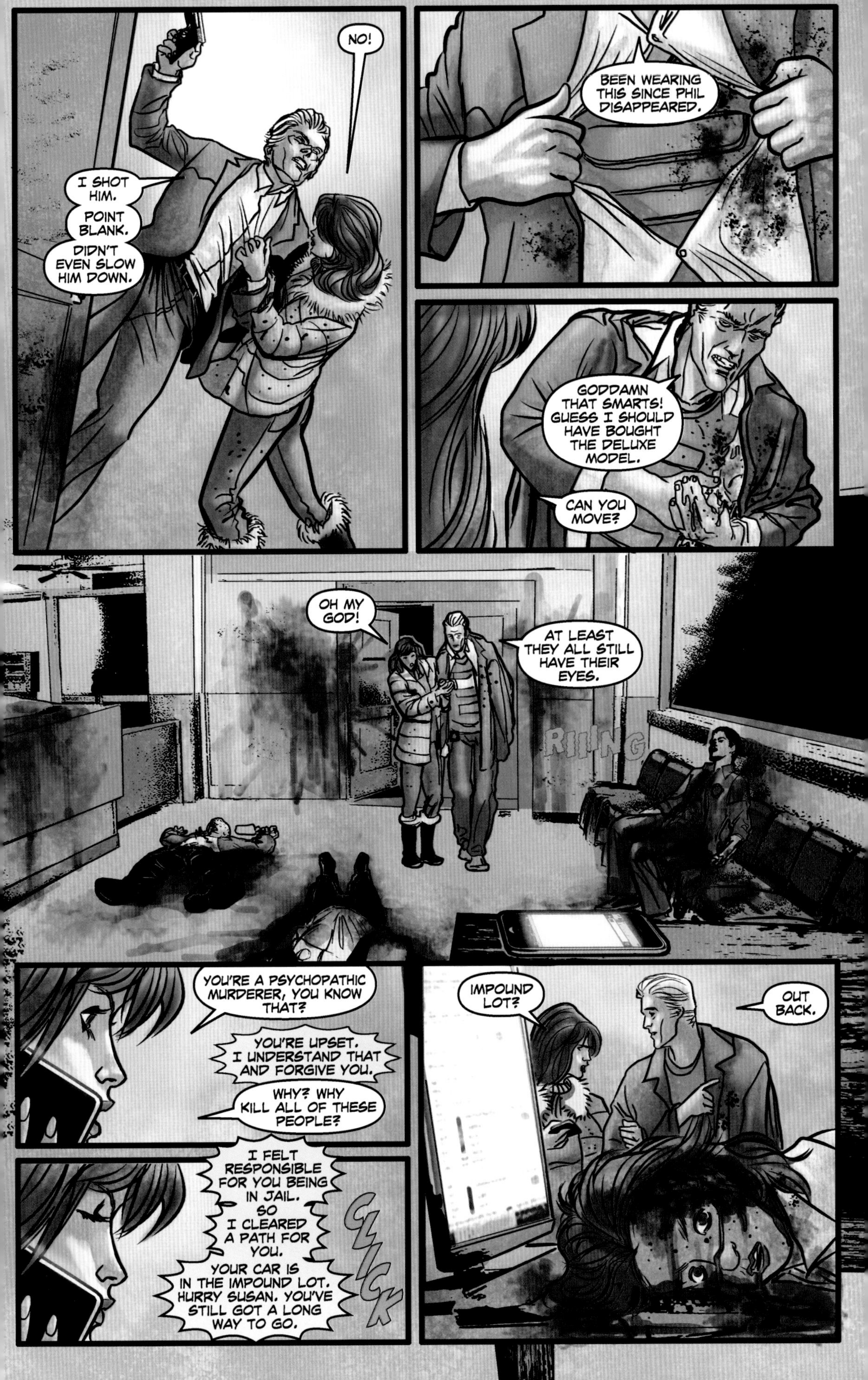
NO!
I SHOT HIM.
POINT BLANK.
DIDN'T EVEN SLOW HIM DOWN.
BEEN WEARING THIS SINCE PHIL DISAPPEARED.
GODDAMN THAT SMARTS! GUESS I SHOULD HAVE BOUGHT THE DELUXE MODEL.
CAN YOU MOVE?
OH MY GOD!
AT LEAST THEY ALL STILL HAVE THEIR EYES.
RIIING
YOU'RE A PSYCHOPATHIC MURDERER, YOU KNOW THAT?
YOU'RE UPSET. I UNDERSTAND THAT AND FORGIVE YOU.
WHY? WHY KILL ALL OF THESE PEOPLE?
I FELT RESPONSIBLE FOR YOU BEING IN JAIL. SO I CLEARED A PATH FOR YOU.
YOUR CAR IS IN THE IMPOUND LOT. HURRY SUSAN. YOU'VE STILL GOT A LONG WAY TO GO.
CLICK
IMPOUND LOT?
OUT BACK.

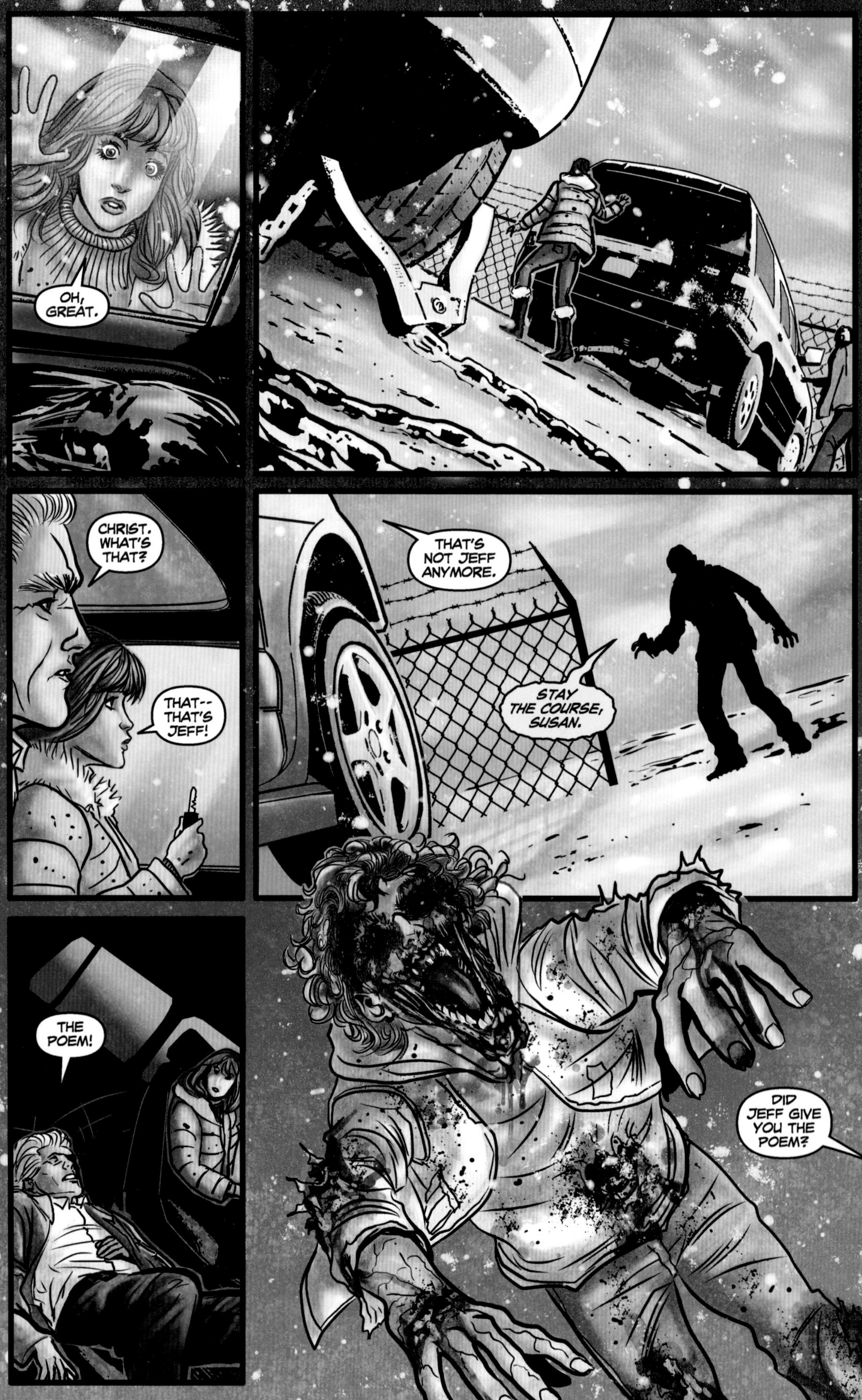

OH, GREAT.
CHRIST. WHAT'S THAT?
THAT-- THAT'S JEFF!
THAT'S NOT JEFF ANYMORE.
STAY THE COURSE, SUSAN.
THE POEM!
DID JEFF GIVE YOU THE POEM?

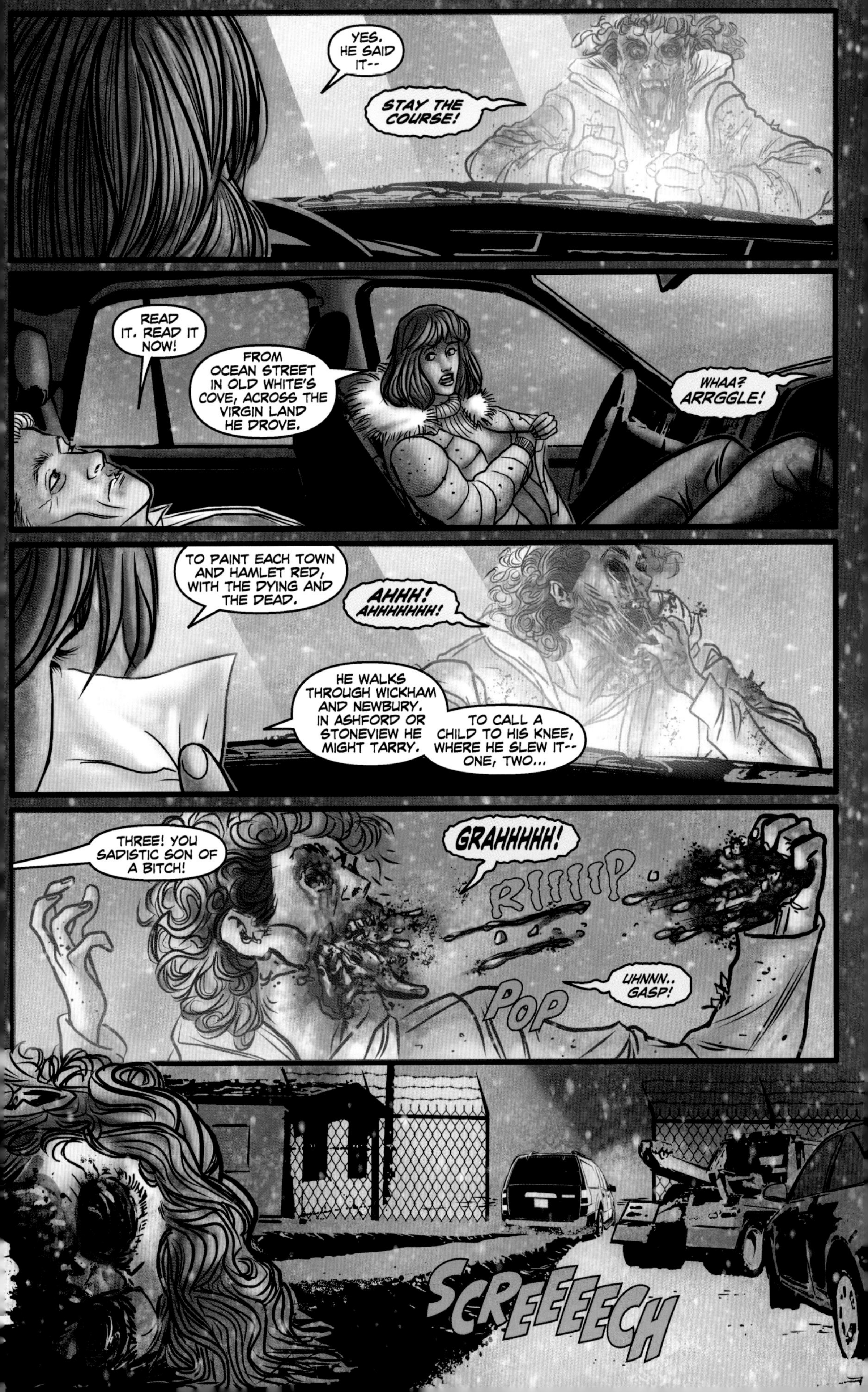
YES. HE SAID IT--
STAY THE COURSE!
READ IT. READ IT NOW!
FROM OCEAN STREET IN OLD WHITE'S COVE, ACROSS THE VIRGIN LAND HE DROVE.
WHAA? ARRGGLE!
TO PAINT EACH TOWN AND HAMLET RED, WITH THE DYING AND THE DEAD.
AHHH! AHHHHHHH!
HE WALKS THROUGH WICKHAM AND NEWBURY. IN ASHFORD OR STONEVIEW HE MIGHT TARRY.
TO CALL A CHILD TO HIS KNEE, WHERE HE SLEW IT-- ONE, TWO...
THREE! YOU SADISTIC SON OF A BITCH!
GRAHHHHH!
RIIIIP
UHNNN.. GASP!
POP
SCREEEECH

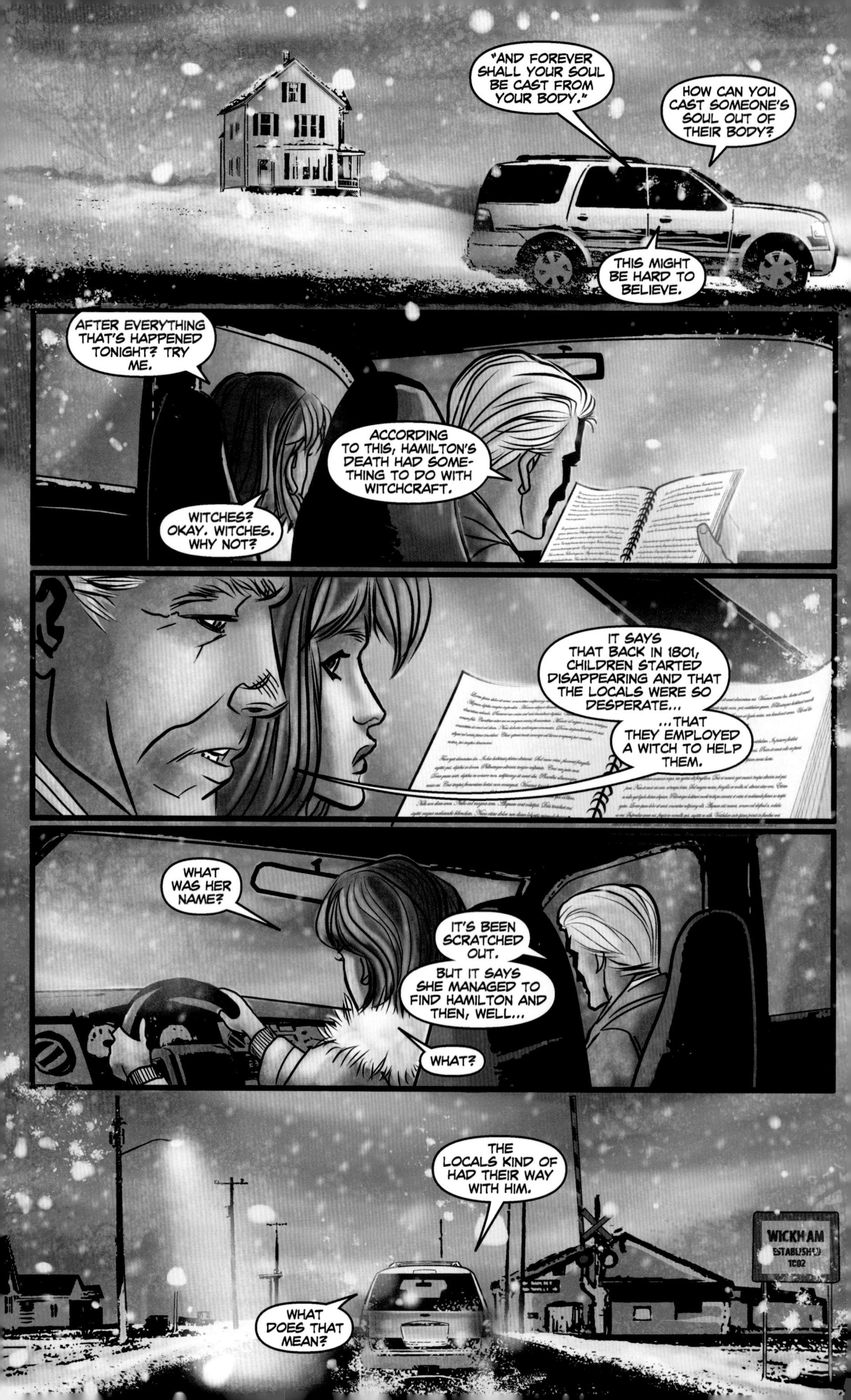
"AND FOREVER SHALL YOUR SOUL BE CAST FROM YOUR BODY."
HOW CAN YOU CAST SOMEONE'S SOUL OUT OF THEIR BODY?
THIS MIGHT BE HARD TO BELIEVE.
AFTER EVERYTHING THAT'S HAPPENED TONIGHT? TRY ME.
ACCORDING TO THIS, HAMILTON'S DEATH HAD SOMETHING TO DO WITH WITCHCRAFT.
WITCHES? OKAY. WITCHES. WHY NOT?
IT SAYS THAT BACK IN 1801, CHILDREN STARTED DISAPPEARING AND THAT THE LOCALS WERE SO DESPERATE...
...THAT THEY EMPLOYED A WITCH TO HELP THEM.
WHAT WAS HER NAME?
IT'S BEEN SCRATCHED OUT.
BUT IT SAYS SHE MANAGED TO FIND HAMILTON AND THEN, WELL...
WHAT?
THE LOCALS KIND OF HAD THEIR WAY WITH HIM.
WICKHAM
WHAT DOES THAT MEAN?

THE LOCALS BURNED HIM, BUT HE CAME BACK TO LIFE!

WHAT?

THEY BURNED HIM AGAIN. THEN DROWNED HIM. BUT HE KEPT COMING BACK.

THE WITCH SAID HE HAD SOME SORT OF "STRANGE MAGIC" IN HIM...

...AND THAT KILLING HIM THE NORMAL WAY WOULDN'T WORK.

SO THEY PULLED THE BASTARD APART AND BURIED THE PIECES ALL OVER NEW ENGLAND.

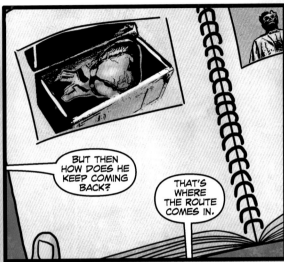

BUT THEN HOW DOES HE KEEP COMING BACK?

THAT'S WHERE THE ROUTE COMES IN.

I KNOW IT'S THE KEY. I JUST DON'T KNOW HOW OR WHY. NEAR AS I CAN TELL, EVEN THOUGH HIS BODY PARTS ARE SEPARATED...

...THEY'RE STILL CONNECTED SOMEHOW.

STRANGE MAGIC.

AND THE PATH HE'S MAKING YOU TAKE...

...IS THE PATH THE HARVESTER TAKES WHEN MURDERING CHILDREN.

YES.

SO HAMILTON IS THE HARVESTER.

I DON'T THINK SO. HIS PARTS ARE INSIDE EACH OF THOSE STATUES... SO HE CAN'T PHYSICALLY BE THE SAME PERSON AS THE HARVESTER.

BUT--

HAMILTON MUST SOMEHOW CONTROL THE DEAD.

LIKE MARILYN AND JEFF.

HE REVIVES THE DEAD BODIES AND USES THEM.

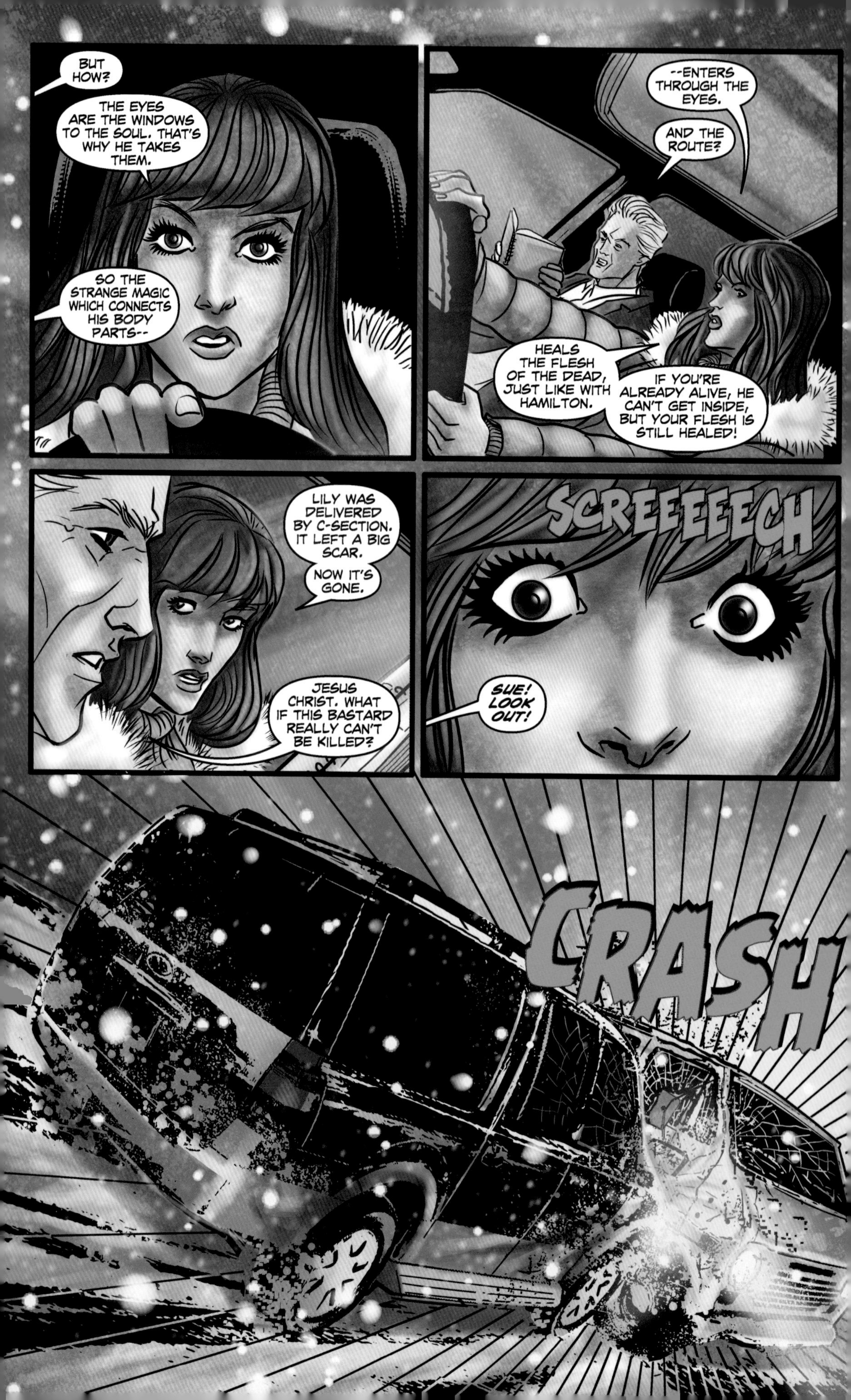

BUT HOW?
THE EYES ARE THE WINDOWS TO THE SOUL. THAT'S WHY HE TAKES THEM.
SO THE STRANGE MAGIC WHICH CONNECTS HIS BODY PARTS--
--ENTERS THROUGH THE EYES.
AND THE ROUTE?
HEALS THE FLESH OF THE DEAD, JUST LIKE WITH HAMILTON.
IF YOU'RE ALREADY ALIVE, HE CAN'T GET INSIDE, BUT YOUR FLESH IS STILL HEALED!
LILY WAS DELIVERED BY C-SECTION. IT LEFT A BIG SCAR.
NOW IT'S GONE.
JESUS CHRIST. WHAT IF THIS BASTARD REALLY CAN'T BE KILLED?
SCREEEEECH
SUE! LOOK OUT!
CRASH

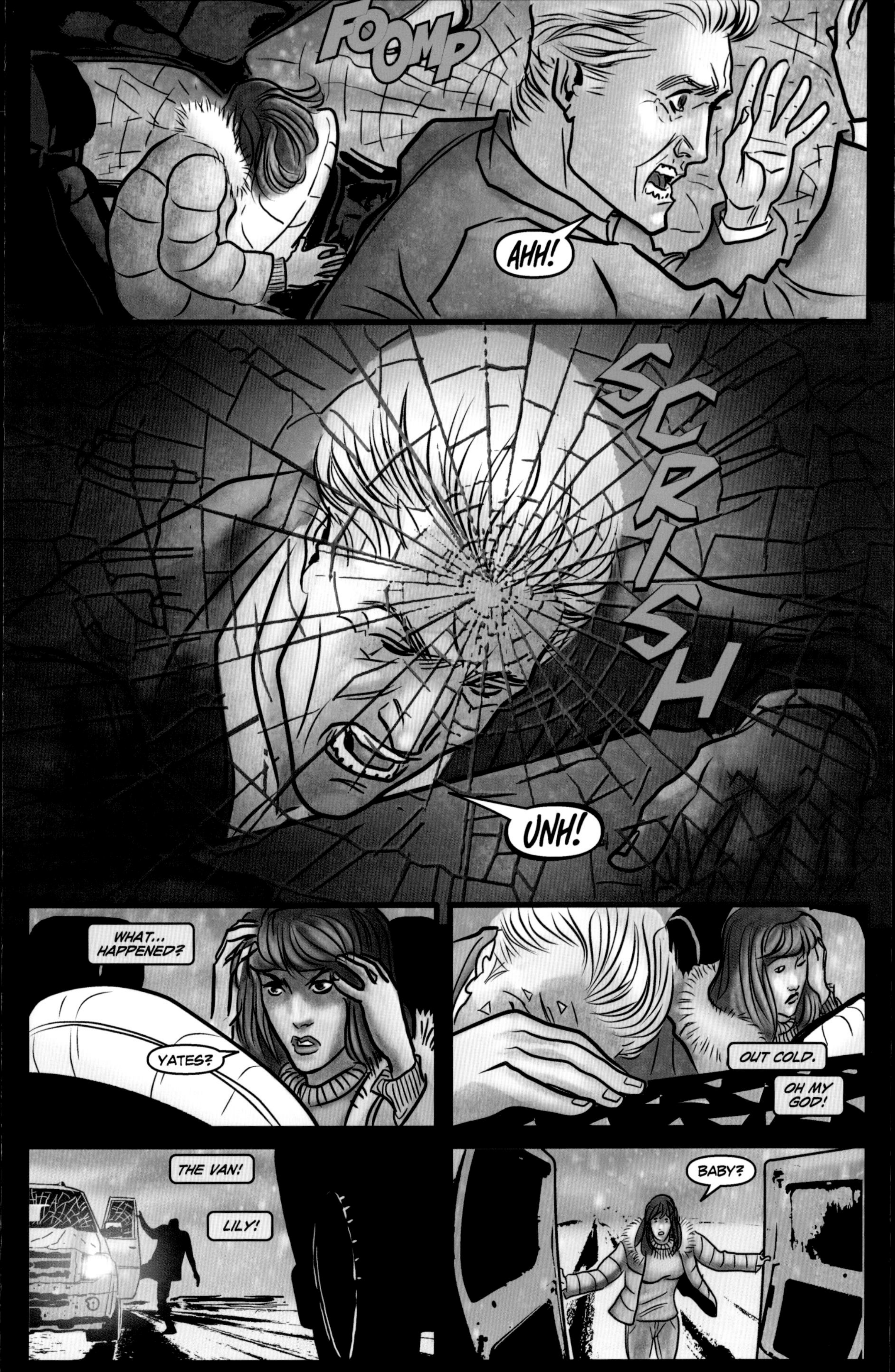
FOOMP
AHH!
SCRISH
UNH!
WHAT... HAPPENED?
YATES?
OUT COLD.
OH MY GOD!
THE VAN!
LILY!
BABY?

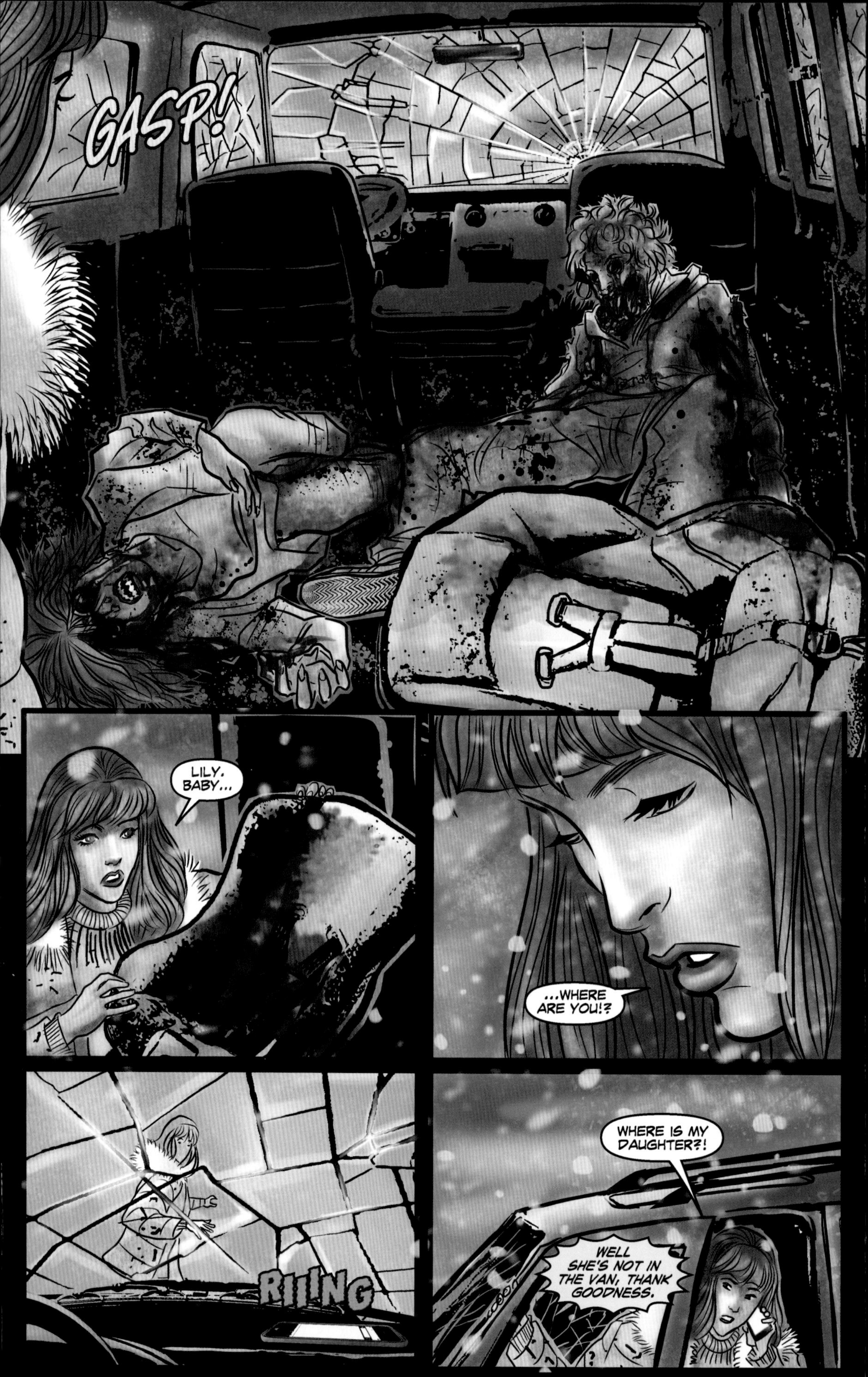
GASP!
LILY. BABY...
...WHERE ARE YOU!?
RIIING
WHERE IS MY DAUGHTER?!
WELL SHE'S NOT IN THE VAN, THANK GOODNESS.

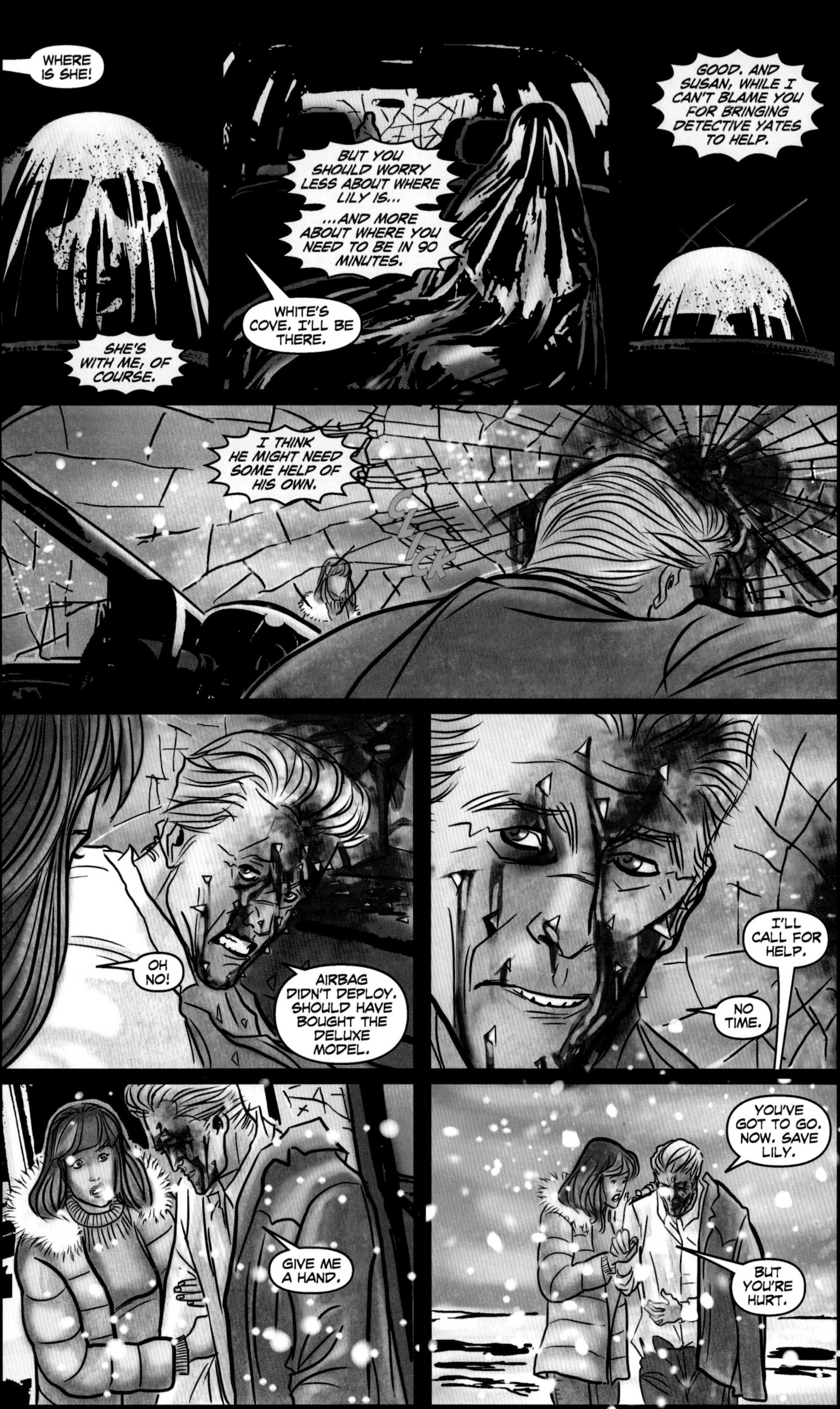
WHERE IS SHE!
SHE'S WITH ME, OF COURSE.
BUT YOU SHOULD WORRY LESS ABOUT WHERE LILY IS...
...AND MORE ABOUT WHERE YOU NEED TO BE IN 90 MINUTES.
WHITE'S COVE. I'LL BE THERE.
GOOD. AND SUSAN, WHILE I CAN'T BLAME YOU FOR BRINGING DETECTIVE YATES TO HELP.
I THINK HE MIGHT NEED SOME HELP OF HIS OWN.
CLICK
OH NO!
AIRBAG DIDN'T DEPLOY. SHOULD HAVE BOUGHT THE DELUXE MODEL.
I'LL CALL FOR HELP.
NO TIME.
GIVE ME A HAND.
YOU'VE GOT TO GO. NOW. SAVE LILY.
BUT YOU'RE HURT.

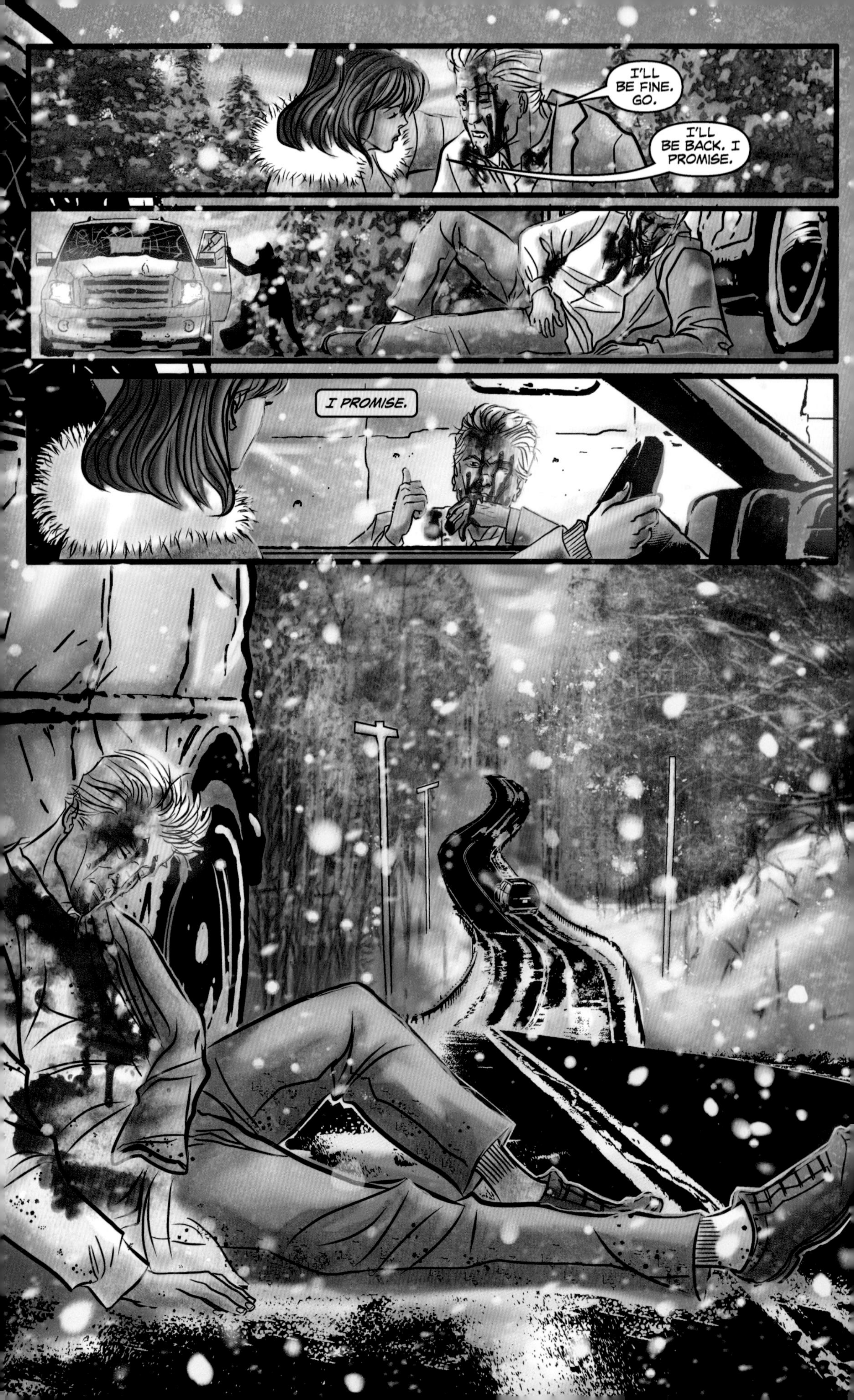
I'LL BE FINE. GO.
I'LL BE BACK. I PROMISE.
I PROMISE.

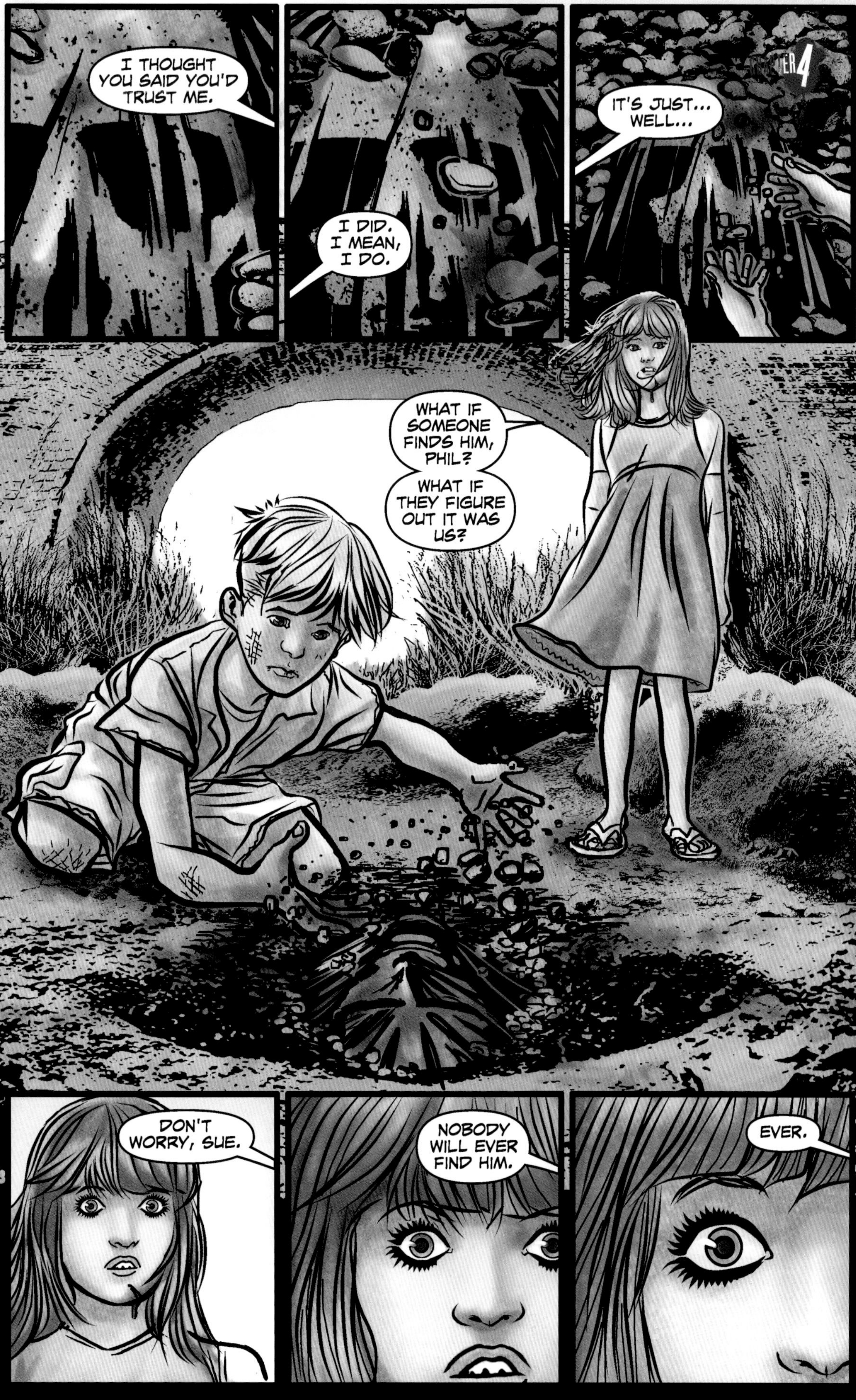

I THOUGHT YOU SAID YOU'D TRUST ME.
I DID. I MEAN, I DO.
IT'S JUST... WELL...
WHAT IF SOMEONE FINDS HIM, PHIL?
WHAT IF THEY FIGURE OUT IT WAS US?
DON'T WORRY, SUE.
NOBODY WILL EVER FIND HIM.
EVER.

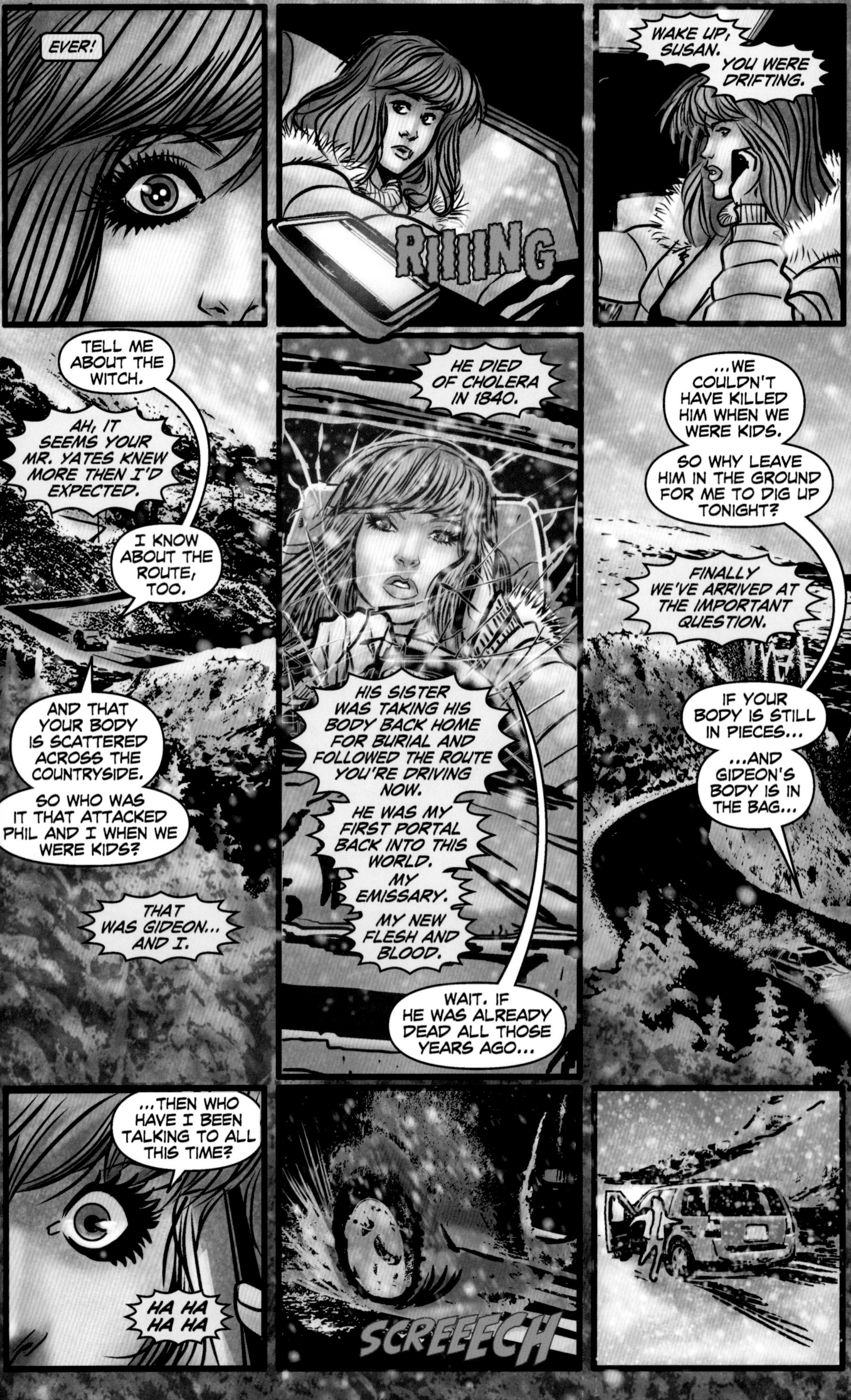
EVER!
RIIIING
WAKE UP, SUSAN.
YOU WERE DRIFTING.
TELL ME ABOUT THE WITCH.
AH, IT SEEMS YOUR MR. YATES KNEW MORE THEN I'D EXPECTED.
I KNOW ABOUT THE ROUTE, TOO.
AND THAT YOUR BODY IS SCATTERED ACROSS THE COUNTRYSIDE.
SO WHO WAS IT THAT ATTACKED PHIL AND I WHEN WE WERE KIDS?
THAT WAS GIDEON... AND I.
HE DIED OF CHOLERA IN 1840.
HIS SISTER WAS TAKING HIS BODY BACK HOME FOR BURIAL AND FOLLOWED THE ROUTE YOU'RE DRIVING NOW.
HE WAS MY FIRST PORTAL BACK INTO THIS WORLD.
MY EMISSARY.
MY NEW FLESH AND BLOOD.
WAIT. IF HE WAS ALREADY DEAD ALL THOSE YEARS AGO...
...WE COULDN'T HAVE KILLED HIM WHEN WE WERE KIDS.
SO WHY LEAVE HIM IN THE GROUND FOR ME TO DIG UP TONIGHT?
FINALLY WE'VE ARRIVED AT THE IMPORTANT QUESTION.
IF YOUR BODY IS STILL IN PIECES...
...AND GIDEON'S BODY IS IN THE BAG...
...THEN WHO HAVE I BEEN TALKING TO ALL THIS TIME?
HA HA HA HA
SCREEECH

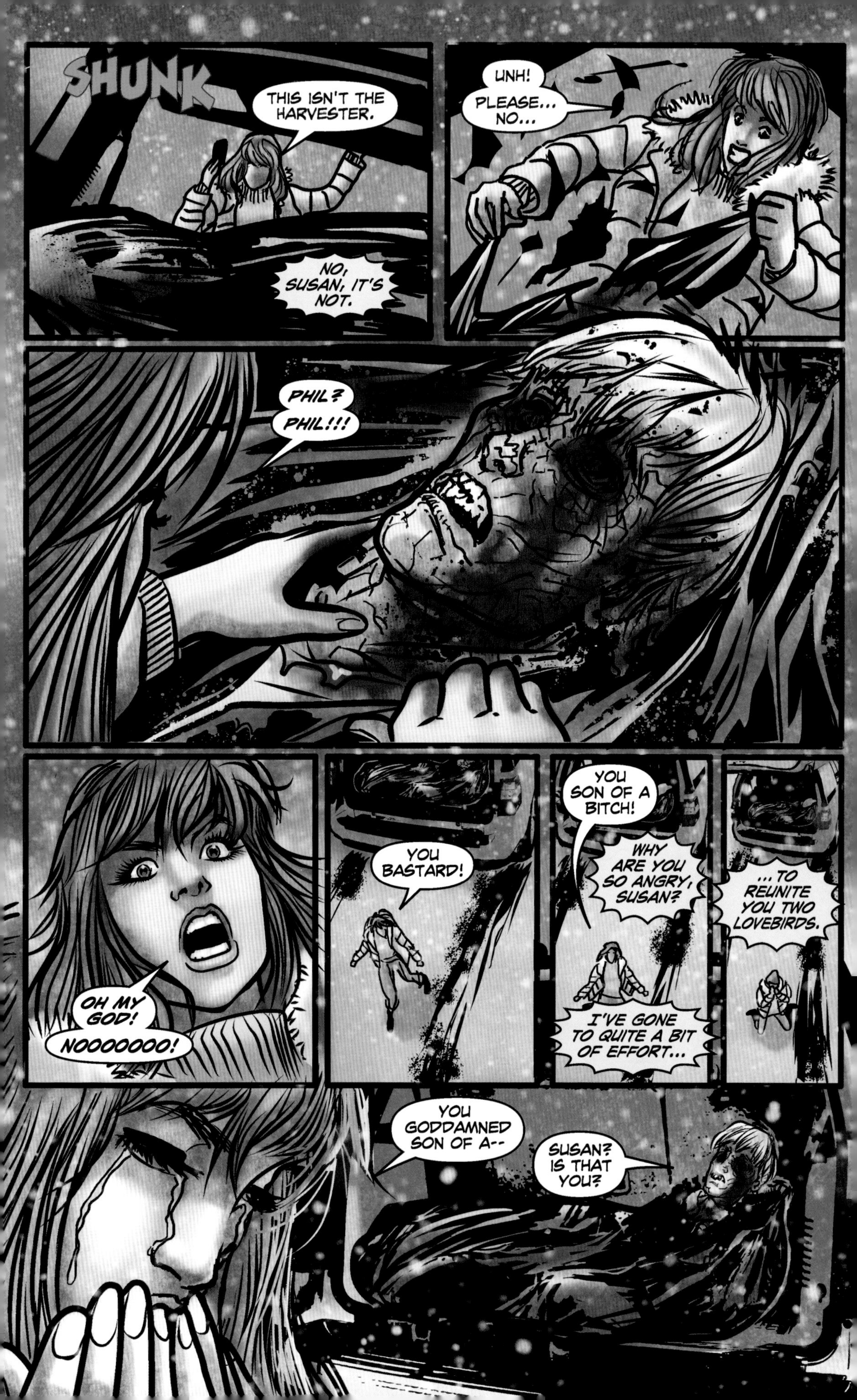
SHUNK
THIS ISN'T THE HARVESTER.
NO, SUSAN, IT'S NOT.
UNH! PLEASE... NO...
PHIL?
PHIL!!!
OH MY GOD!
NOOOOOOO!
YOU BASTARD!
YOU SON OF A BITCH!
WHY ARE YOU SO ANGRY, SUSAN?
I'VE GONE TO QUITE A BIT OF EFFORT...
...TO REUNITE YOU TWO LOVEBIRDS.
YOU GODDAMNED SON OF A--
SUSAN? IS THAT YOU?

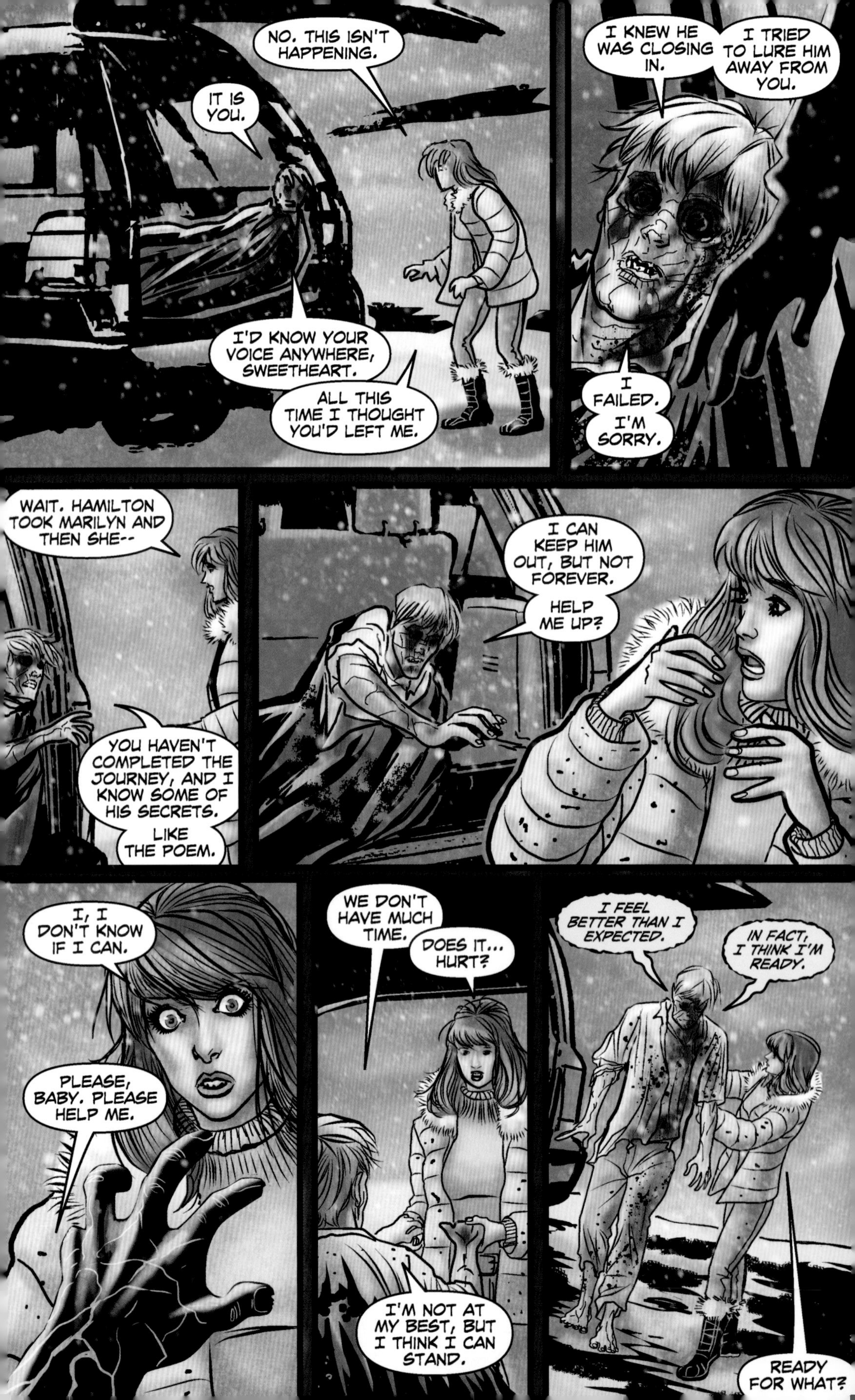
NO. THIS ISN'T HAPPENING.
IT IS YOU.
I'D KNOW YOUR VOICE ANYWHERE, SWEETHEART.
ALL THIS TIME I THOUGHT YOU'D LEFT ME.
I KNEW HE WAS CLOSING IN.
I TRIED TO LURE HIM AWAY FROM YOU.
I FAILED.
I'M SORRY.
WAIT. HAMILTON TOOK MARILYN AND THEN SHE--
YOU HAVEN'T COMPLETED THE JOURNEY, AND I KNOW SOME OF HIS SECRETS.
LIKE THE POEM.
I CAN KEEP HIM OUT, BUT NOT FOREVER.
HELP ME UP?
I, I DON'T KNOW IF I CAN.
PLEASE, BABY. PLEASE HELP ME.
WE DON'T HAVE MUCH TIME.
DOES IT... HURT?
I'M NOT AT MY BEST, BUT I THINK I CAN STAND.
I FEEL BETTER THAN I EXPECTED.
IN FACT, I THINK I'M READY.
READY FOR WHAT?

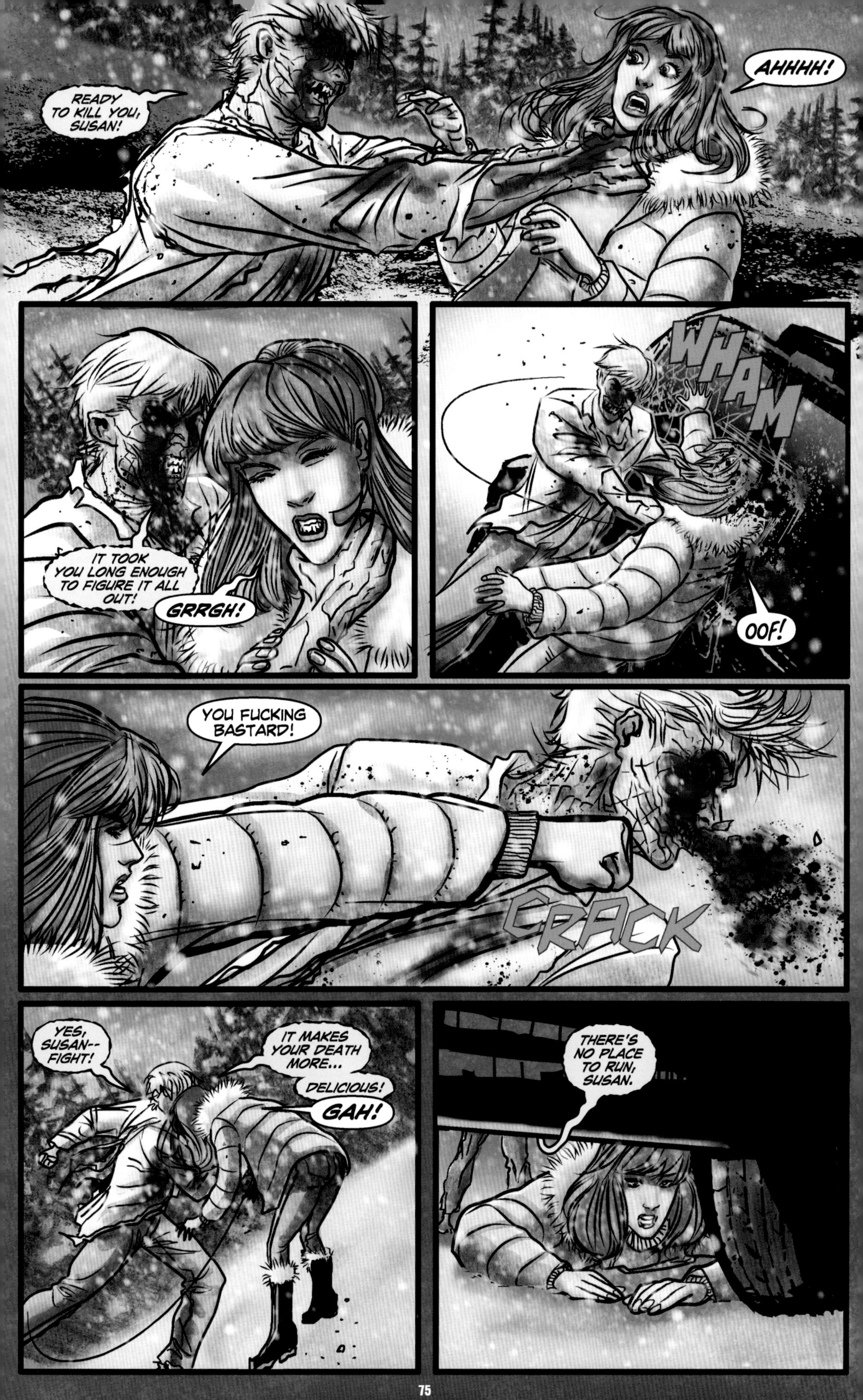
READY TO KILL YOU, SUSAN!
AHHHH!
IT TOOK YOU LONG ENOUGH TO FIGURE IT ALL OUT!
GRRGH!
WHAM
OOF!
YOU FUCKING BASTARD!
CRACK
YES, SUSAN-- FIGHT!
IT MAKES YOUR DEATH MORE...
DELICIOUS!
GAH!
THERE'S NO PLACE TO RUN, SUSAN.

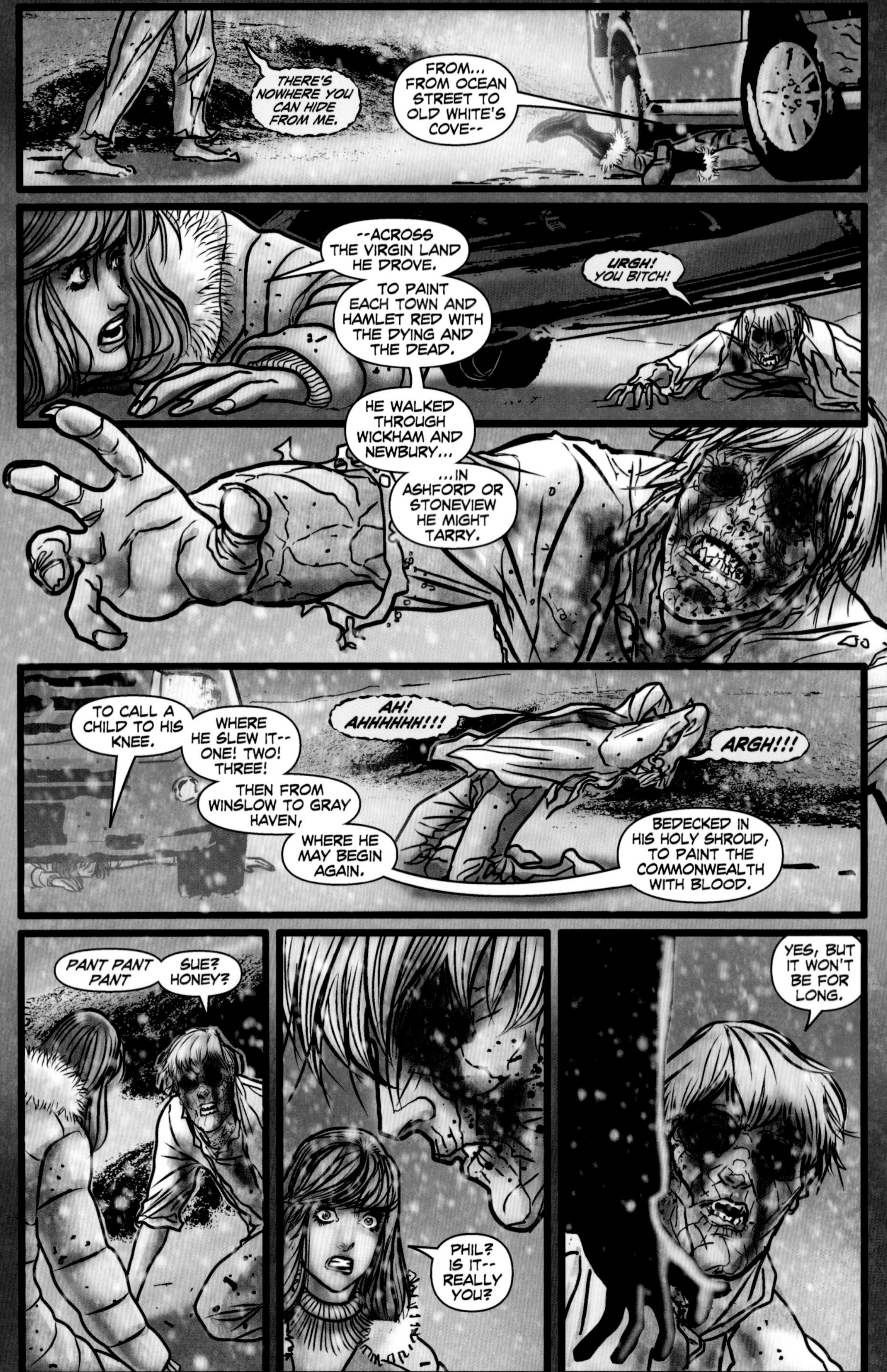
THERE'S NOWHERE YOU CAN HIDE FROM ME.
FROM... FROM OCEAN STREET TO OLD WHITE'S COVE--
--ACROSS THE VIRGIN LAND HE DROVE.
TO PAINT EACH TOWN AND HAMLET RED WITH THE DYING AND THE DEAD.
URGH! YOU BITCH!
HE WALKED THROUGH WICKHAM AND NEWBURY...
...IN ASHFORD OR STONEVIEW HE MIGHT TARRY.
TO CALL A CHILD TO HIS KNEE.
WHERE HE SLEW IT-- ONE! TWO! THREE!
THEN FROM WINSLOW TO GRAY HAVEN,
WHERE HE MAY BEGIN AGAIN.
AH! AHHHHHH!!!
ARGH!!!
BEDECKED IN HIS HOLY SHROUD, TO PAINT THE COMMONWEALTH WITH BLOOD.
PANT PANT PANT
SUE? HONEY?
PHIL? IS IT-- REALLY YOU?
YES, BUT IT WON'T BE FOR LONG.

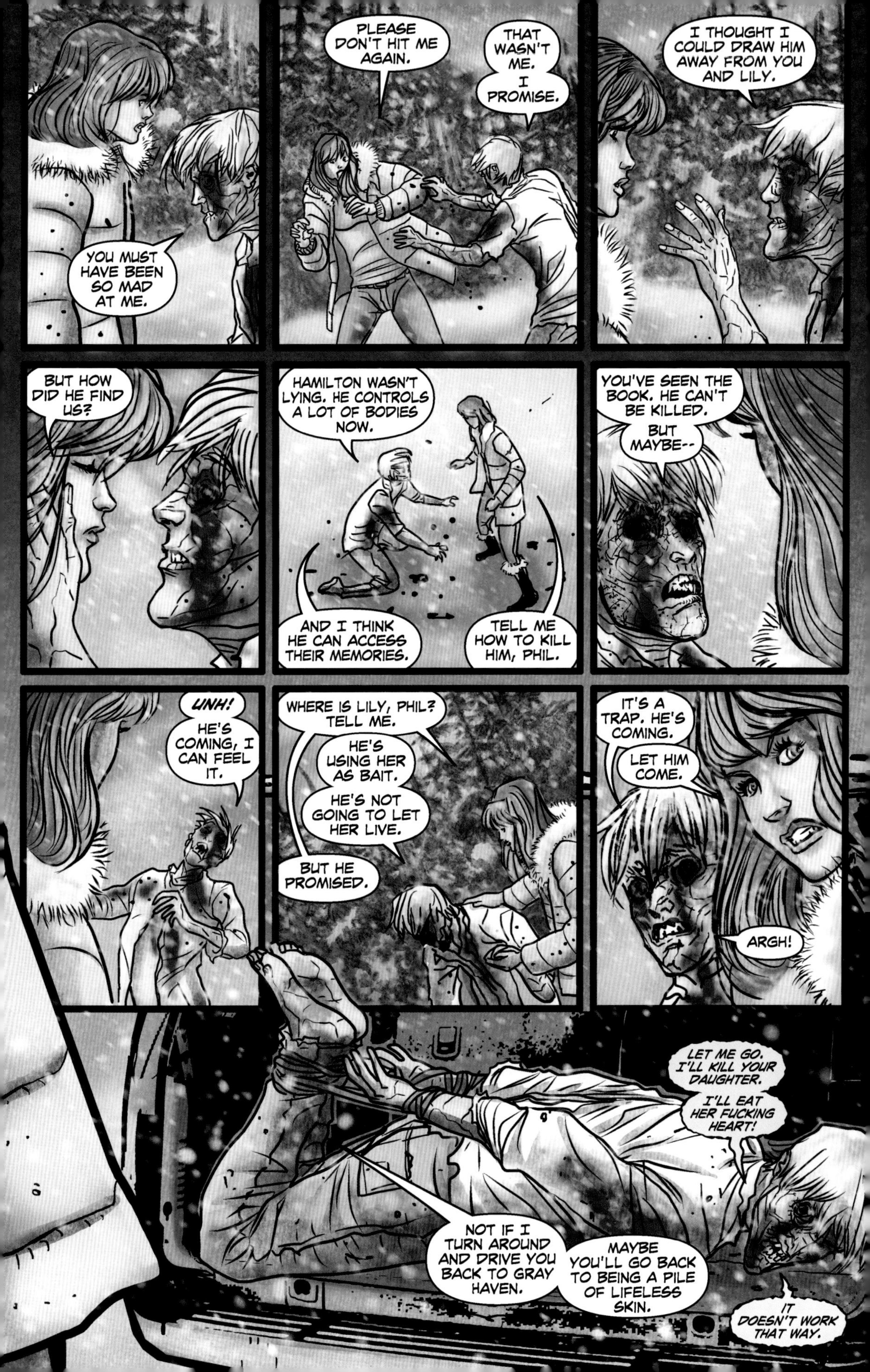
YOU MUST HAVE BEEN SO MAD AT ME.
PLEASE DON'T HIT ME AGAIN.
THAT WASN'T ME.
I PROMISE.
I THOUGHT I COULD DRAW HIM AWAY FROM YOU AND LILY.
BUT HOW DID HE FIND US?
HAMILTON WASN'T LYING. HE CONTROLS A LOT OF BODIES NOW.
AND I THINK HE CAN ACCESS THEIR MEMORIES.
TELL ME HOW TO KILL HIM, PHIL.
YOU'VE SEEN THE BOOK. HE CAN'T BE KILLED.
BUT MAYBE--
UNH!
HE'S COMING, I CAN FEEL IT.
WHERE IS LILY, PHIL? TELL ME.
HE'S USING HER AS BAIT.
HE'S NOT GOING TO LET HER LIVE.
BUT HE PROMISED.
IT'S A TRAP. HE'S COMING.
LET HIM COME.
ARGH!
LET ME GO. I'LL KILL YOUR DAUGHTER.
I'LL EAT HER FUCKING HEART!
NOT IF I TURN AROUND AND DRIVE YOU BACK TO GRAY HAVEN.
MAYBE YOU'LL GO BACK TO BEING A PILE OF LIFELESS SKIN.
IT DOESN'T WORK THAT WAY.

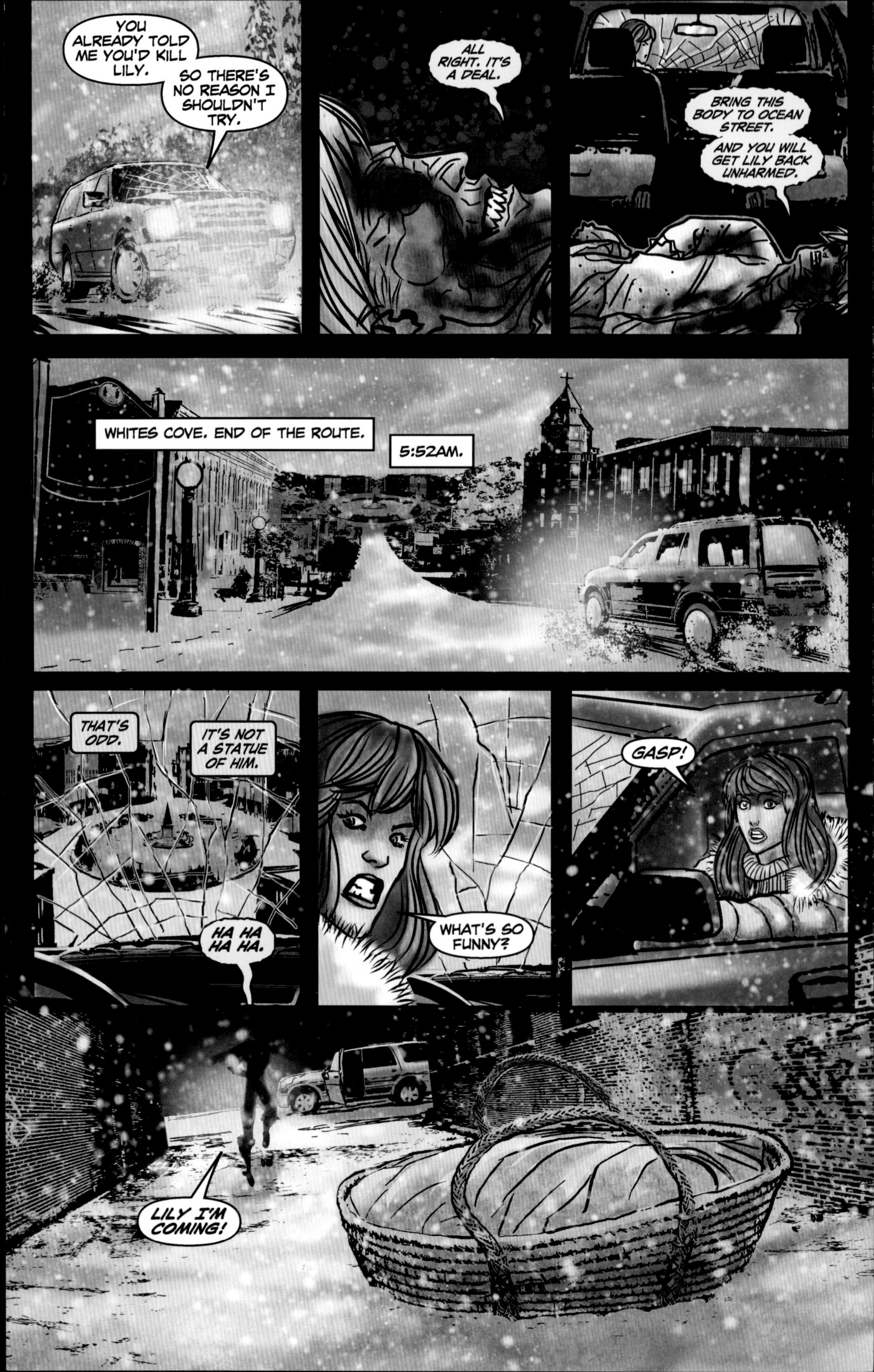
YOU ALREADY TOLD ME YOU'D KILL LILY.
SO THERE'S NO REASON I SHOULDN'T TRY.
ALL RIGHT. IT'S A DEAL.
BRING THIS BODY TO OCEAN STREET.
AND YOU WILL GET LILY BACK UNHARMED.
WHITES COVE. END OF THE ROUTE.
5:52AM.
THAT'S ODD.
IT'S NOT A STATUE OF HIM.
HA HA HA HA.
WHAT'S SO FUNNY?
GASP!
LILY I'M COMING!

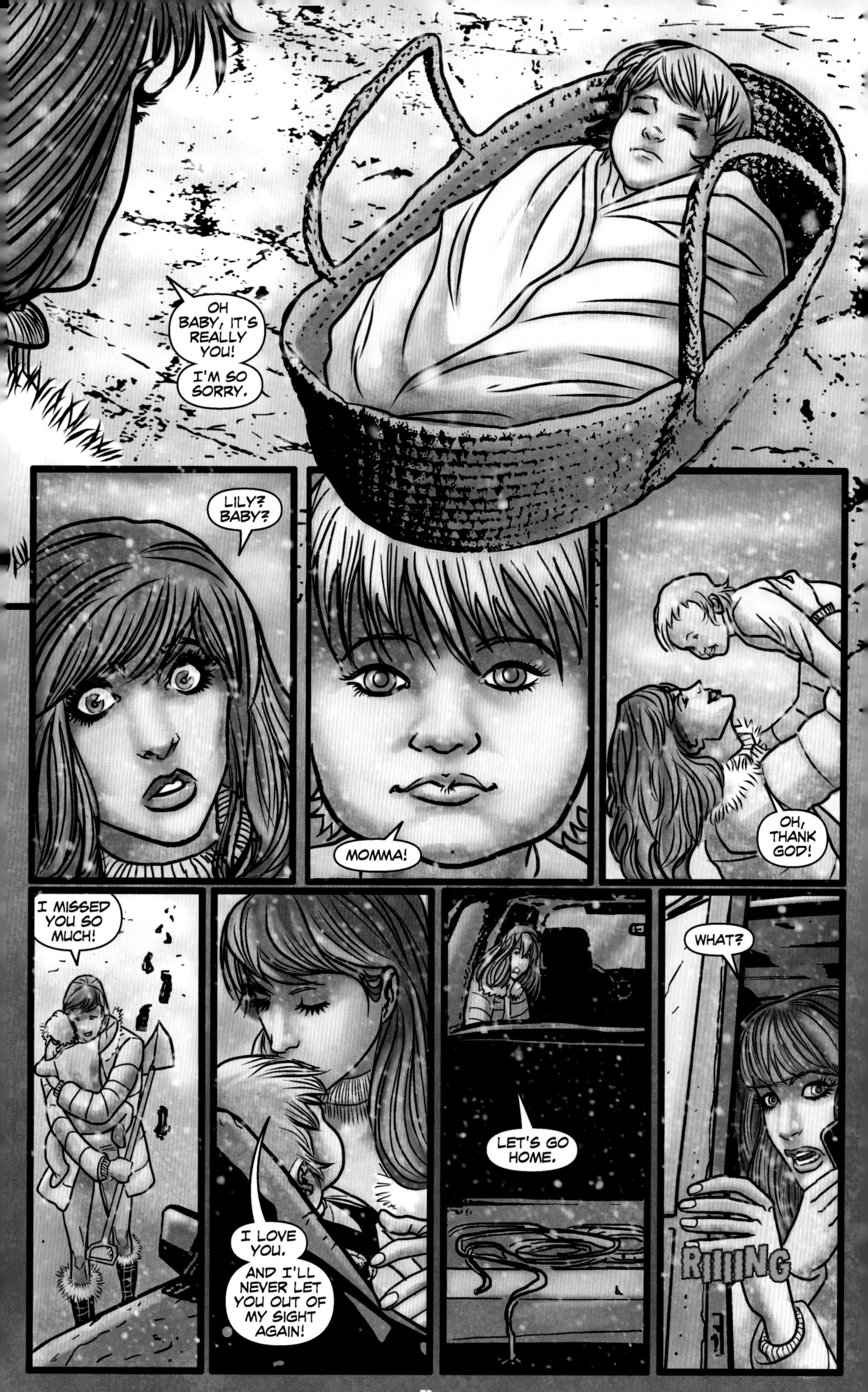
OH BABY, IT'S REALLY YOU!
I'M SO SORRY.
LILY? BABY?
MOMMA!
OH, THANK GOD!
I MISSED YOU SO MUCH!
I LOVE YOU.
AND I'LL NEVER LET YOU OUT OF MY SIGHT AGAIN!
LET'S GO HOME.
WHAT?
RIIIING

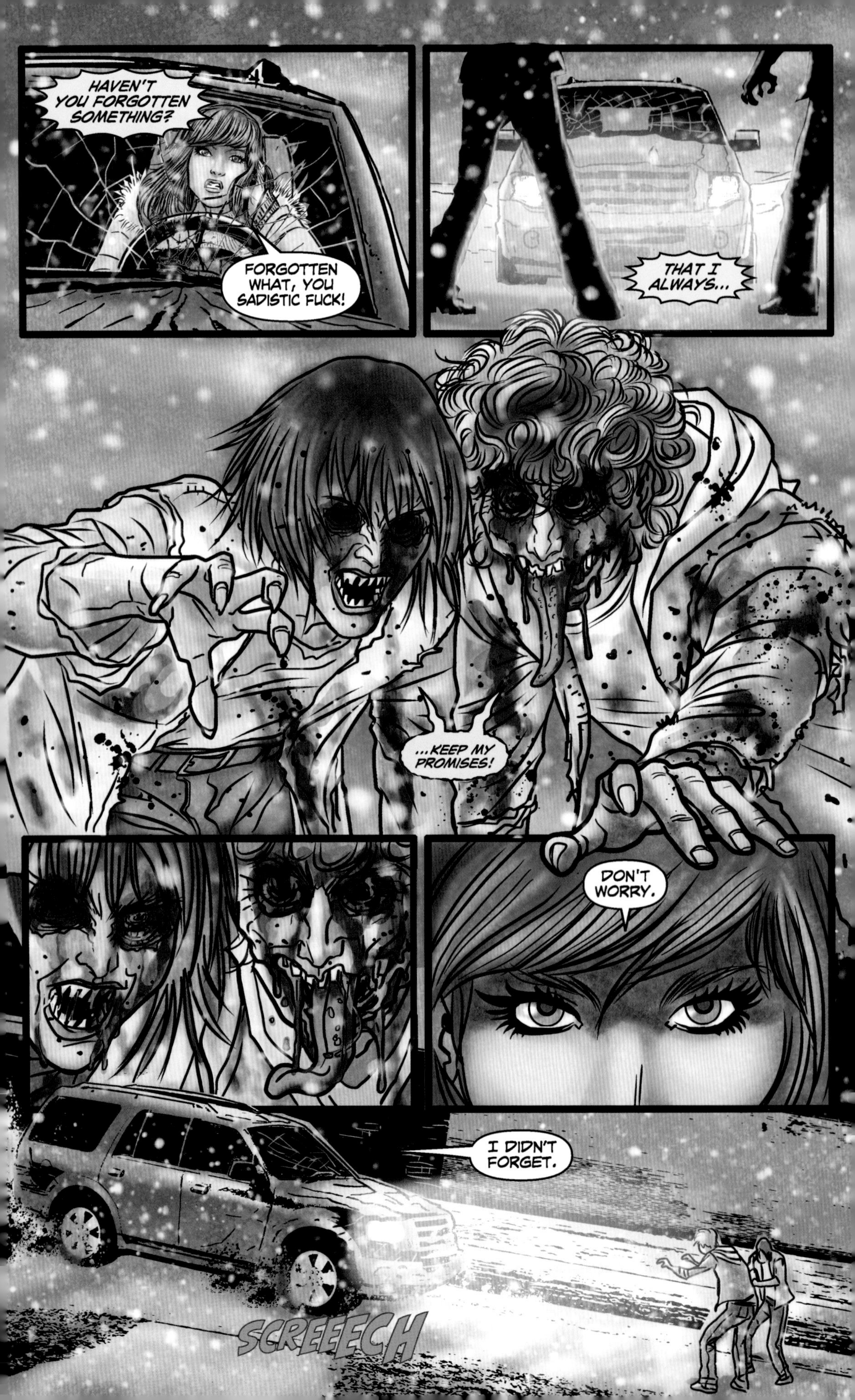
HAVEN'T YOU FORGOTTEN SOMETHING?
FORGOTTEN WHAT, YOU SADISTIC FUCK!
THAT I ALWAYS...
...KEEP MY PROMISES!
DON'T WORRY.
I DIDN'T FORGET.
SCREEECH

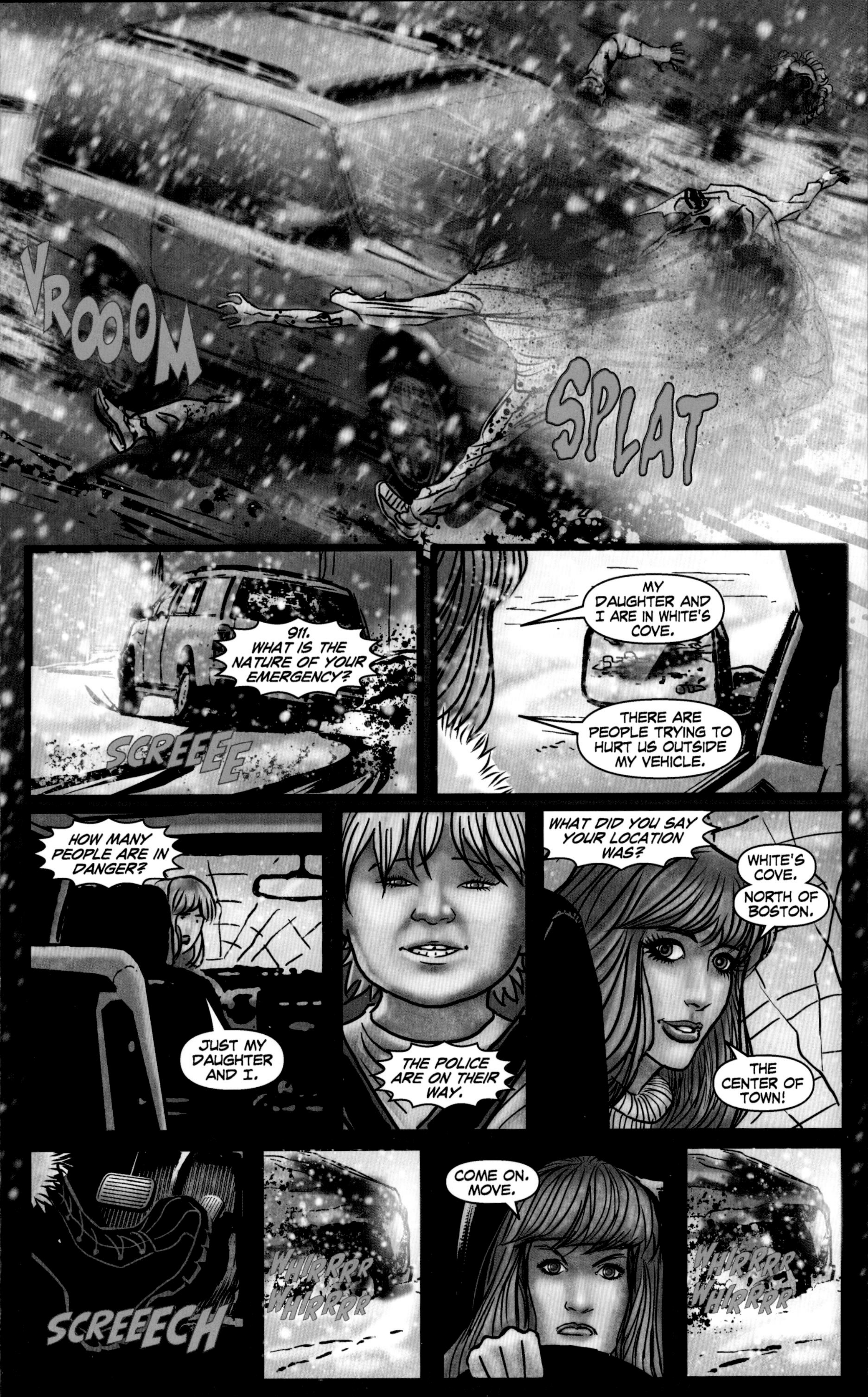
VROOOM
SPLAT
911. WHAT IS THE NATURE OF YOUR EMERGENCY?
SCREEEEE
MY DAUGHTER AND I ARE IN WHITE'S COVE.
THERE ARE PEOPLE TRYING TO HURT US OUTSIDE MY VEHICLE.
HOW MANY PEOPLE ARE IN DANGER?
JUST MY DAUGHTER AND I.
THE POLICE ARE ON THEIR WAY.
WHAT DID YOU SAY YOUR LOCATION WAS?
WHITE'S COVE.
NORTH OF BOSTON.
THE CENTER OF TOWN!
SCREEECH
WHIRRRR WHIRRRR
COME ON. MOVE.
WHIRRRR WHIRRRR

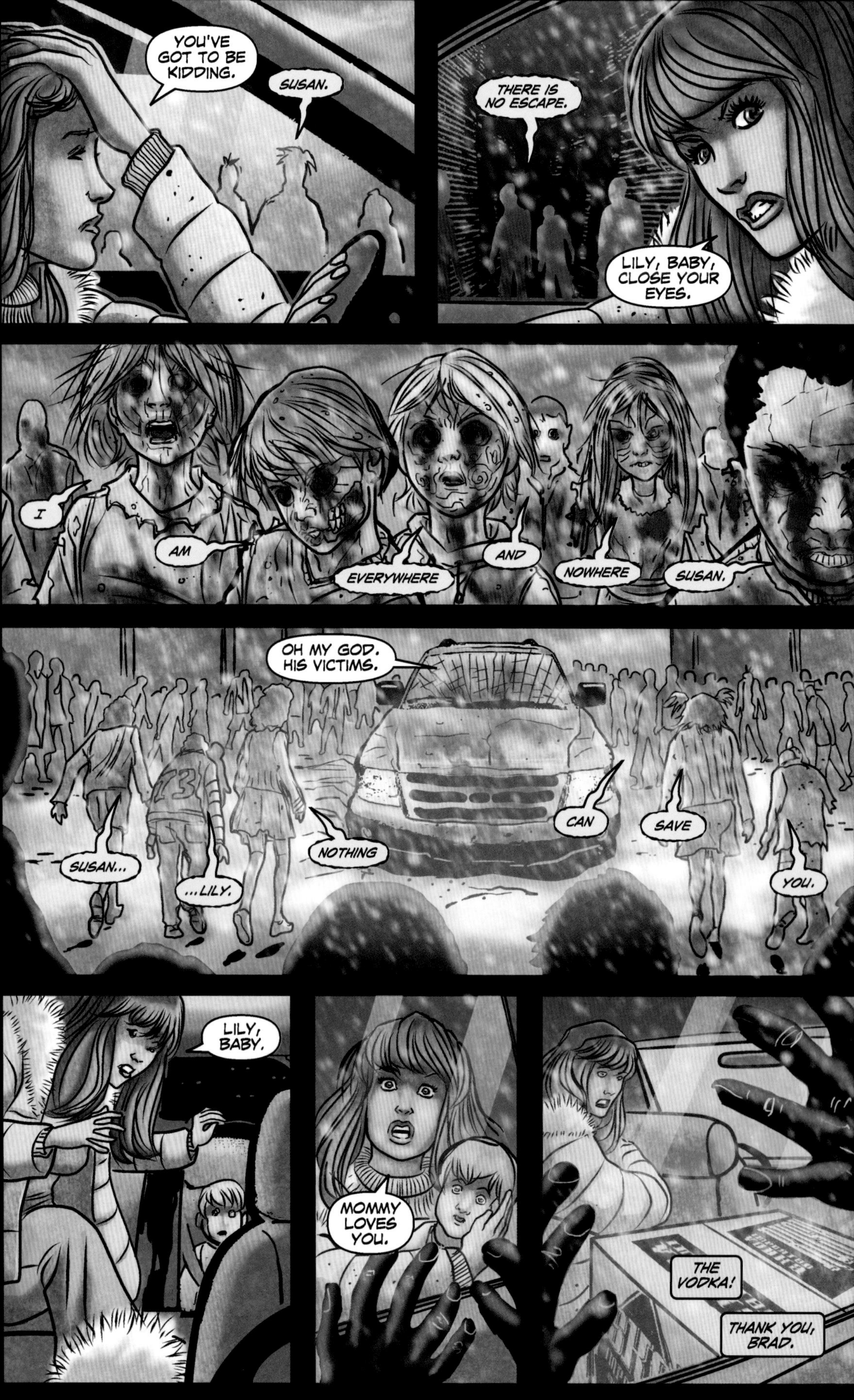
YOU'VE GOT TO BE KIDDING.
SUSAN.
THERE IS NO ESCAPE.
LILY, BABY, CLOSE YOUR EYES.
I
AM
EVERYWHERE
AND
NOWHERE
SUSAN.
OH MY GOD. HIS VICTIMS.
SUSAN...
...LILY.
NOTHING
CAN
SAVE
YOU.
LILY, BABY.
MOMMY LOVES YOU.
THE VODKA!
THANK YOU, BRAD.

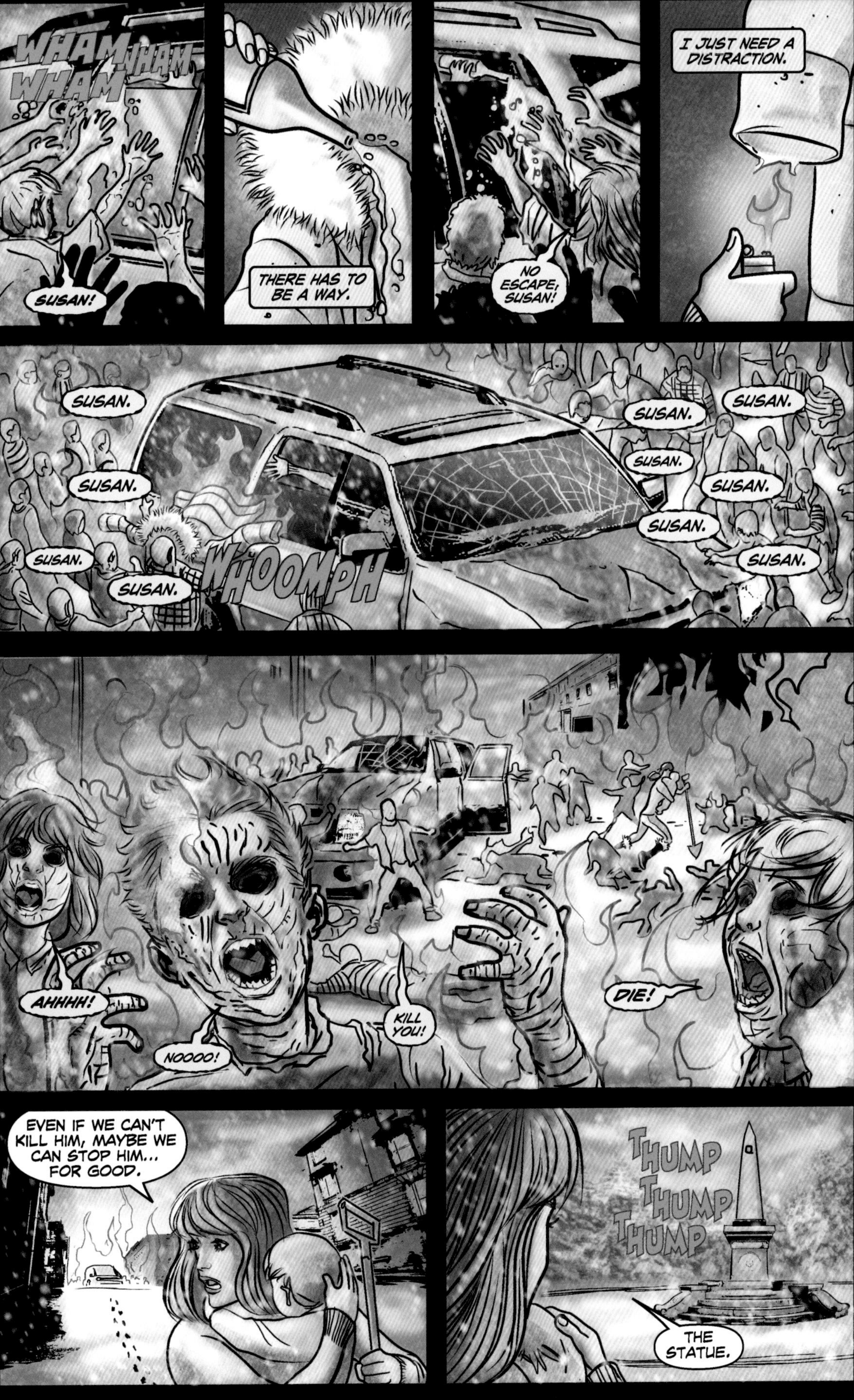
WHAM WHAM WHAM
SUSAN!
THERE HAS TO BE A WAY.
NO ESCAPE, SUSAN!
I JUST NEED A DISTRACTION.
SUSAN.
SUSAN.
SUSAN.
SUSAN.
WHOOMPH
SUSAN.
SUSAN.
SUSAN.
SUSAN.
SUSAN.
SUSAN.
AHHHH!
NOOOO!
KILL YOU!
DIE!
EVEN IF WE CAN'T KILL HIM, MAYBE WE CAN STOP HIM... FOR GOOD.
THUMP THUMP THUMP
THE STATUE.

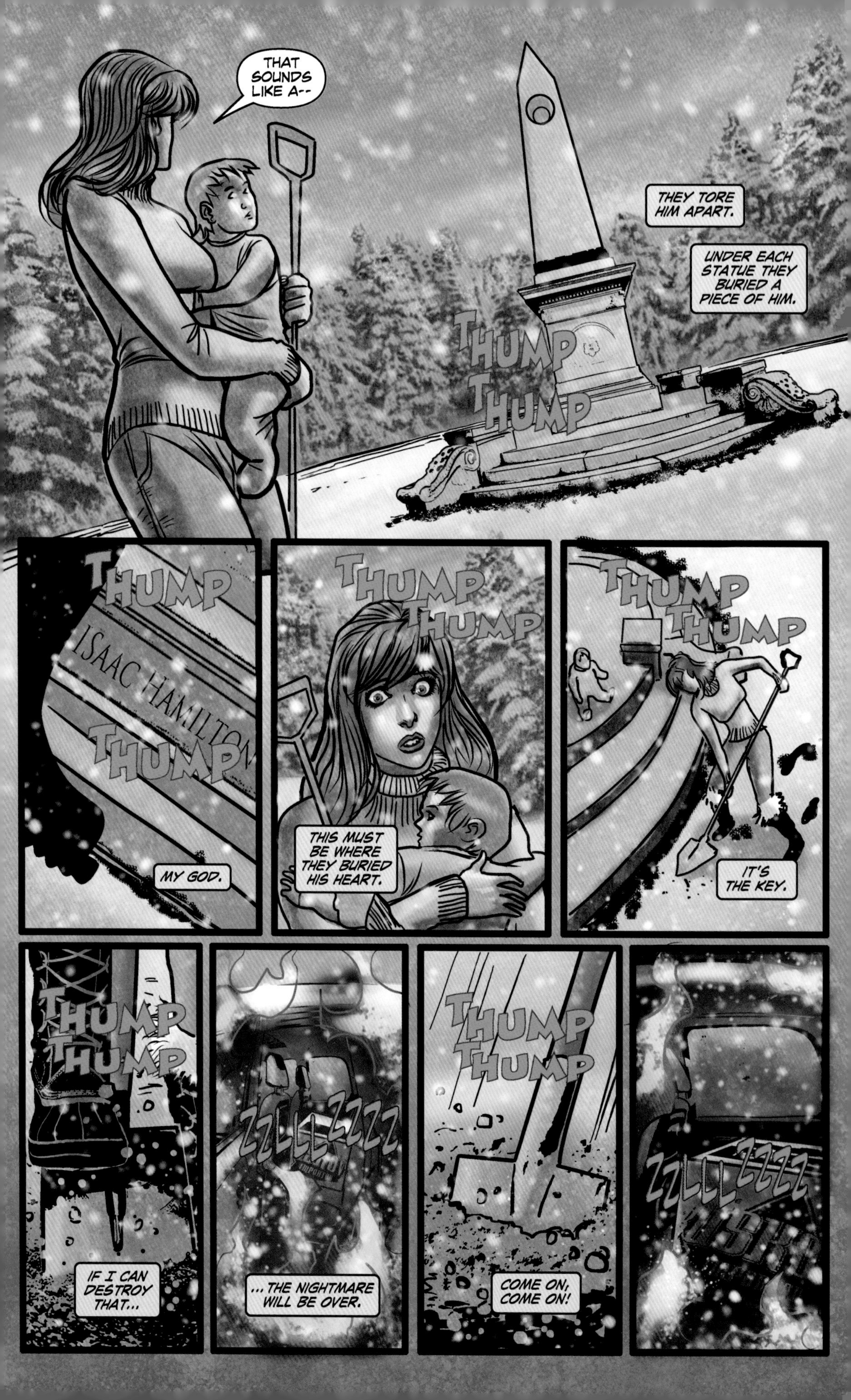
THAT SOUNDS LIKE A--
THEY TORE HIM APART.
UNDER EACH STATUE THEY BURIED A PIECE OF HIM.
THUMP THUMP
THUMP
ISAAC HAMILTON
THUMP
MY GOD.
THUMP THUMP
THIS MUST BE WHERE THEY BURIED HIS HEART.
THUMP THUMP
IT'S THE KEY.
THUMP THUMP
IF I CAN DESTROY THAT...
ZZLLLZZZZ
...THE NIGHTMARE WILL BE OVER.
THUMP THUMP
COME ON, COME ON!
ZZLLLZZZZ

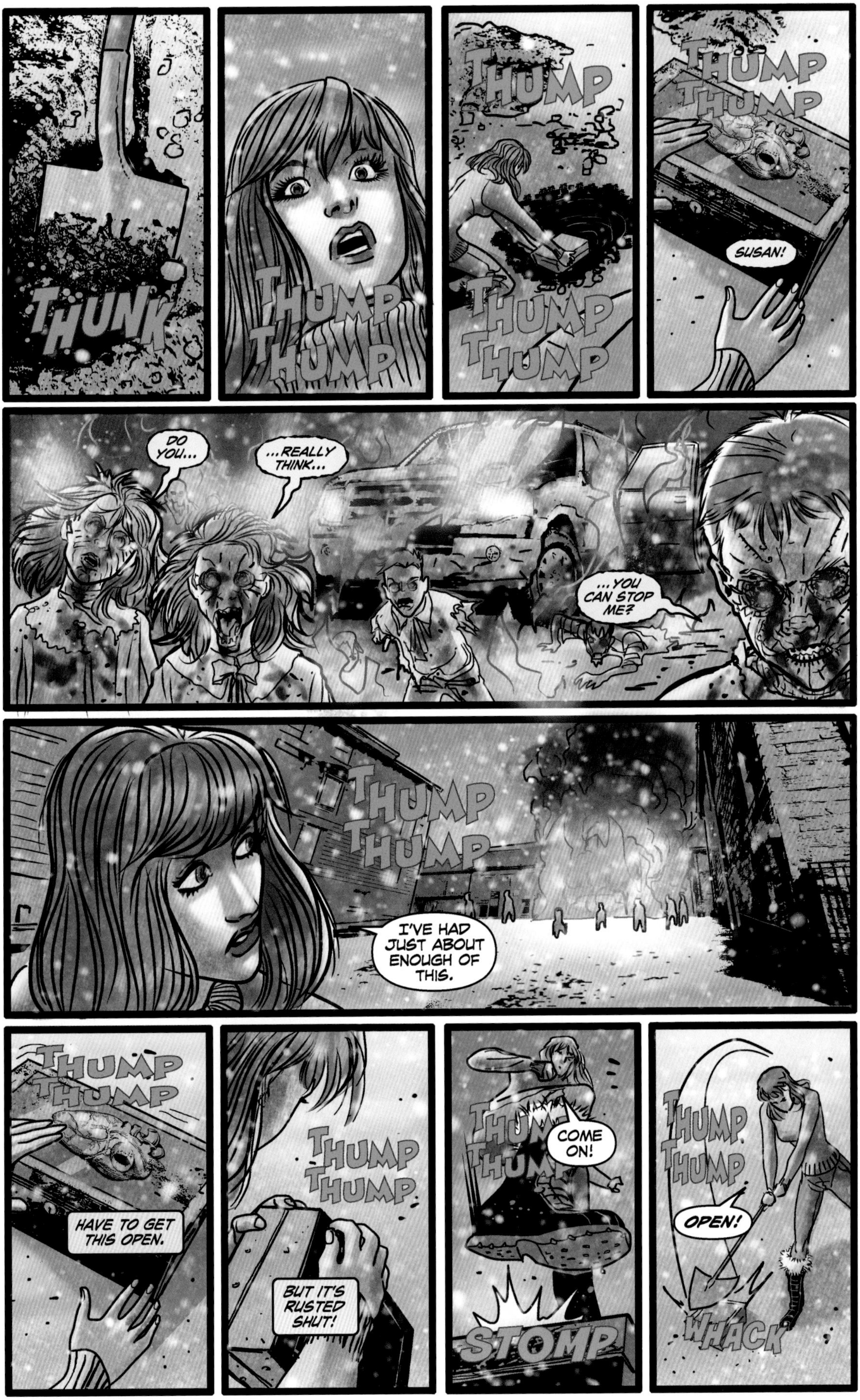
THUNK
THUMP THUMP
THUMP
THUMP THUMP
THUMP THUMP
SUSAN!
DO YOU...
...REALLY THINK...
...YOU CAN STOP ME?
THUMP THUMP
I'VE HAD JUST ABOUT ENOUGH OF THIS.
THUMP THUMP
HAVE TO GET THIS OPEN.
THUMP THUMP
BUT IT'S RUSTED SHUT!
THUMP THUMP
COME ON!
STOMP
THUMP THUMP
OPEN!
WHACK

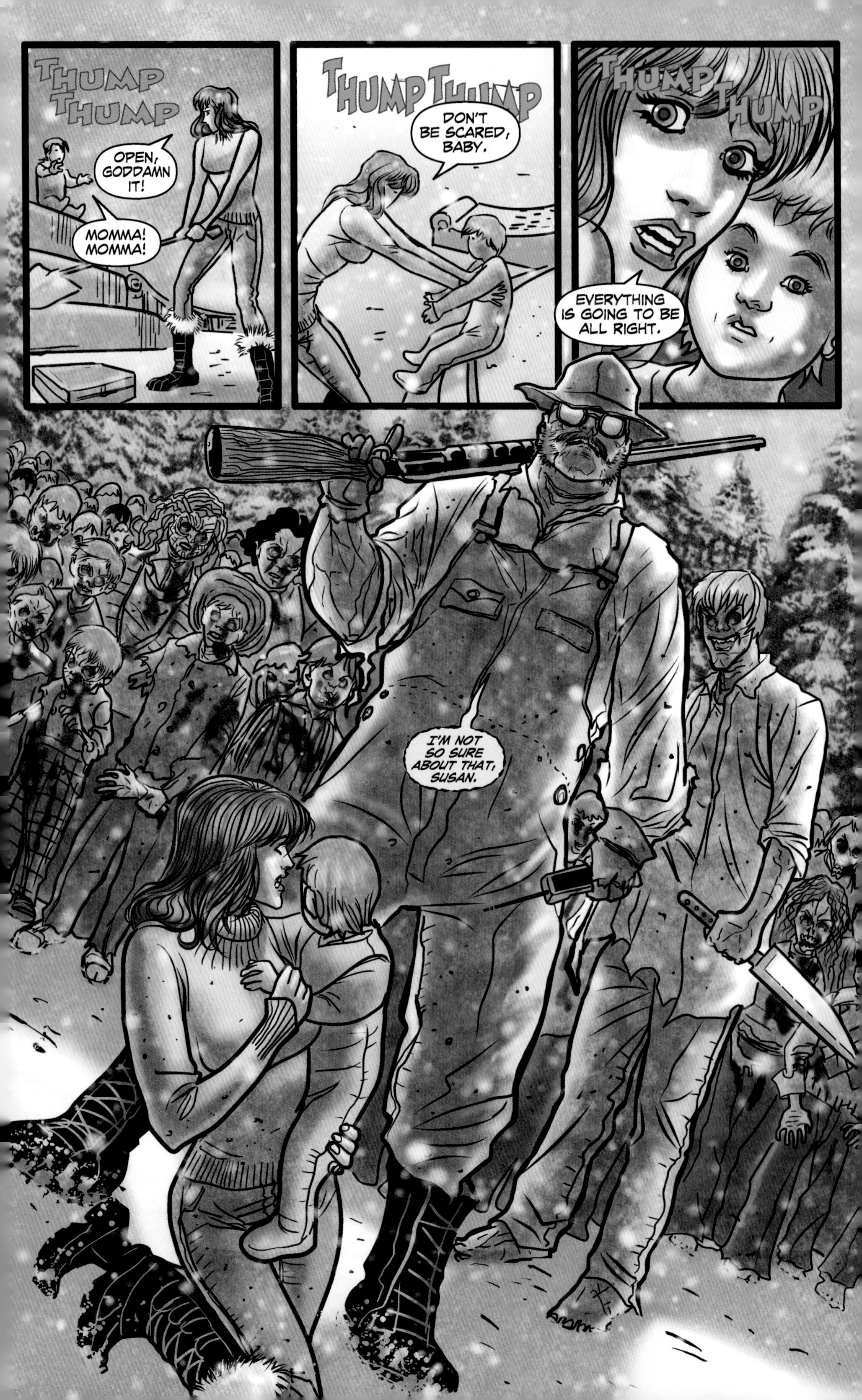
THUMP THUMP
OPEN, GODDAMN IT!
MOMMA! MOMMA!
THUMP THUMP
DON'T BE SCARED, BABY.
THUMP THUMP
EVERYTHING IS GOING TO BE ALL RIGHT.
I'M NOT SO SURE ABOUT THAT, SUSAN.

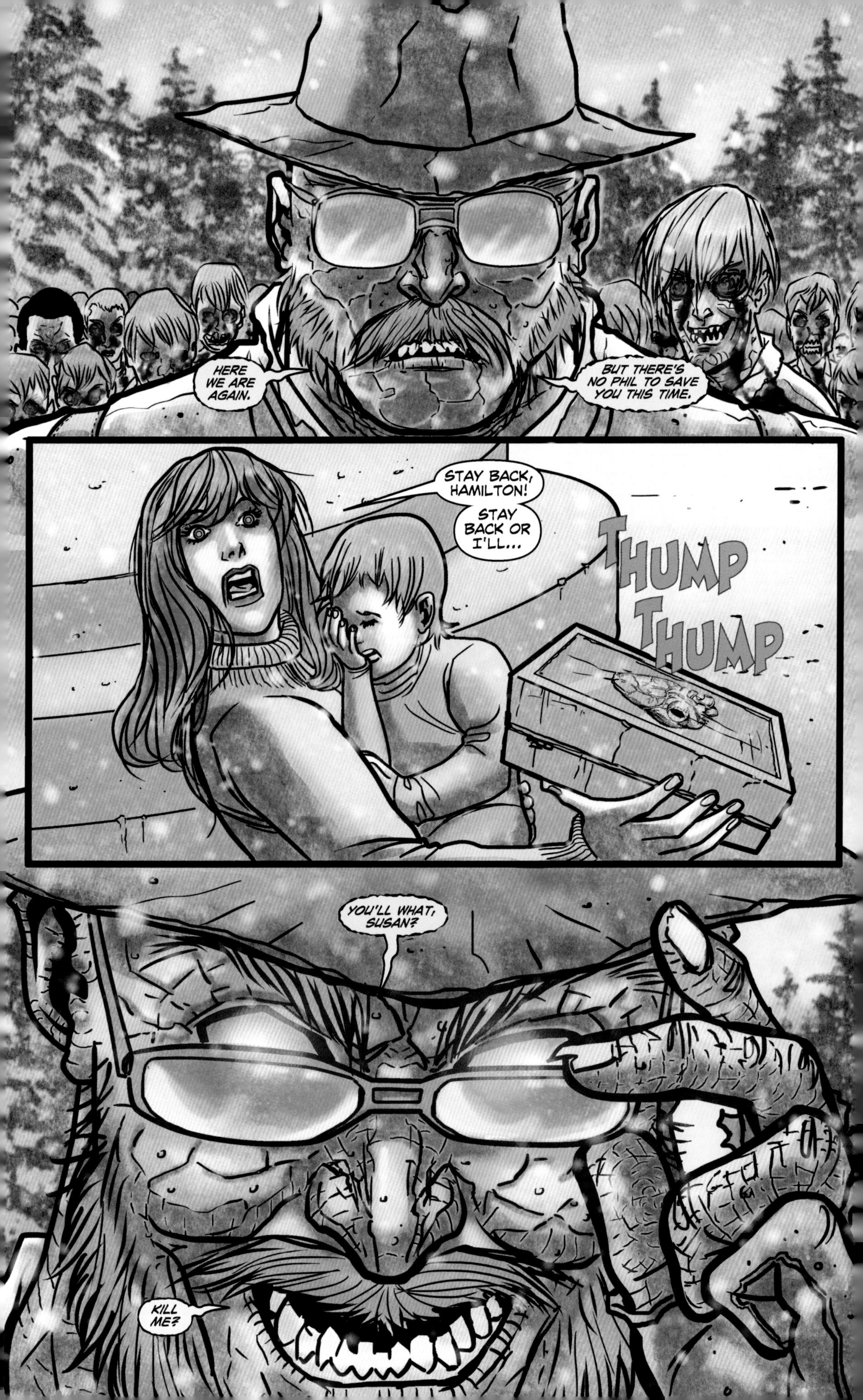
HERE WE ARE AGAIN.
BUT THERE'S NO PHIL TO SAVE YOU THIS TIME.
STAY BACK, HAMILTON!
STAY BACK OR I'LL...
THUMP THUMP
YOU'LL WHAT, SUSAN?
KILL ME?

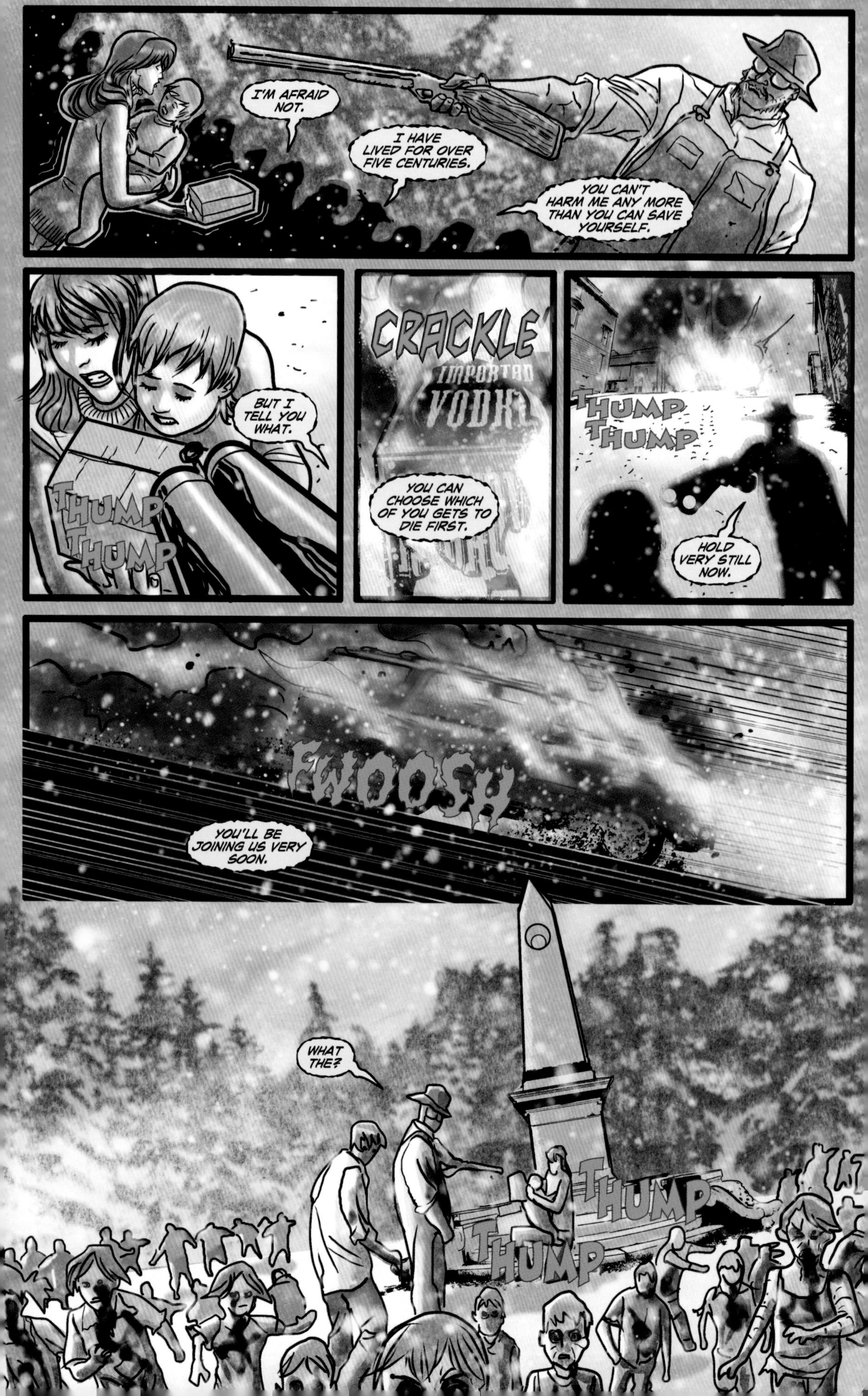

I'M AFRAID NOT.
I HAVE LIVED FOR OVER FIVE CENTURIES.
YOU CAN'T HARM ME ANY MORE THAN YOU CAN SAVE YOURSELF.
BUT I TELL YOU WHAT.
THUMP THUMP
CRACKLE
IMPORTED
YOU CAN CHOOSE WHICH OF YOU GETS TO DIE FIRST.
THUMP THUMP
HOLD VERY STILL NOW.
FWOOSH
YOU'LL BE JOINING US VERY SOON.
WHAT THE?
THUMP THUMP

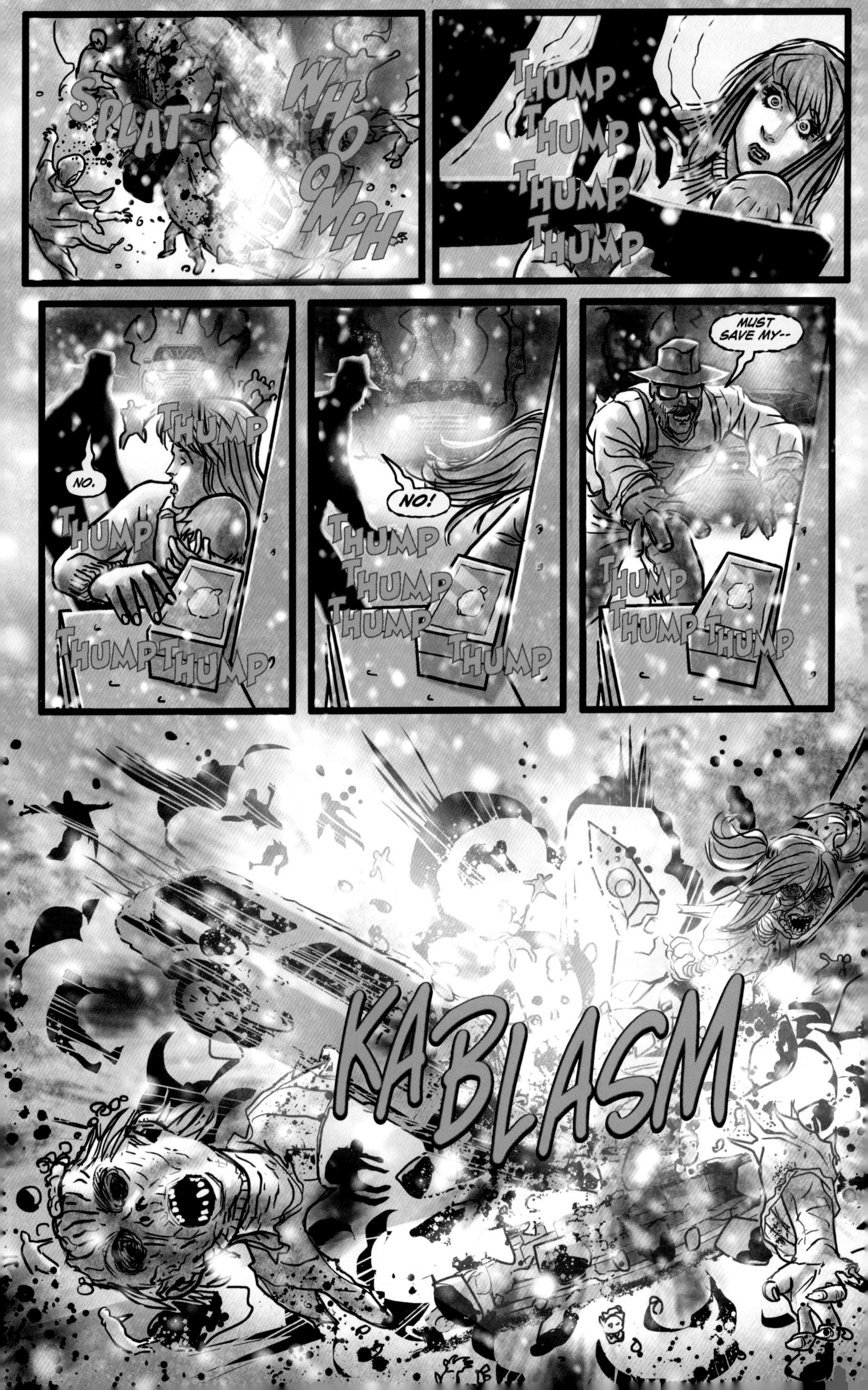

SPLAT
WHOOOMPH
THUMP
THUMP
THUMP
THUMP
THUMP
NO.
THUMP
THUMP
THUMP
NO!
THUMP
THUMP
THUMP
THUMP
MUST SAVE MY--
THUMP
THUMP
THUMP
KABLASM

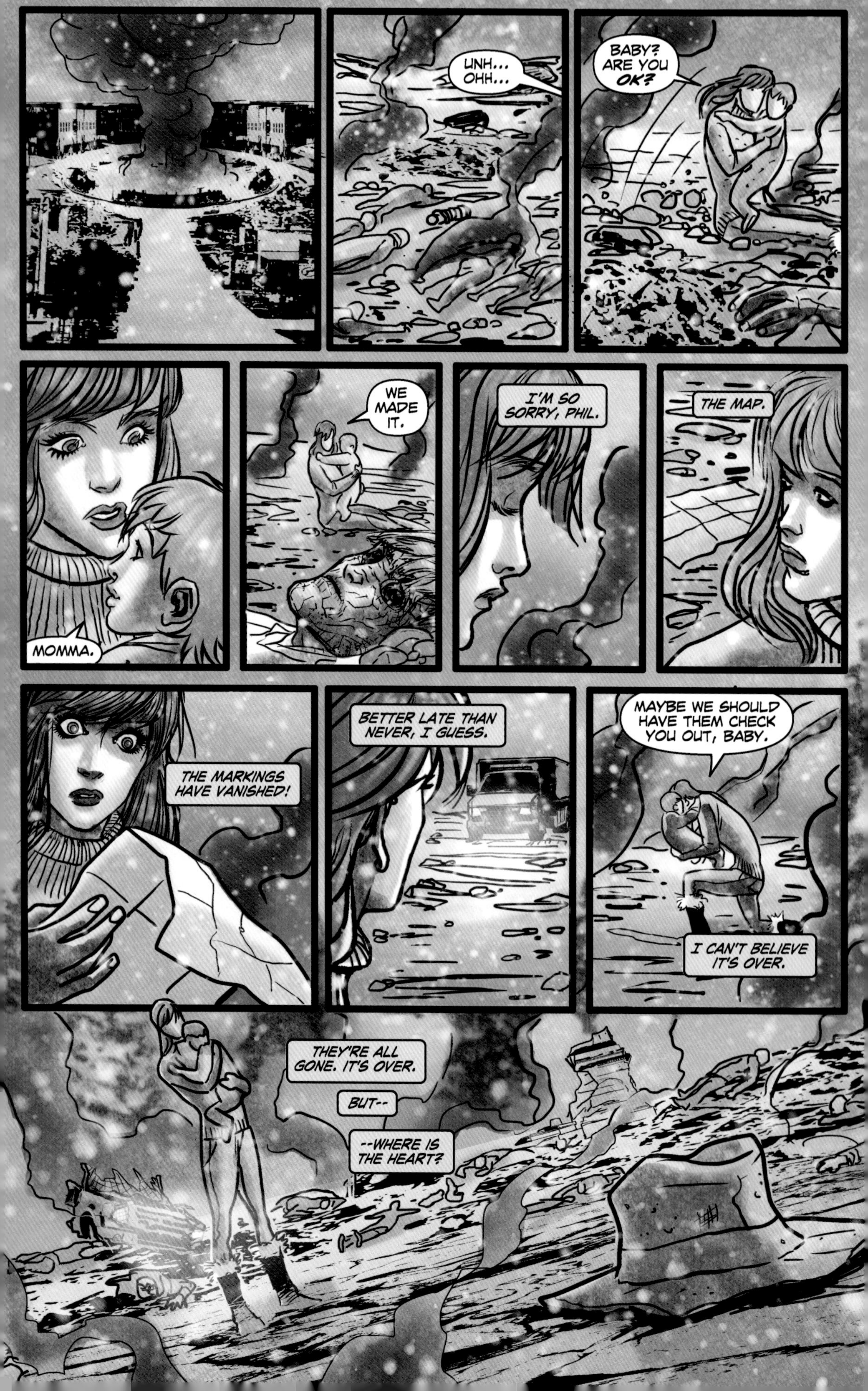
UNH... OHH...
BABY? ARE YOU OK?
MOMMA.
WE MADE IT.
I'M SO SORRY, PHIL.
THE MAP.
THE MARKINGS HAVE VANISHED!
BETTER LATE THAN NEVER, I GUESS.
MAYBE WE SHOULD HAVE THEM CHECK YOU OUT, BABY.
I CAN'T BELIEVE IT'S OVER.
THEY'RE ALL GONE. IT'S OVER.
BUT--
--WHERE IS THE HEART?

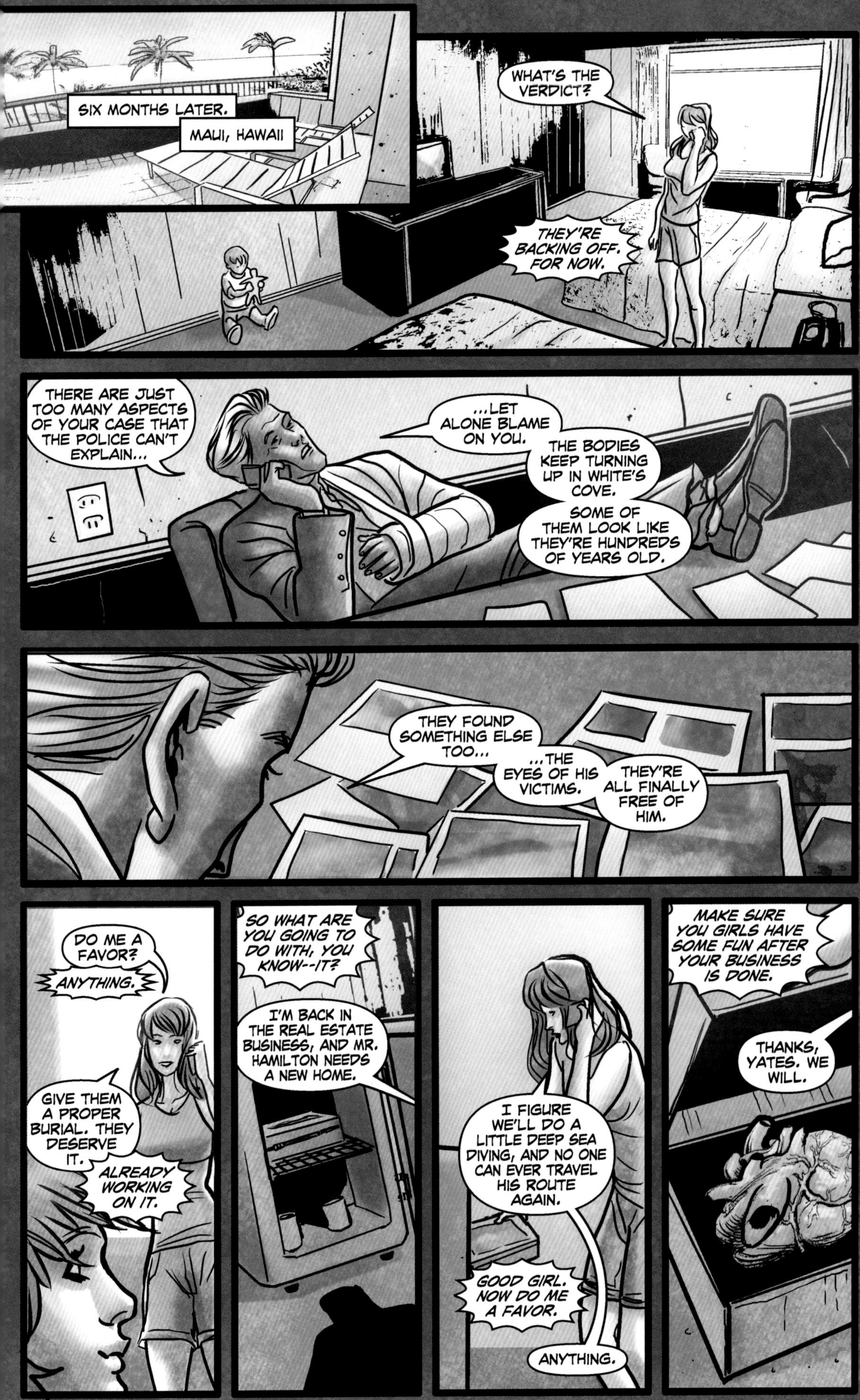
SIX MONTHS LATER.
MAUI, HAWAII
WHAT'S THE VERDICT?
THEY'RE BACKING OFF. FOR NOW.
THERE ARE JUST TOO MANY ASPECTS OF YOUR CASE THAT THE POLICE CAN'T EXPLAIN...
...LET ALONE BLAME ON YOU.
THE BODIES KEEP TURNING UP IN WHITE'S COVE.
SOME OF THEM LOOK LIKE THEY'RE HUNDREDS OF YEARS OLD.
THEY FOUND SOMETHING ELSE TOO...
...THE EYES OF HIS VICTIMS.
THEY'RE ALL FINALLY FREE OF HIM.
DO ME A FAVOR?
ANYTHING.
GIVE THEM A PROPER BURIAL. THEY DESERVE IT.
ALREADY WORKING ON IT.
SO WHAT ARE YOU GOING TO DO WITH, YOU KNOW--IT?
I'M BACK IN THE REAL ESTATE BUSINESS, AND MR. HAMILTON NEEDS A NEW HOME.
I FIGURE WE'LL DO A LITTLE DEEP SEA DIVING, AND NO ONE CAN EVER TRAVEL HIS ROUTE AGAIN.
GOOD GIRL. NOW DO ME A FAVOR.
ANYTHING.
MAKE SURE YOU GIRLS HAVE SOME FUN AFTER YOUR BUSINESS IS DONE.
THANKS, YATES. WE WILL.

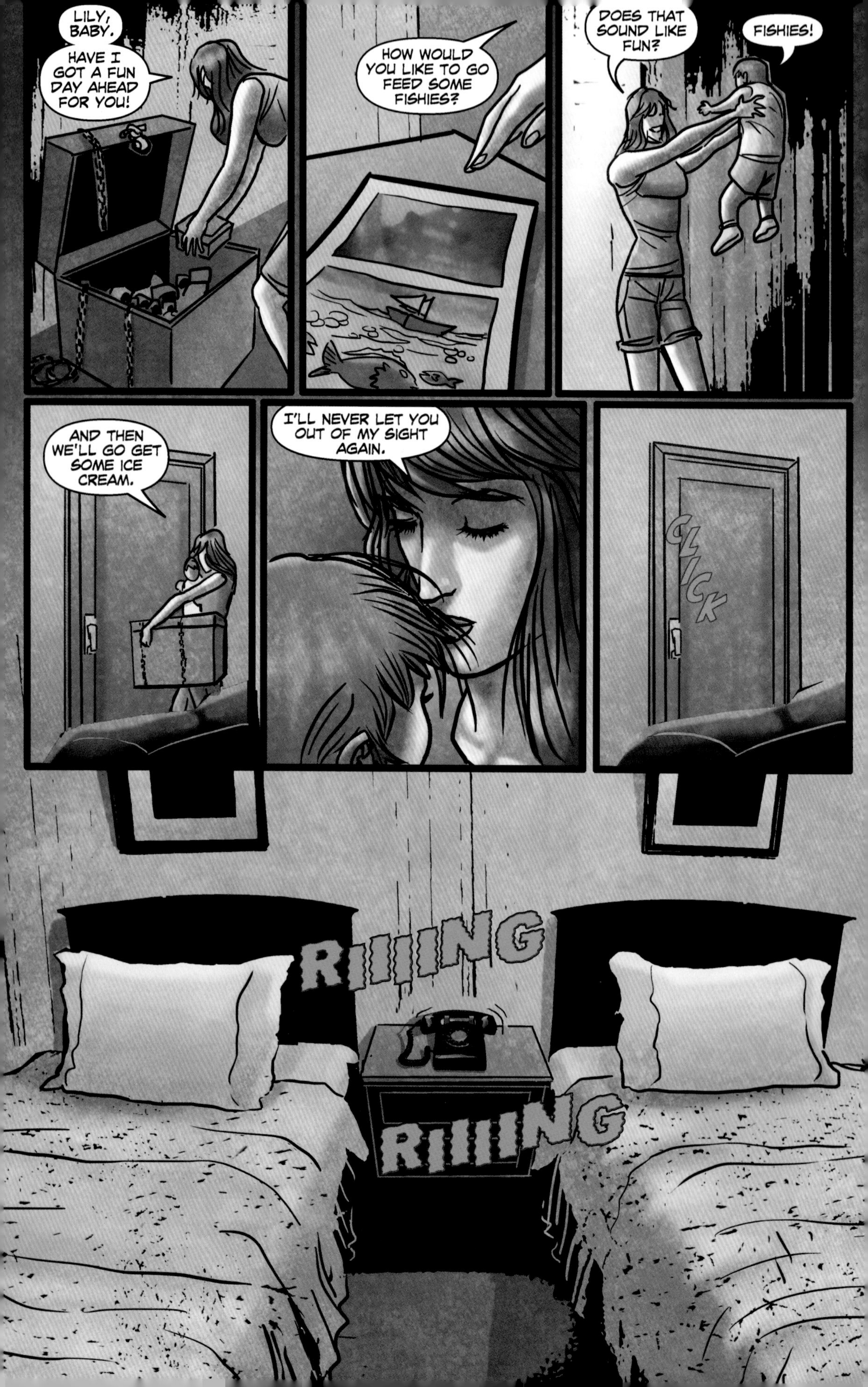
LILY, BABY.
HAVE I GOT A FUN DAY AHEAD FOR YOU!
HOW WOULD YOU LIKE TO GO FEED SOME FISHIES?
DOES THAT SOUND LIKE FUN?
FISHIES!
AND THEN WE'LL GO GET SOME ICE CREAM.
I'LL NEVER LET YOU OUT OF MY SIGHT AGAIN.
CLICK
RIIIING
RIIIING

Art Gallery

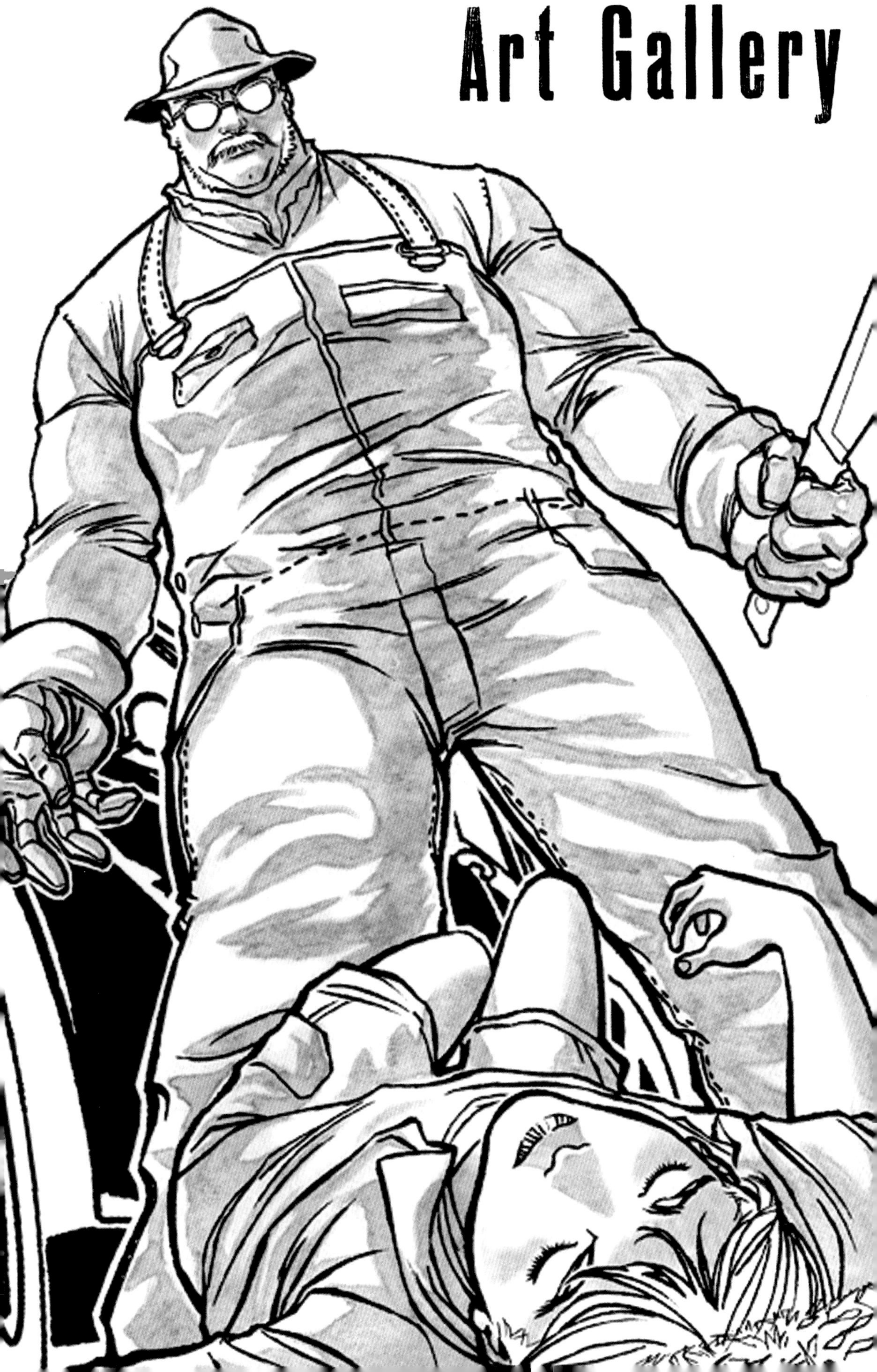

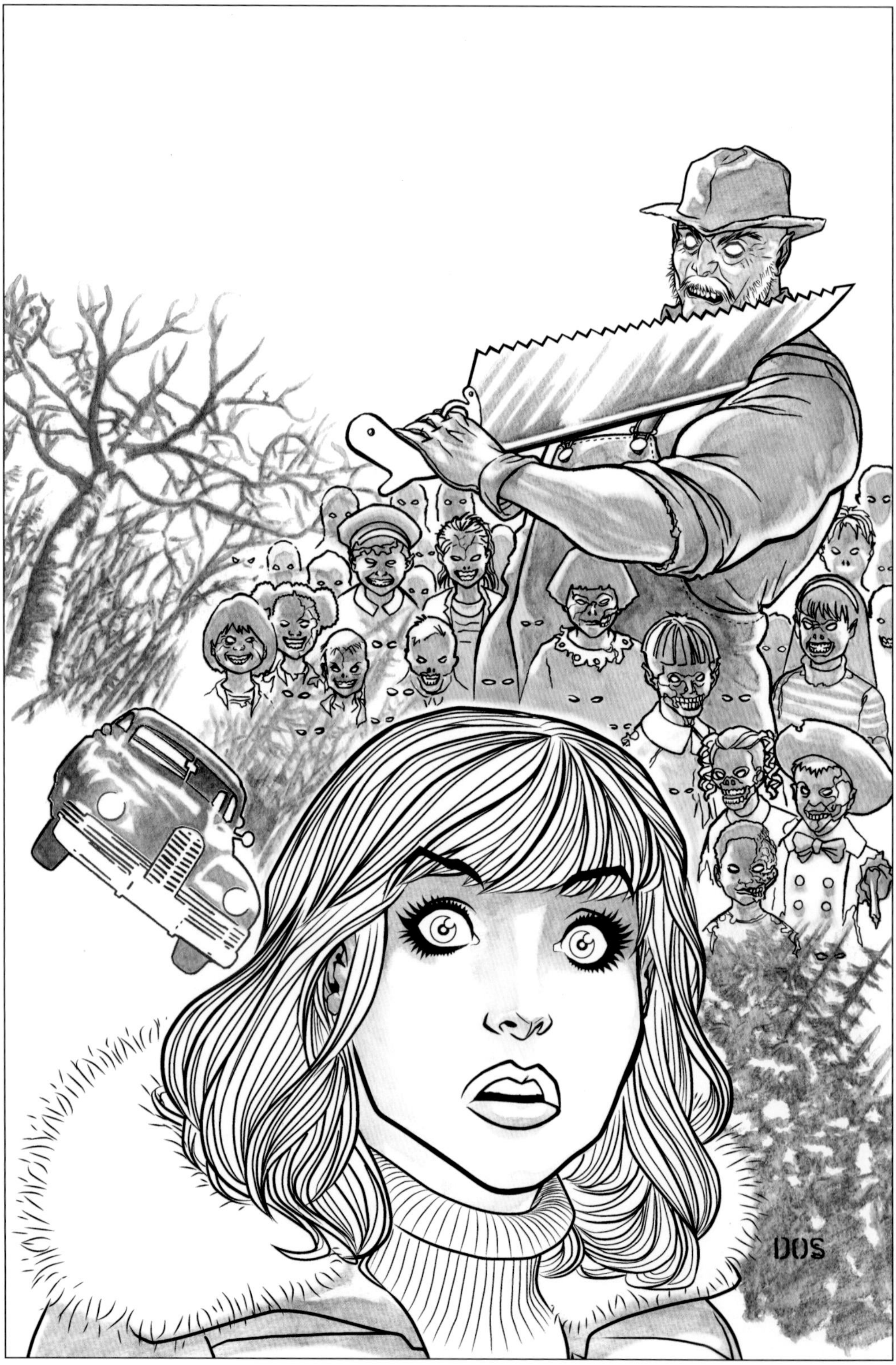
DOS

Previous page: Dietrich Smith

This page and next: David Petersen

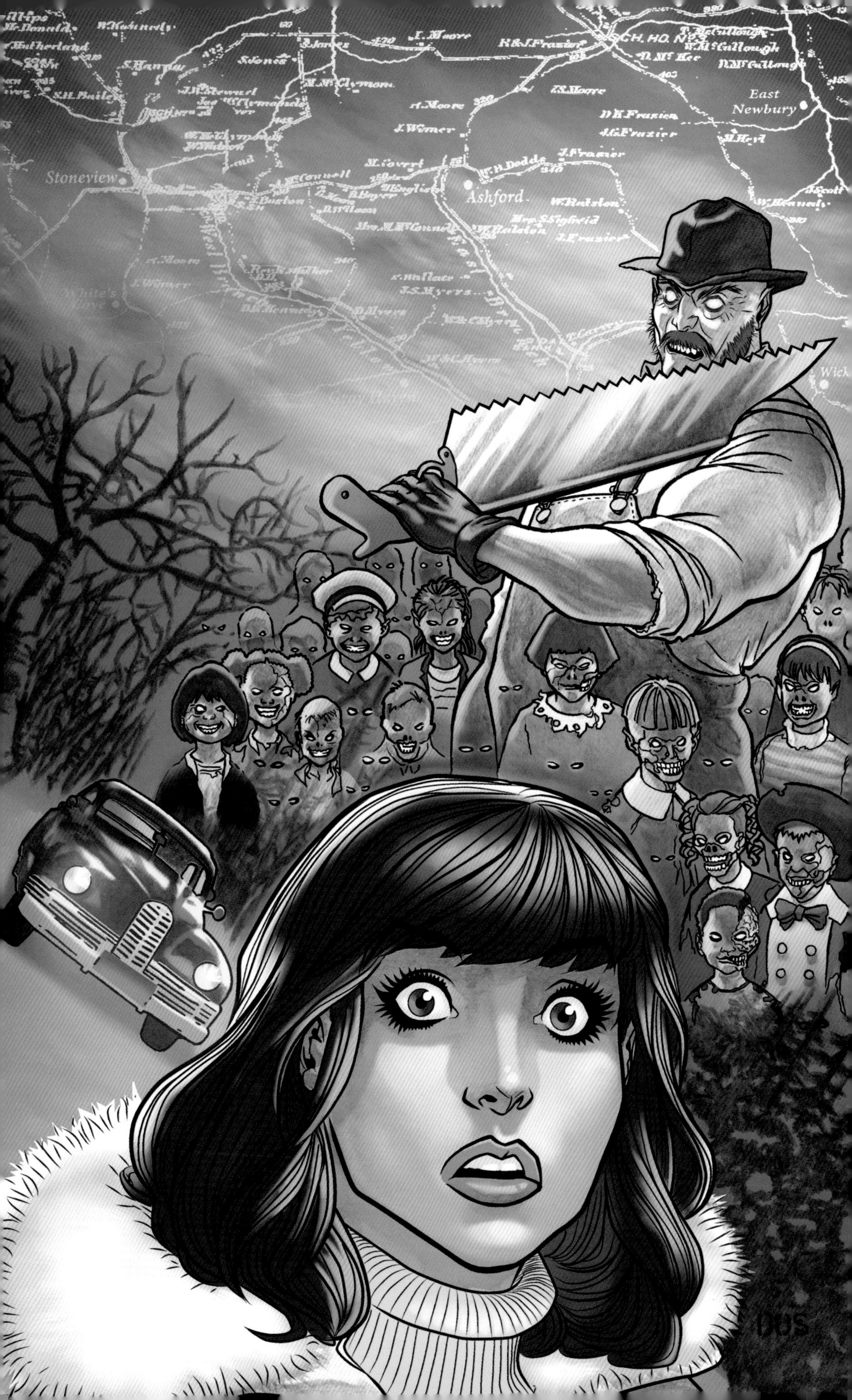
East
Newbury
Stoneview
Ashford

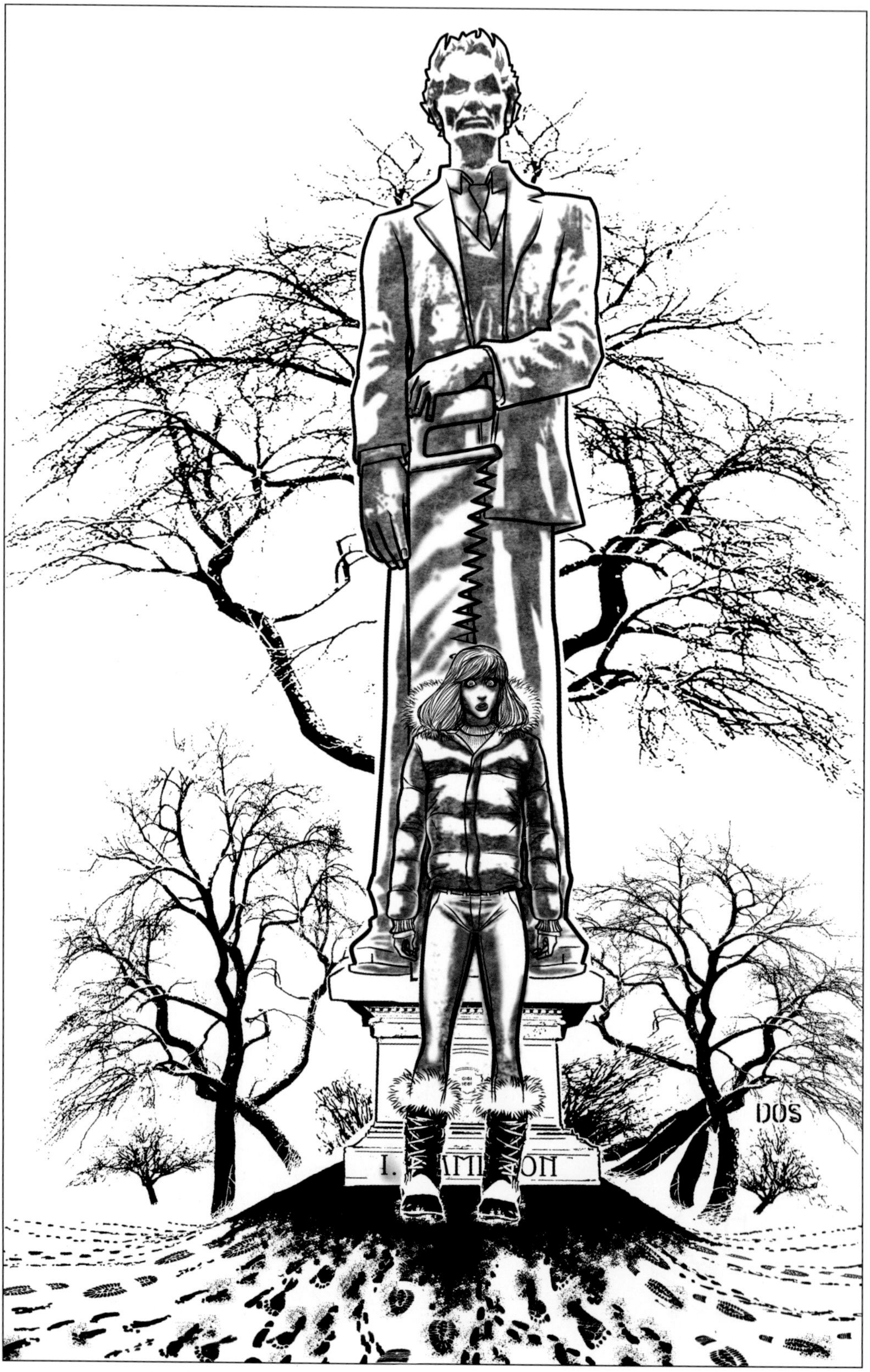
DOS

This page and next: David Petersen

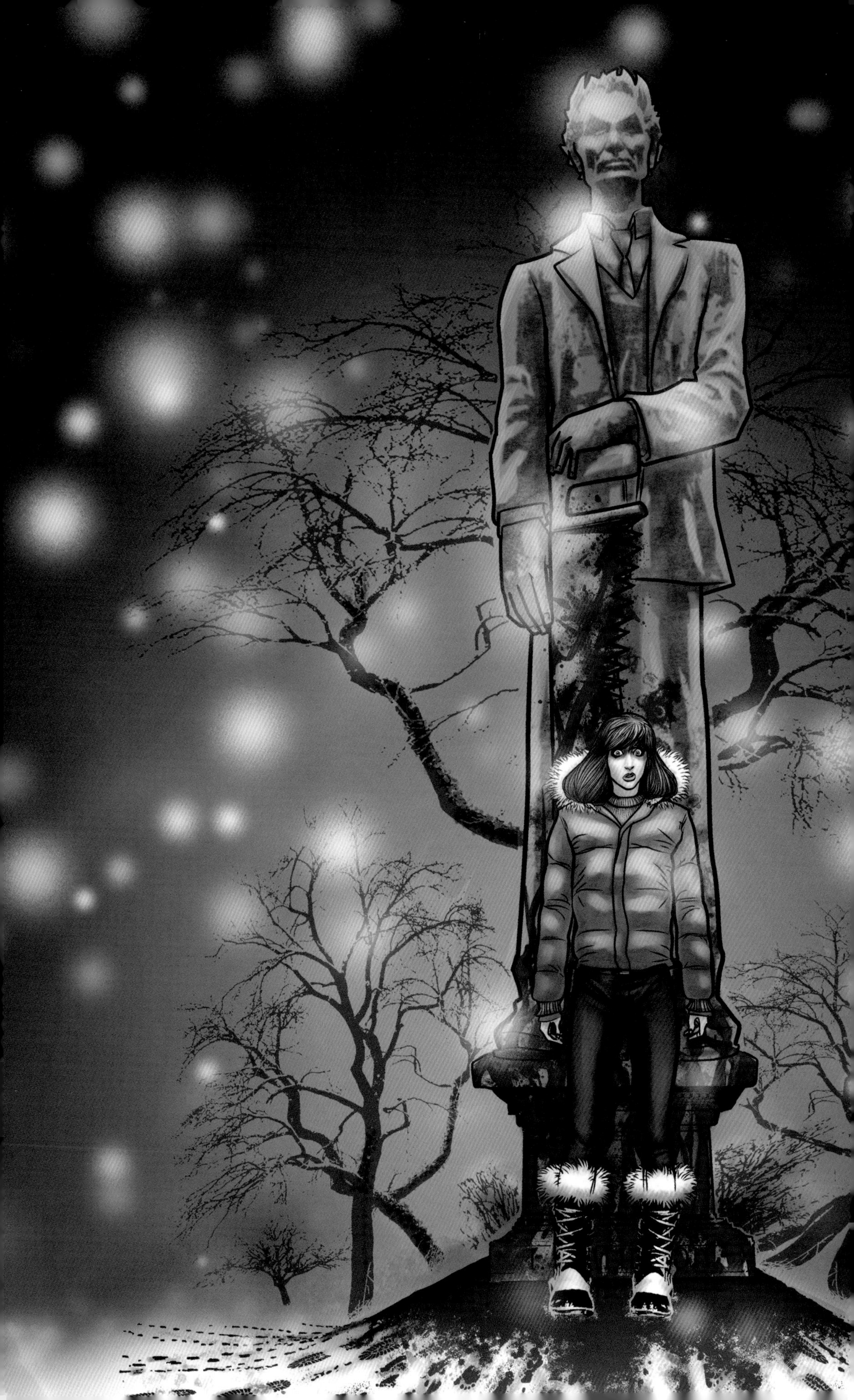

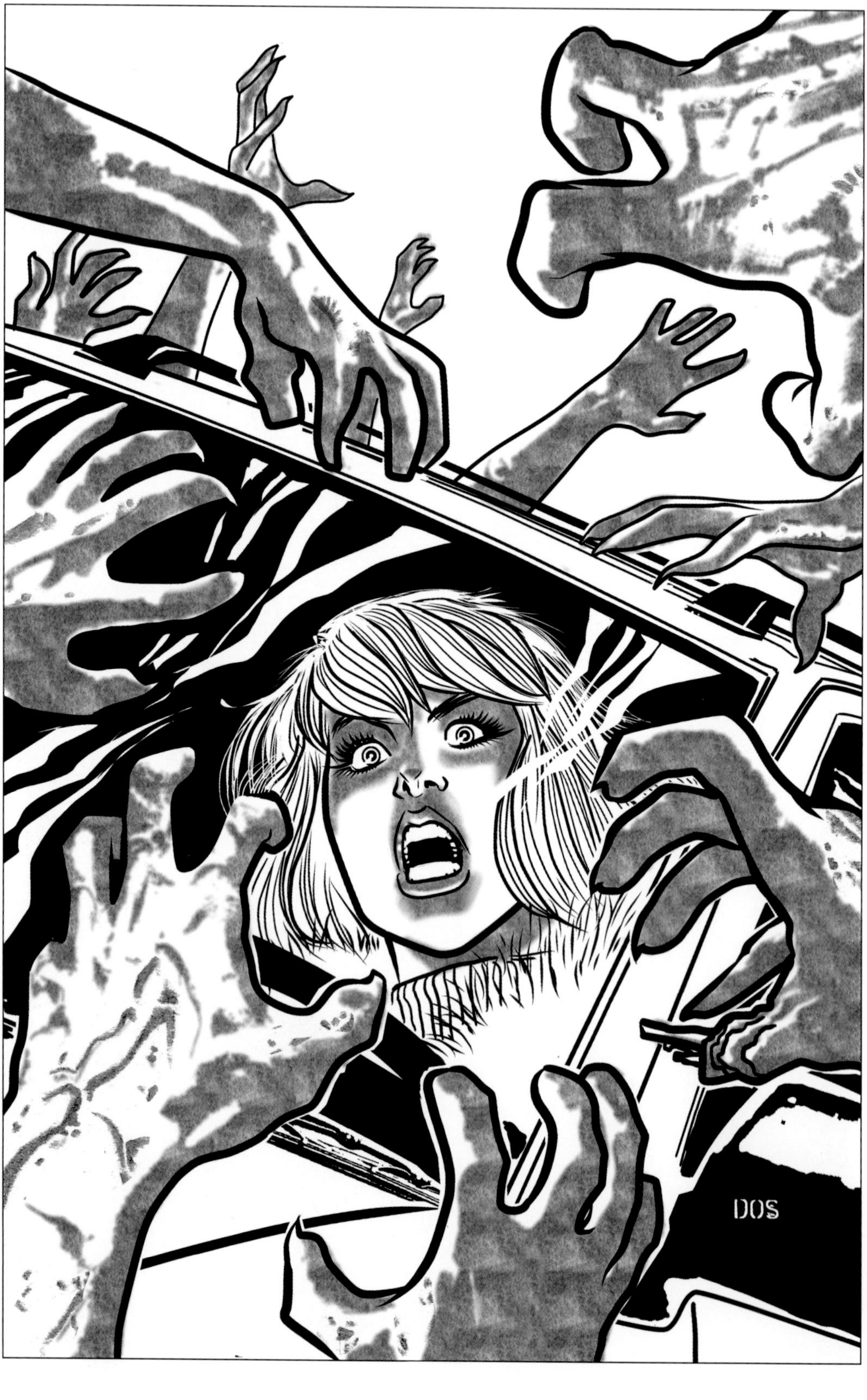
DOS

This page and next: David Petersen

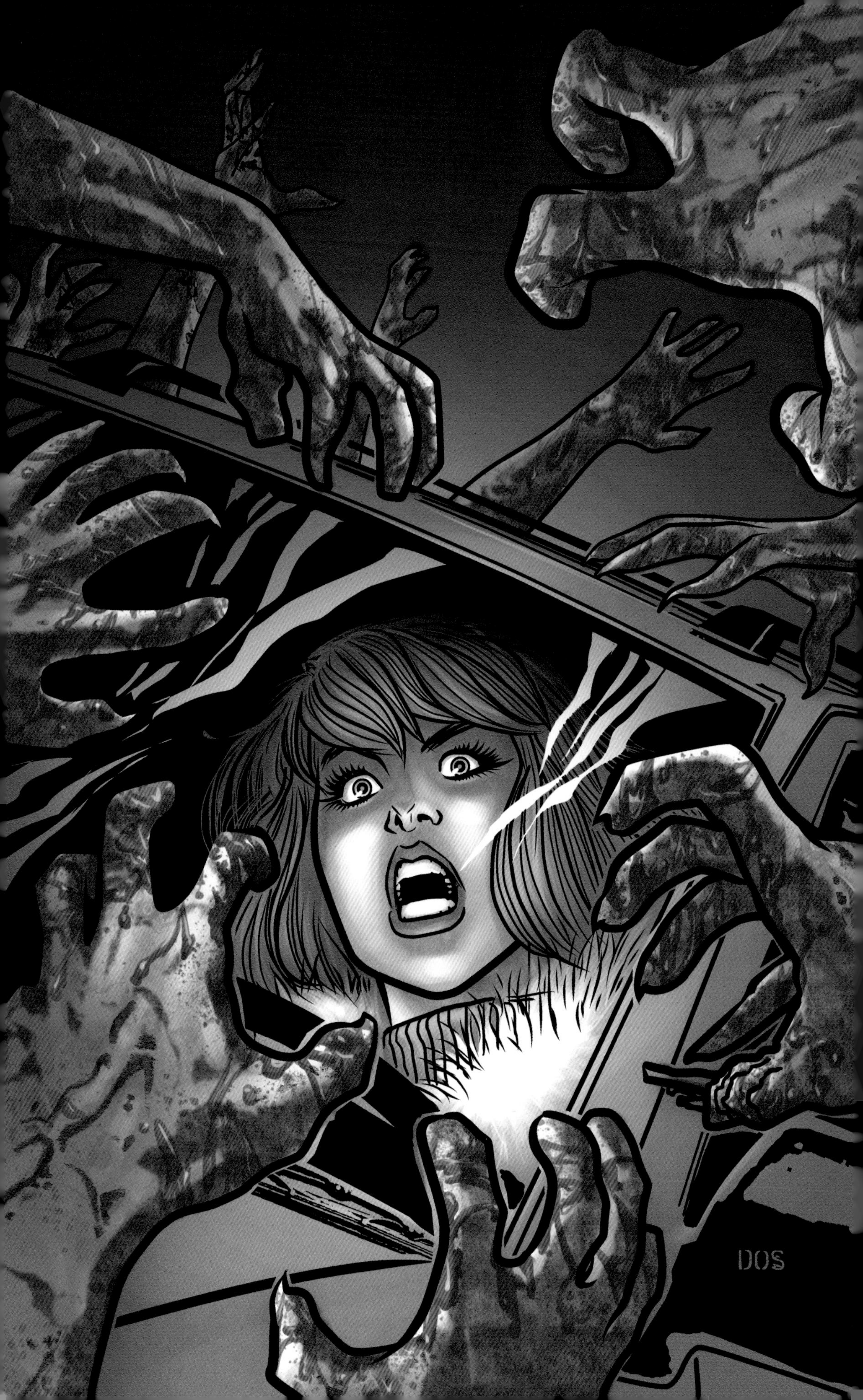
DOS

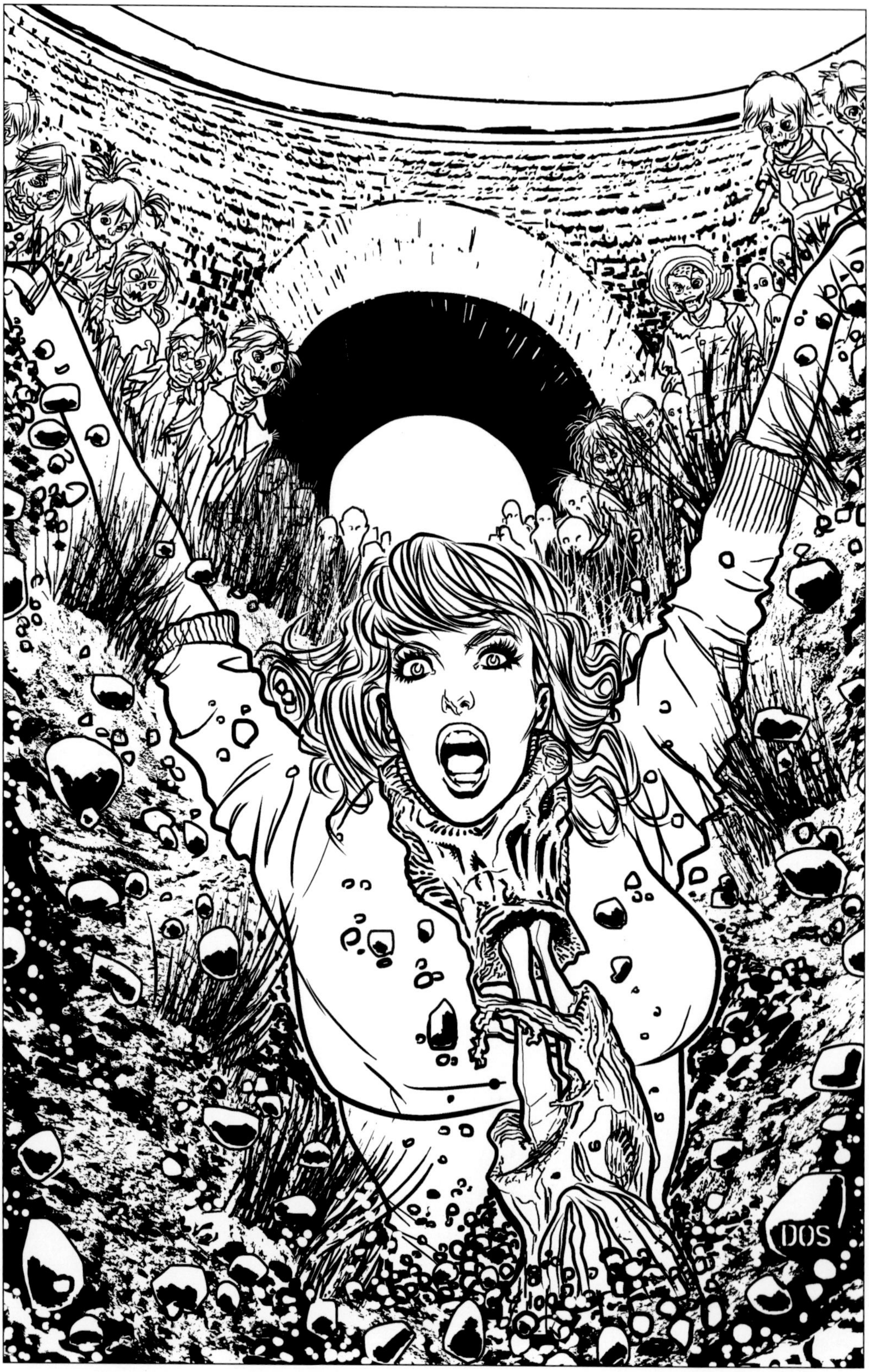
DOS

This page and next: David Petersen

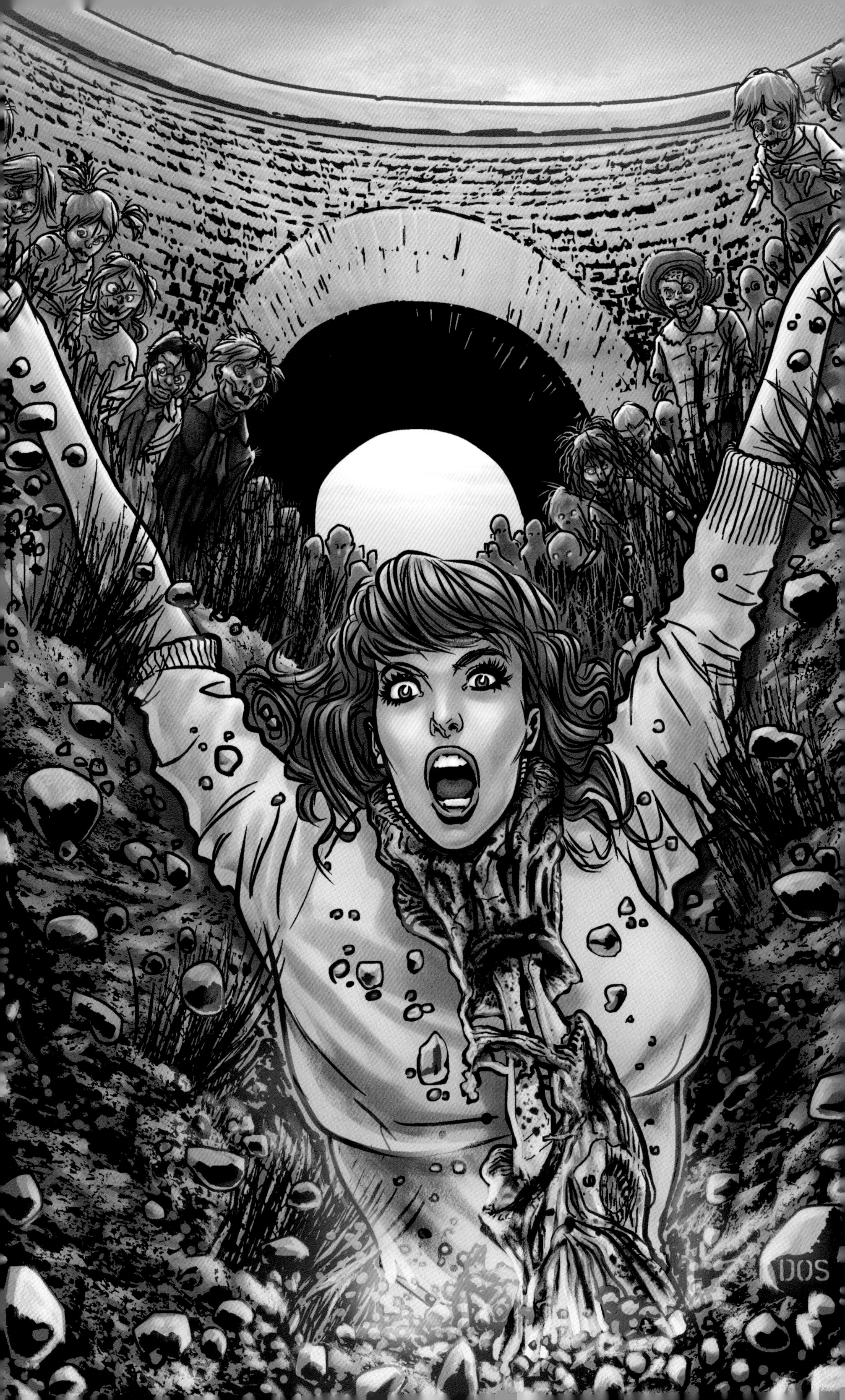
DOS

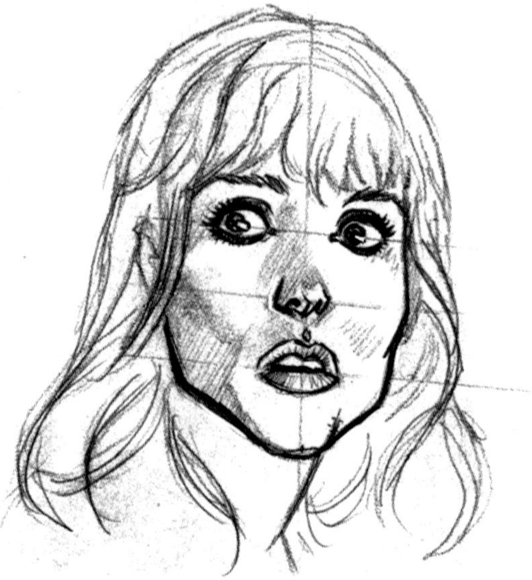

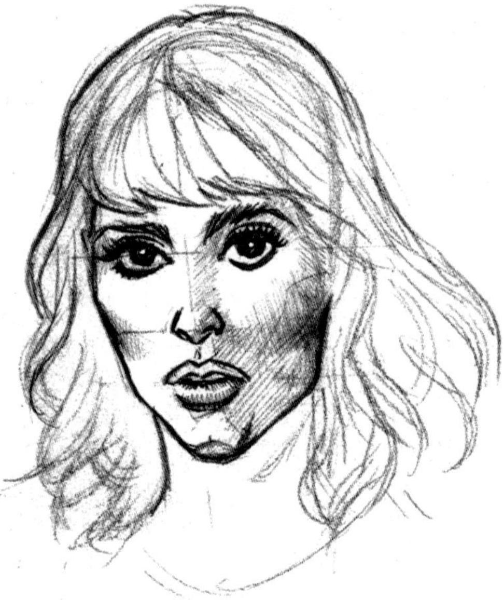

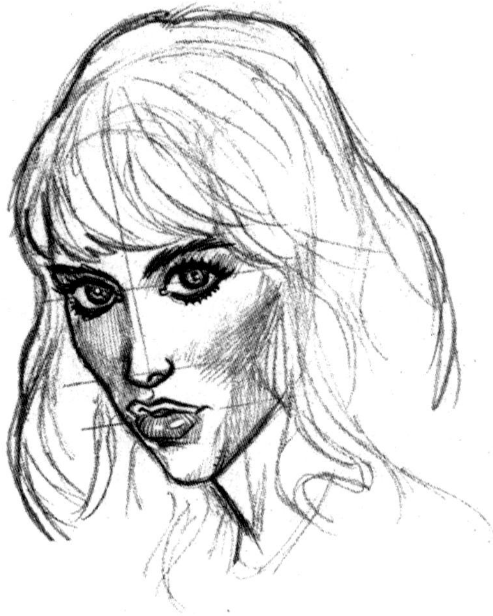

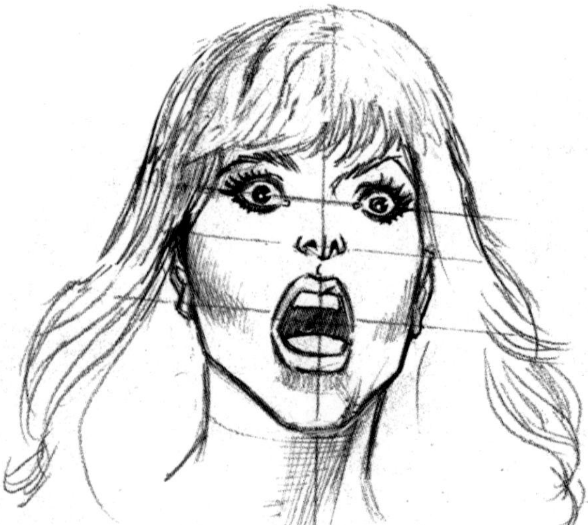

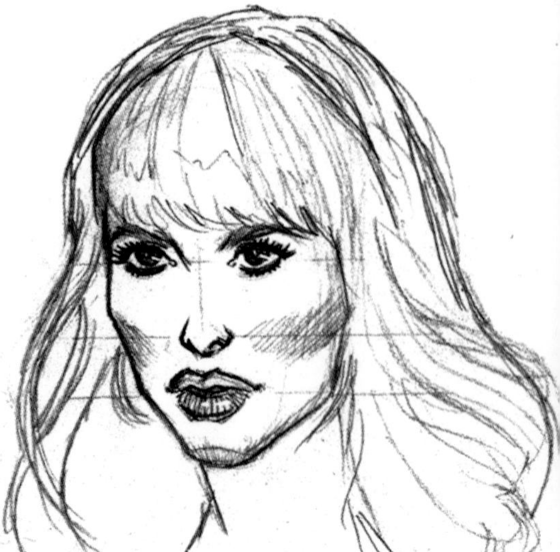

This page and next: Dietrich Smith

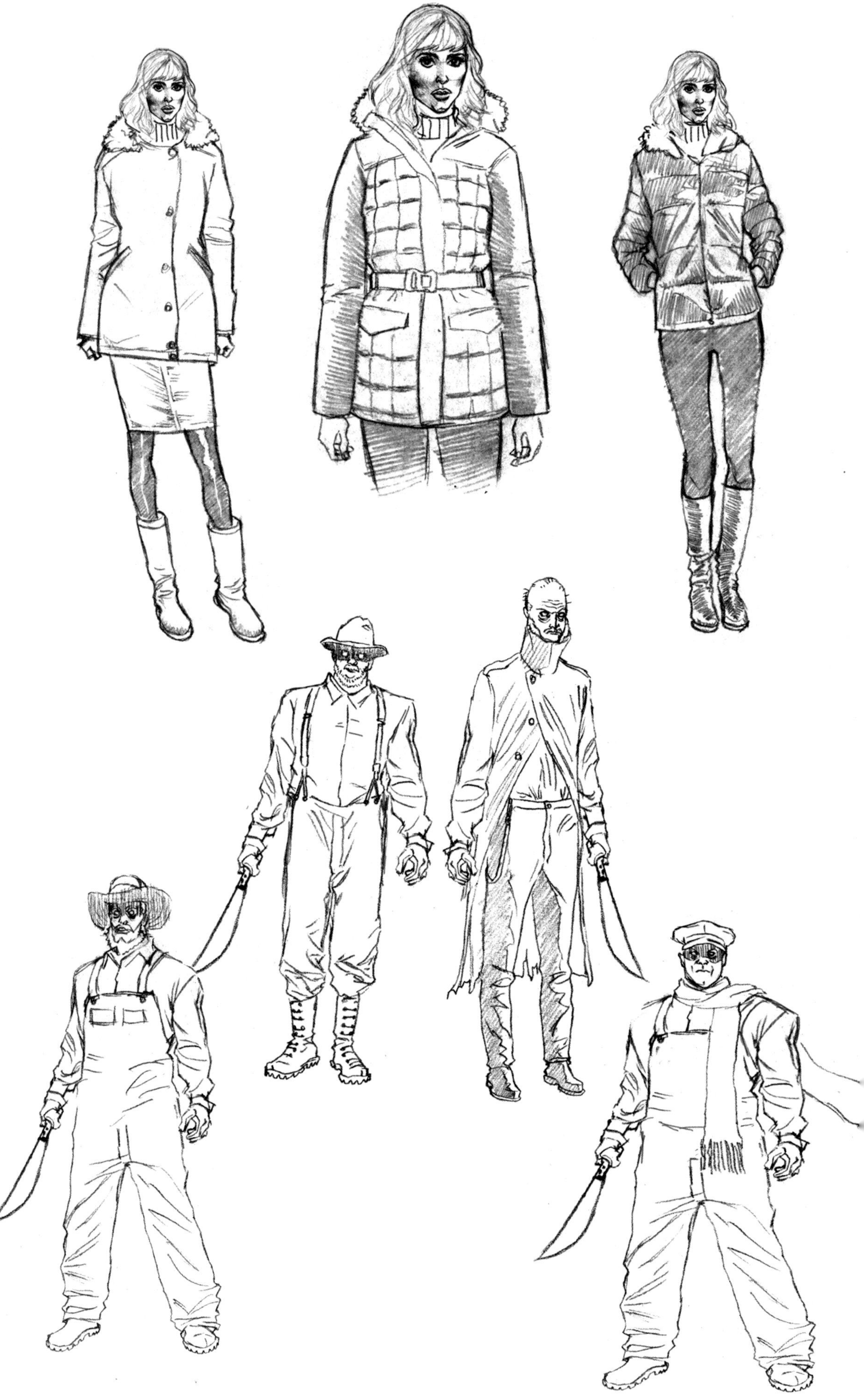

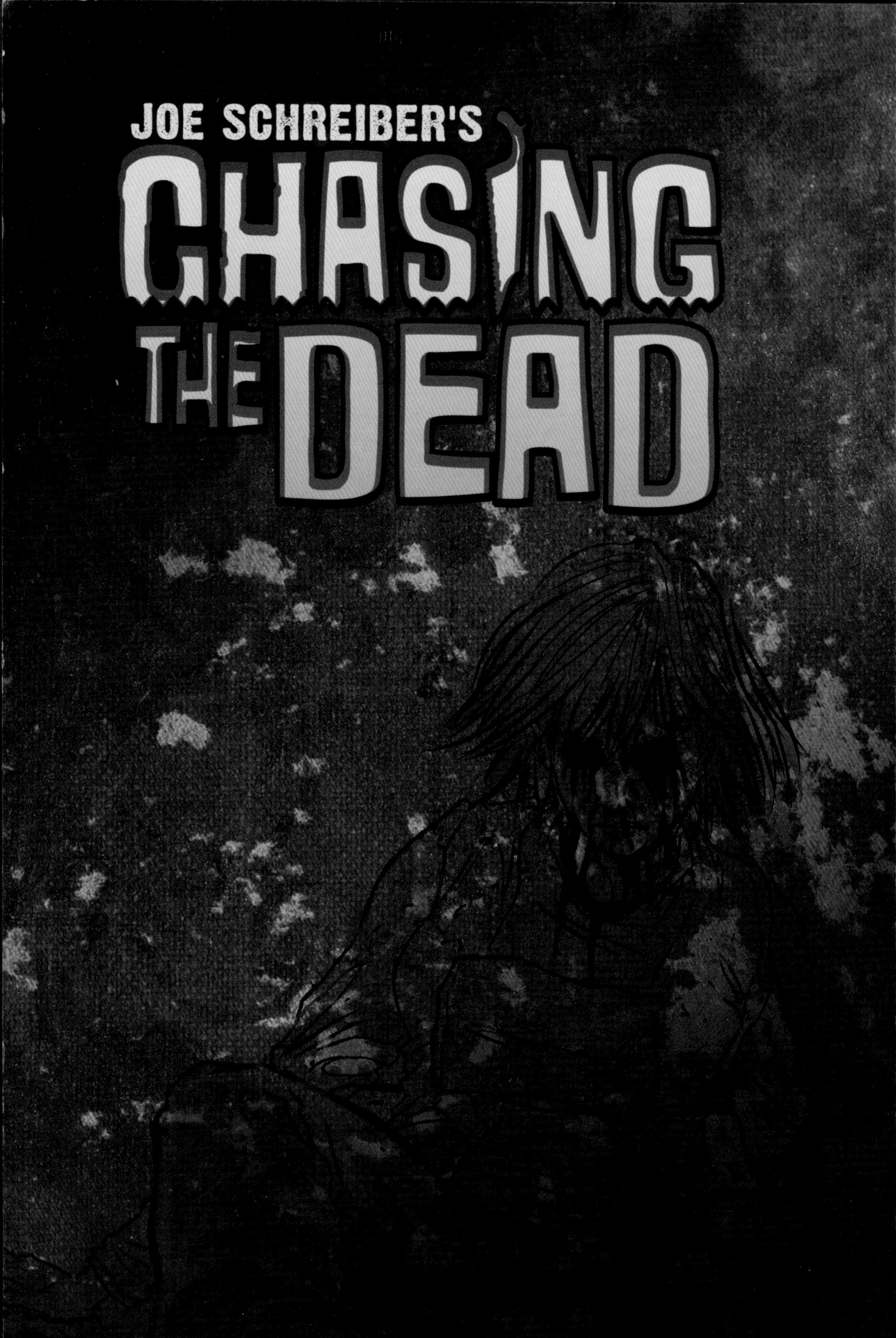
JOE SCHREIBER'S
CHASING
THE DEAD